Formation Theology
Volume Four

LIVING OUR
CHRISTIAN FAITH
AND
FORMATION TRADITIONS

Other Books by Adrian van Kaam and Susan Muto

Aging Gracefully

Am I Living a Spiritual Life?

Christian Articulation of the Mystery

The Commandments:
Ten Ways to a Happy Life and a Healthy Soul

Commitment: Key to Christian Maturity

Divine Guidance:
Seeking to Find and Follow the Will of God

Dynamics of Spiritual Direction

The Emergent Self

Epiphany Manual on the Art and Discipline of
Formation-in-Common

Formation Guide for Becoming Spiritually Mature

Foundations of Christian Formation

Growing through the Stress of Ministry

Harnessing Stress: A Spiritual Quest

Healthy and Holy Under Stress: A Royal Road to Wise Living

The Participant Self

The Power of Appreciation:
A New Approach to Personal and Relational Healing

Practicing the Prayer of Presence

Praying the Lord's Prayer with Mary

Readings from A to Z: The Poetry of Epiphany

Songs for Every Season

Stress and the Search for Happiness

Tell Me Who I Am

Dear Fr. John,
We are so grateful for your friendship and prayers,

Formation Theology
Volume Four

LIVING OUR CHRISTIAN FAITH AND FORMATION TRADITIONS

Susan Muto
Adrian van Kaam
Susan Muto

EPIPHANY ASSOCIATION
Pittsburgh, Pennsylvania

Imprimatur: Most Reverend Paul J. Bradley, V.G., D.G.
Bishop of Pittsburgh
June 30, 2006

Nihil Obstat: Reverend Joseph J. Kleppner, S.T.D., Ph.D.
Censor Librorum

The *Nihil Obstat* and the *Imprimatur* are declarations that the work is considered to be free from doctrinal or moral error. It is not implied that those who have granted the same agree with the contents, opinions, or statements expressed.

©2007 Epiphany Association
820 Crane Avenue
Pittsburgh, Pennsylvania 15216-3050

All rights reserved. No part of this book may be reproduced, stored in a retrieval system, or transmitted, in any form or by any means, electronic, mechanical, photocopying, recording, or otherwise, without written permission of the Epiphany Association.

The Scripture quotations contained herein are from the New Revised Standard Version Bible: Catholic Edition, copyright ©1993 and 1989 by the National Council of the Churches of Christ in the U.S.A. Used by permission. All rights reserved.

ISBN: 1880982-37-4

Library of Congress Catalog #2006935296

Printed in the United States of America

CONTENTS

Acknowledgments

Introduction by Susan Muto 13
   Mentors on a Mission 14
   Foundational Faith Formation 17
   Becoming Epiphanic People 19
   Founding Intuitions 20
   Continuity Out of Chaos 21
   Seeing Psychology as a Human Science 22
   Implications for Education 24
   Necessary Critique of Existential Psychology 27
   New Research Efforts 29
   Applied Research and Beyond 31
   Beginning Shift to Formation 32
   Return to Full Time Study of Formation 33
   Directives from Formation Traditions 35

1. Origin of Formation Traditions 39
   Directives Bestowed on Us
      in Our Human Field of Formation 42
   Telling Our Formation Story 43
   Role of Memory, Imagination, and Anticipation 44
   Disclosures of Form-Traditional Directives 46

2. Emergence of Christian Formation Traditions 49
   Formative Reading as Preservative 51

Differentiating and Integrating Structures
    of Our Christian Traditions .54
Actualization of Our Christian Traditions 55

3. Formation Traditions as Bridges
to Human and Christian Living .57
Horizontal and Vertical Interformation 60
Human Nature and Formation Traditions 62
Influence of Traditions on Our Nature 63

4. Traditional Formation in Pluritraditional Settings 67
Accelerating Emergence of Pluritradionality 69
Impact of Traditional Plurality 71
Personal and Institutional Aspects
    of Formation Traditions 73
Connections with the Pyramid Structure 74
Infiltration by New Traditions 75

5. Formation Theology and
Transformational Traditions 79
Inexhaustibility of the Mystery .84
Articulation of the Historical Humanity
    of Jesus Christ 86

6. Integrating Our Christian
Faith and Formation Traditions 89
Seminal Messages of the Revelation 90
Fertile Ground of Our Faith 92
Practice of Christian Formation .94

7. Symbolic Transmission of a Living Tradition 97
Centrality of Christian Classics .99
Normative Event of Jesus Christ 100
Wellspring of Classical Wisdom 102

8. Traditions and Transformation 107
   Unparalleled Achievement of Christ's Life 109
   Womanly Words of Wisdom 110
   Following the Threefold Path 112
   Crossing the Bridge 113
   Walking in the Truth 114
   Becoming Living Prayer 118

9. Foundations of Our Faith
and Formation Traditions 123
   Appeal to the Heart 124
   Appraising Formation Events 125
   God's Ongoing Creation
      and Coformation of Our Life 128
   Centrality of Traditional Ecclesial Appraisals 129

10. Traditions Enhancing Christian Formation 133
   Our Traditional View of the World 136
   Principle of Pneumatic Formability 137
   Pre-Revealed and Revealed
      Foundations of Formation 138

11. Tradition and Our Communal Life as Christians ...141
   Responding to Transformative Direction 142
   Remembering Our Mission and Ministry 144

12. Fruits of Transformative Participation
in Our Traditions 149
   From Formative to Transformative Presence 151
   From Transformative Love to the Life of Prayer 153

13. Tradition and Transfiguration
of the People of God 157
   Retelling Our Story 159
   Restoration of Traditional Meaning 162

14. Aids to Articulating Our Christian Traditions 165
    Traditions as Formative 166
    Classical Articulations 167
    Attention to Articulation 168
    Continuity of the Classics 169
    Classical Articulation and
        the History of Spirituality .171

**15. Integrative Field of Our
    Faith and Formation Traditions** 175
    Center of Our Formation Field 176
    Spheres and Dimensions of Our Formation Field 177
    Our Interformational Sphere .178
    Danger of Denying the Power of Traditions 179
    A Crucial Problem 182
    Expressions of Our Love-Will 183

**16. Teaching the Classics in Service
    of Our Traditions** 187
    Teachings from an Ancient Master 189
    Influence of Dionysius 191
    Ways of Knowing God 192

17. Teachings from a Medieval Master 197
    Influence of Julian 200
    Gifted Character of Julian's *Showings* 201
    Julian's Doctrine of the Spiritual Life 203

18. Teachings from a Contemporary Master 209
    Characteristics of Practical Mysticism 213
    Exercise of Christian Commitment 216

19. Social Conscience and Traditional Formation 219
    Appraisal in Service of Christian Fidelity 221
    Situations as Passing and Persistent 223
    Types of Passing Formation Situations 224

    Secondary Periods of Formation 225
    Flow of Ongoing Formation 226

**20. Commitment to Our Faith and
Formation Traditions** 231
    Influence of Syncretic Formation Traditions 232
    Responding to Divine Formation Traditions 233

**21. Challenge of Adhering to Our Faith
and Formation Traditions** 239
    Linguistic and Traditional Limits 241
    Physical Sciences in Relation to Our Field of Life 242
    Functional and Transcendent Directives 243
    Exploration of Directives 244
    Actualization of Traditional Directives 245
    Ascending Hierarchy of Directives 246

22. Heart of Faith Formation 249
    Functioning in Faith 251
    Integrative Directives 252
    Thematic and Concrete Directives 253
    Transformative Foundations 254
    Conclusion 255

Afterword by Susan Muto 257
Notes 263
Bibliography 269
Index 281
About the Authors 291

ACKNOWLEDGMENTS

This culminating text in our Formation Theology Series is the fruit of painstaking efforts made on our behalf by our Epiphany Academy staff, students, colleagues, and benefactors, each of whom we honor in spirit, naming in particular our production assistants, Mary Lou Perez and Vicki Bittner, and our editorial consultants, Rev. Joseph Kleppner, S.T.L., Ph.D. and Msgr. Albert Kuuire, S.T.D., Ph.D.

Unwavering support for these publications continues to come from our Board of Directors, headed by David Natali, M.D., and our core and adjunct faculty in Pittsburgh and in Indianapolis.

May all of us and every reader of this volume grow in lasting and living appreciation for the treasury of faith and traditional formation entrusted to us by the grace of God.

INTRODUCTION
by
Susan Muto, Ph.D.

At the start of this volume on Christian faith and formation traditions, it makes good sense to return to the historic roots of formative spirituality and to describe its emergence scientifically, anthropologically, and theologically. The story starts in earnest during World War II and continues to the present day, first on the continent and then in the United States. One might say its initial chapters were written from 1944 to 1945, during the last year of the war, when people in the North and West of the Netherlands experienced the infamous Hunger Winter. Here, according to my colleague and co-author, Father Adrian van Kaam, begins the narrative of a life's work that is still unfolding. What happened is part of the historical record of an infamous era. The Allied Troops were defeated in the Battle of Arnhem. German troops entrenched themselves in these areas of Holland, showing no mercy to anyone. Stocks of food were taken away. Thousands of able-bodied men were transported to work camps. Others were rounded up for execution or sent directly to concentration camps and certain death. Famine caused countless people to die of hunger. Those who survived had to escape to the countryside. Father van Kaam, who happened to be at home in the Hague on vacation, was among those trapped by the Nazis. He was as shocked by their cruel treatment as anyone could be. As a twenty-four year old theology student in the last year before his ordination to the priesthood, he found himself among these displaced persons in a small village called Nieuwkoop. Desperate as he himself felt, still more frantic people hiding with him came to him for counsel. After all, he was soon to be a "man of the cloth." They turned to him for spiritual help. He was humbled by their trust. The questions they asked planted in his heart the first seeds of formative thinking and set him on a new course for the rest of his life. Many had lost their homes, their professions, their confidence in a benevolent mystery that would sustain them. Wives were without husbands, children without their parents and friends. Whole Jewish families were sent to the gas chambers. The cozy form they had given to their lives in better times fell apart. What could be done to help these broken souls find some meaning in their misery? Their future seemed hopeless. Trust in the basic goodness of life had to be rekindled, but how would this be possible? People from various religious and ideological traditions experienced the "More Than" in different ways. However they named the mystery, this connection was their only bridge between the abyss of chaos characterized by this heinous, pain-filled point in time and some reason to go on living. The reply Father van Kaam gave to some of his compatriots was the only answer he could find for himself. It was: "to close our ears to the rumors of disaster and try to hear inwardly the barely audible music of a deeper harmony amidst such horrific suffering."

Such whispers of hope do not come in dramatic disclosures but through the openings of our everyday life. Even in this diaspora of desperate people, whose lives were threatened by the enemy's destruction of the dikes that kept the lowlands from sinking into the sea, the sound of goodness restored could be heard. The shining forth of transcendent meaning in daily life occurred in nondescript events, in little things like needle and thread, in signs of love that kept the flame of faith burning like the last embers of a dying fire.

Mentors on a Mission

During these long hours of hiding, Father van Kaam recalled many episodes of his young adult life and none more precious than the memory of his soul-friend at home in the Hague and in the Spiritan community, Marinus Scholtes (1919-1941). Not only did they share the experience of being students in the senior seminary program of the Spiritans in Weert; they also grew up in two neighboring parishes in Den Haag, the seat of the Dutch government and its parliament. During their Christmas, Easter, and summer recesses at home, ten years before the Hunger Winter, they spent time together and in the company of other young people and supportive adults with whom they could share their growing interest in spiritual formation. How could the ageless truths they found in scripture and the masters apply to their lives as laity, clergy, and religious? Some older members of the group, living as professionals in the market place, had similar questions. Others with academic affiliations as faculty members and students at the University of Leiden were interested in finding ways to combine their life of faith with their everyday tasks in family, church, and society. Out of these relationships was born the prototype of our present-day Epiphany Association.

A particularly dear friend of Father van Kaam's was Gerard Bol, a doctoral student in literature, who worked with Professor Pieter Nicolaas van Eyck, a poet and well-known expert in the writings of the 16th century Flemish-Dutch mystic Hadewijch. Another key companion of his was Adriaan Langelaan, who held a director's position in the Hague division of the Bank of Amsterdam. He and his wife, Marie, joined in these animated conversations, centered on the inspiration to live a simple unobtrusive life in the world in imitation of the hidden life of Jesus of Nazareth—the very ideal that gave birth in 1979 to our Epiphany mission and ministry in the United States and throughout the world.

In the period prior to the outbreak of the war, within this trustworthy circle of friends, all felt safe to engage in heartfelt discussions of their faith and formation experiences. As it turned out, none of them were called as laity to identify with one or the other special spirituality that might lead to one's joining a particular religious community, Third Order or Secular Institute. Examples of such "special schools of spirituality" abounded, including, to name a few, the Benedictine, Franciscan, Ignatian, Carmelite, Montfortan, Spiritan, and Salesian. For those seekers spontaneously attracted to these particular traditions there was no problem. They felt at home in them both spiritually and apostolically.

These early Epiphany pioneers, already drawn by grace to a deeper spiritual formation, had thought that the best way to follow this inner appeal was to join one of these orders, institutes, or congregations. They mistook the general invitation to maturation in Christ for a vocation to enter into a closely knit religious or lay community, seeing this adherence as a necessary means to holiness. Gerard Bol was one of them. Spiritually inclined and hungering for formation-in-depth, he had entered the Dutch novitiate of the Jesuits. However, the novice master made it clear after some months that he was called to a profound spiritual life in the world. He explained to him that the general call to ecclesial holiness was not the same as a vocation to a particular type of spirituality within the walls of a specific religious order.

Lay members of this "little Epiphany" came to see and appreciate that specialized spirituality groups, sanctioned and promoted by the Church, celebrate in their own fashion the fundamental principles of faith formation. They follow their rules and constitutions in accordance with the particular charism of the religious or lay organization to which they belong.

The question these friends asked themselves was how one could give effective personal and ecclesial form to one's life of faith without joining any special group? They admitted that it would be hazardous were they to attempt to do so on their own. How right they were in this matter would be confirmed for Father van Kaam by his experience of the great mix of people hiding with him during the Hunger Winter. Had anyone tried to impose on them a special spirituality, his own included, they might have felt more lost than found. He had to root his counsel in what he had learned years ago about the experiential wisdom found in all traditions of effective faith formation. The good results that followed, spiritually, psychologically, and physically, made him doubly grateful to his gifted mentors and especially to Marinus.

Foundational Faith Formation

These early Epiphany Associates turned to the Bible and the literature of spirituality for insight into what Father van Kaam later named "foundational faith formation" rooted in the theology of divine information or Revelation. Informational theology was, of course, not only factual but also inclusive of general formational principles. The question of most concern for the Dutch group was: how could the faith cognition to which they were already committed as Christians be complemented by an experiential theology of formation applicable to their familial, social, sacramental, and moral life? This theology of faith formation would of necessity have to include dialogue with the many pretheological disciplines of human development, which were becoming increasingly familiar to them, especially after the war.

Noteworthy, too, was the fact that the vacuum of experiential faith formation, created by the devastation that encompassed Europe, had been filled by an increasing number of approaches to spirituality. Some remained faithful to, others cut themselves off from, the institutional Church to which they might belong. Each emphasized its own approaches to prayer and action, its own devotional preferences and styles of life. The concrete implementation of people's faith could only take place amidst the many religious and ideological forces playing on their life. Cooperation without compromise became a real challenge. One had to adapt to new insights in such a way that they did not erode fidelity to one's own faith tradition.

This predicament led many to ponder if it were possible for specialized patterns of faith formation to replace for all the faithful a foundational approach that respected and served people in all walks of life. Specialized schools of spirituality held some, but not all of the answers to their basic hunger for spiritual deepening. Was there a way to encourage diverse individuals and groups of people to pursue effective, experiential modes of transformation that would nourish everyone's heart, mind, and soul? Nothing was accomplished by trying to impose on others who did not feel at home with such models, a particular style of prayer or a ready-made program of formation. Some might choose to adhere, beyond the foundations of the faith, to a special way of formation, but this adherence could prove to be for others more of a hindrance than a help to Christian maturity.

Some members of this prototype Epiphany group wondered if their concerns were symptomatic of a growing desire on the part of many people to find an effective way of living with God without feeling guilty that they were not called, for example, to a religious community with its own rules and ways of initiation. Their need for a basic theology of human and Christian formation that would serve to illumine the inhumane shadows of oppression they faced daily became acute. Could they find a way to personalize the foundations of what they believed without necessarily having to cross over the bridge of a special spirituality?

More often than not they were told that in matters of faith formation they should seek counsel from spiritual guides trained to extol the way of formation communicated to members of their congregations, who were willing to pass this knowledge on to them. As a result, many lay faithful were left with the impression that to follow the foundational formation principles of the Church they had to accept as their own the styles and emphases of that particular director's spirituality.

Father van Kaam understood the dilemma his friends and later students were facing. They turned to him for counsel pertaining to a way of faith formation that would be helpful to all believers, whether or not they followed the rubrics of a special school of spirituality. They responded enthusiastically to the notion of a theology of experiential faith formation that would enable them to embody their beliefs in everyday life. They wanted the basic doctrines and classical expressions of their faith to come alive in a new way. They knew that these timeless truths spanned the ages while still giving voice to their deepest concerns during and after the war that tore them apart.

INTRODUCTION / 19

Becoming Epiphanic People

Direction-in-common sessions were a tried and true way of helping those in hiding to maintain their sanity. Father van Kaam recalls with special fondness one occasion on which he asked them to picture in their mind's eye a beautiful scene: that of Japanese girls shaping and arranging flowers and setting up in exquisite silence lovely tea ceremonials. For a moment everyone left the chaos of a country under cruel occupation. They went on an imaginative journey to a place where these women were totally at peace with what they were doing. They not only gave form to flowers and the sipping of tea; they also became symbols of how to gather dispersed lives around a deeper center. By being present to the simple task at hand, they experienced what they were doing as an epiphany reminiscent of a higher scheme of things. They gathered together not only these choice blossoms but also, in appreciation of them, their own thoughts and feelings, their remembrances of the past and hopes for the future. As time passed by on their imaginative journey to this place where they found these women totally at peace with what they were doing, they became whole again. Having had to endure so much suffering, they began to find ways to reshape their limited lives and those of their deprived compatriots in simple ways conducive to tranquillity amidst turbulence.

We, too, become split, tense and broken when we cease being simply in the situation where we find ourselves. The secret of not falling apart, of not losing our sense of life's meaning despite the density of the mystery that surrounds us, is to try to be present to the small things and unpretentious deeds that make up our day-to-day life. During these endless hours of hiding together, Father van Kaam concluded, "It was not a luxury but a necessity to live each moment as an epiphany of a concealed symphony always playing in the universe and uniting us to one another through our faith and formation traditions. Only in a community bound by love were we able to live distinctively human and courageous lives."

"Epiphanic people," Father van Kaam taught, "try to pay attention to everyday life as a manifestation or gift of an ever present mystery transforming cosmos and humanity, even in the worst of times." He recalls that victims of the Hunger Winter tried to listen attentively not only to enemy movements but also to the sounds of the wind in the rafters of the attics of the farms in which they hid; to rain drops on the haystacks in which they buried themselves when army units passed by; to footsteps of farm hands in the stable feeding the cows; to voices of children in the kitchen; and to the whirring, churning machines making buttermilk. They learned to be attentive to hopeful symbols like a blade of grass, a humming insect, a small sparrow, the shape of a buttercup, the weather-beaten faces of old workers, the flowing lines of furniture or dress. To be present in this way helped everyone to gather themselves together in the here and now, to live fully where they were, never rushing ahead to what may happen tomorrow or sinking back in a past that was no longer there.

For all who worked in the resistance, such full presence, also to the battle for justice, made them more effective. Ineffectiveness of mission was often due to not being wholly with what one had to do within the limits of his or her commitment. When resistance fighters saw their task as a noble sharing in the lasting cry of humanity for justice, their involvement grew by leaps and bounds. They did a better job. As a result, many of them survived the war.

Founding Intuitions

Out of these and similar experiences erupted the founding intuitions for a universal human science of formation, serving an anthropology and eventually a theology that together would comprise an empirical-experiential, truly comprehensive approach to the meaning of life and world. It would be designed to make sense to a significant number of people facing crises of transcendence and adhering to a wide variety of religious or ideological faith and formation traditions. Its aim, only possible with the help of grace, would be to work to reverse the bellicose role of distorted formation traditions, as distinguished from their underlying foundational faith traditions. Such distortions had already enflamed populations to the point of sparking a firestorm of self-righteous aggression, leading to pogroms, wars, concentration camps, genocide, and persecutions.

This founding intuition would require a lifetime of elaboration. Influencing it would be many discussions and encounters with adherents of various belief systems. They lived for the most part by some transcendent formation tradition or at least by some pretranscendent developmental perspective that helped them to make sense of their experiences. Methods of articulation and elucidation would have to be found to name these events.

During the Hunger Winter it became clear that people of various backgrounds could share with one another certain foundational principles and dynamics pertaining to the formation of life and world. Such foundations were meaningful to all because of their shared human nature *as formational*. From 1946, the year of his ordination, onward, Father van Kaam began in earnest the multifaceted projects of research and publication that were to become his life's work.

Continuity Out of Chaos

After the war and the conclusion of his theological and philosophical studies, Father van Kaam was appointed professor of philosophical anthropology at his Dutch seminary in Gemert. The two fields he was assigned to teach enabled him to elaborate the foundational principles of the formation science he had conceived in seed form during the Hunger Winter. These fields were, respectively, Thomistic philosophy and the philosophy of logic and science. The first discipline enabled him to grasp the hypothetical presuppositions necessary to inaugurate a truly humane science of formation. The second facilitated his working out of the principles that must guide the strict methodology required by such a new approach to formative human experiences and their transcendent orientation.

His interests bore lasting fruit when he met a Belgian supervisor of education, Ms. Maria Schouwenaars. She invited him to expand his commitments by teaching in the Dutch Life Schools of Formation for Young Adults, which she had initiated in her home country. To better aid this endeavor, he went on to study pedagogy and andragogy at the graduate Hoogveld Institute of the University of Nijmegen, integrating the information he received there with his own emergent discipline of transcendent human formation and its sustaining science and anthropology. The Life Schools made it possible for him to explore his original ideas in a theoretical and practical manner with students aged 18-24, who followed his courses in applied formation. He showed them how to integrate what they learned with their representative vocations to the single and married life and to the avocations that supported them.

The originality and importance of this work came to the attention of the then Secretary of State of the Vatican, Monsignor Giovanni Baptista Montini (later Pope Paul VI). He asked the Vatican representative in the Netherlands to speak in confidence to Father van Kaam's provincial superior, Father Henri Strick, C.S.Sp., to consider releasing him for this work on a full-time basis and eventually to think of his teaching formative spirituality at the university level. This opportunity was readily granted to him by his superiors and was soon to be fulfilled in a providential way. His first step was to follow his provincial's request that he spend a year in Paris, researching the life of the Venerable Francis Libermann, one of the beloved founders of the Spiritans. The fruit of this research was his masterful biography, *A Light to the Gentiles*. The next step of this faith journey would bring him from Europe to America, which would become his second home just as English would become his second language.

Seeing Psychology as a Human Science

In 1954 Father van Kaam accepted the invitation extended to him by the then president of Duquesne University in Pittsburgh, Pennsylvania, Father Vernon Gallagher, C.S.Sp., to teach what he assumed would be foundational formation. Soon after he arrived, he found that the plan the president had in mind was for him to make himself available for the initiation of a program that turned out to be as new to him as to those who would follow it. He had for a time to change fields and become involved in what he came to call "psychology as a human science." The president who invited him to do so happened to be a person accomplished in art appreciation and English literature. His sensitivity to the human predicament aroused in him a concern for fostering on a Catholic campus, under the jurisdiction of the Holy Ghost Fathers, an exclusively positivistic approach to psychology, however prevalent or popular it might be at that time. Fearing its effect on the human spirit, he sought a way to foster a more humane yet still scientifically responsible study of psychology. The positivistic approach operated in accordance with the methods of the physical sciences. Important as the offerings of this type of psychology were, both he and Father van Kaam shared the opinion that it should be complemented by a distinctively human approach, one which would acknowledge both the transcendent dimension and relative freedom of the human person.

Having arrived at Duquesne with the expectation to continue his research and teaching in the field of human and spiritual formation, Father van Kaam found that psychology would, at least temporarily, have to become an added new field of specialization and endeavor. This commitment necessitated graduate studies, among others, in clinical psychology at Case Western Reserve University in Cleveland, Ohio; in counseling and therapy training under Carl Rogers at the University of Chicago; and in personality theory and psychotherapy under Abraham Maslow, Kurt Goldstein, and Andreas Angyal at Brandeis University.

By the year 1958, Father van Kaam had obtained a Ph.D. in psychology from Case Western University. The title of his dissertation was "The Experience of Really Feeling Understood by a Person: A Phenomenological Study of the Necessary and Sufficient Constituents of this Experience as Described by 360 Subjects in Chicago and Pittsburgh." After earning his doctoral degree, he organized, in keeping with the original request of the president of Duquesne, a new curriculum designed to foster "psychology as a human science." He also tried to take up again his chief interest in the work of spiritual formation by starting to teach a series of courses on the transcendent emergence of the human spirit within a special division of the psychology department, named "religion and personality." He had to function for the time being as primarily a professor in the humane approach to psychology he had initiated, but he never forfeited his first commitment to formative spirituality. Therefore, as part of his work in the psychology department, he addressed the notion of a distinctively human approach to life as distinguished from a merely pretranscendent view of human development.

Implications for Education

At that time in the United States at least two circles of psychologists and existential thinkers had developed similar approaches to the person as free and insightful. One circle revolved around Viktor Frankl, the other around Rollo May. Other psychologists concerned about human freedom, decision-making, and insights of a more transcendent nature moved towards establishing an approach to psychology that was more humanistic. This movement was represented, among others, by Gordon Allport, Carl Rogers, Kurt Goldstein, Andreas Angyal, Rudolf Dreikurs, Heinz Ansbacher, Abraham Maslow, Clark Moustakas, and Sidney Jourard.

Maslow, Rogers, and May were especially open and generous to Father van Kaam. They established a working relationship with him, indeed a friendship, in spite of their divergent belief systems and formation traditions. Rollo May fostered his election to the council of the Association of Existential Psychology and Psychiatry. He also made him the first editor of their journal. Carl Rogers invited him to be part of an intimate group of professors and staff members gathering at his home in the evening for a variety of discussions and allowing him to express in open discourses his critical objections to a mere client-centered approach to counseling as wholly non-directive.

Maslow's trust in him was especially touching. In spite of the fact that he disagreed with many of his basic presuppositions, Maslow invited him to teach his courses at Brandeis during his sabbatical year, giving him the freedom to communicate his own views. He responded in turn to the invitation to speak to Father van Kaam's students at Duquesne. He told Maslow at that time of his theory of limited form-traditional direction developed during the Dutch phases of the initiation of his new theory and science of formation. They argued back and forth. Though initially disagreeing with him, Maslow listened intently and, at a certain moment, seemed to lean in the direction of his colleague. Later Father van Kaam learned that Maslow's concern for his beloved granddaughter made him aware of the dangers of premature non-directive self-actualization. He also became aware that decision-making beyond the region of one's knowledge, expertise, and life experience could lead to the counter-productive result of fostering an exclusively non-directive approach to the education of children.

The moment of crisis came for Maslow in the aftermath of the failure of the well intentioned attempts by Carl Rogers and his colleagues to introduce traditionless non-directive education, premature fully independent decision-making, and total self-actualization in a number of schools offered to them for experimentation in California. Unfortunate consequences, combined with serious complaints by parents and children, convinced the experts involved that the outcomes of this experiment were not going to be all that encouraging. To the dismay of Maslow and other critics of these systems, a number of schools, educational institutes, and programs began blindly to imitate these non-directive educational processes. It was too late to control the damage that had been done. William Coulson, whose critiques never wavered, traveled far and wide to warn educators and parents that he himself, like Maslow and later Rogers, had been too optimistic in their expectations of what such an education, loosened from any directive content, might really do to the school systems and the pupils in them.

As one of his colleagues later revealed, Maslow, driven by his sense of responsibility, expanded and edited two volumes of journals to undo the harm that had been done unwittingly. They were published posthumously, no longer supported by the grants that had widely spread his former contributions. These journals were largely ignored by many of his followers. They were not even mentioned or given equal time in posthumous reviews of his works.

Initially Maslow was not too sure that this shift of interest would be understood. As a heart patient he probably was also afraid that others, finding his journals in case of his death, would not welcome their publication. At least he knew where Father van Kaam stood. His formation theory of personality insisted on the desirability of a life open to transcendent direction. The last time Maslow visited him he begged him to take under his wing the manuscripts he was writing. He gave his friend the key to a box filled with these writings which he intended to send to him through the intermediary of a student of his who had now become, on his advice, a member of the graduate program in psychology that Father van Kaam had established at Duquesne University. Maslow asked him not to divulge the contents of the box before his death. In case he survived long enough he asked him to return the box to him so that he himself could begin work on their editing and possible publication.

Father van Kaam found a safe hiding place for the box in the basement of Trinity Hall, the priest residence on campus where he lived. A few years later Maslow called him and asked him to send the box on to him with the help of the same graduate student. He was now ready to make these notes public, together with many others he had collected. That was probably the beginning of the twenty last months of his life, which were spent in preparation of his journals for publication. This publication, as reported in detail by William Coulson, confirmed, at least indirectly, Father van Kaam's own theory of the need for a formative direction of life illumined by consonant faith and formation traditions.

Necessary Critique of Existential Psychology

Having been assigned to develop one of the first academic programs in psychology as a human science, Father van Kaam strove to explain the difference between his own understanding of the essence-existence structure and the implicit assumptions of certain existential and humanistic psychologists. Another concern of his was the lack of attention to transscientific disciplines in search of meaning as distinct from pretranscendent sciences of measurement. Regrettable also was the tendency to limit one's openness to other perspectives in the field of psychology itself as well as to related disciplines and faith traditions.

For psychology to become a fully human science, a suitable methodology would have to be found to illumine what was typically human or transcendent, no matter from what source of knowledge such insights and findings might come. His contacts with colleagues and students proved that humanistic existential psychology had already received recognition in the United States. Evidence enough could be found in the publication of books, articles, and journals like the *Review of Existential Psychology and Psychiatry*, which he served as an editor. Once the metalanguage of this field became familiar to a growing number of researchers and practitioners, it would be easier to initiate a new academic program specializing in psychology as a human science while taking into account the work done by many other scholars in the United States and abroad whose works were becoming known, among others, through the Duquesne University Press under the direction of Father Henry Koren, C.S.Sp., Ph.D.

Father van Kaam never doubted the need to engage in critical, creative dialogue with such already existing approaches. He tried to reform and broaden them from within by using their own metalanguage while giving it a wider scope and meaning. Then certain findings already tested in other schools and clinics could serve the project of establishing a new mode of psychology at Duquesne that would be both existential and phenomenological rather than simply positivistic or behavioristic or merely humanistic.

The proof that this work of critical dialogue remained as open as possible resided in the contacts and close friendships Father van Kaam maintained at that time with Carl Rogers at the University of Chicago, Rudolf Dreikurs at the Alfred Adler Institute, and Kurt Goldstein, Andreas Angyal, and Abraham Maslow at Brandeis University. He was also invited to serve on the editorial board of the *Journal of Individual Psychology*, edited by Heinz Ansbacher. He kept in touch with the existential psychological movement in America by attending monthly meetings in New York of the Association of Existential Psychology and Psychiatry, organized and chaired by Rollo May. Important contacts in Europe were established with Viktor Frankl, whose guest he was in Vienna, Austria.

Some followers of the existential and humanistic movements were also influenced by Eastern traditions like Zen Buddhism. To explore this wave of interest called for more first-hand information. For this reason, Father van Kaam traveled to the Far East, visited the Buddhist University of Tokyo, spent time in a Buddhist monastery in Eheie, and consulted during this phase of travel Western experts in Buddhism working in Japan, like Father William Johnson, S.J.

Growing familiarity with these movements did not diminish Father van Kaam's reservations about their underlying assumptions. However, these firsthand encounters provided him with the information he needed to understand their terminology and to comprehend their interpretation of the human person. His acquaintance with leaders in many diverse yet related fields confirmed his original observation that existential psychology, as taught at that time in the United States, had restricted itself mainly to philosophical, literary, psychotherapeutic, and psychoanalytic approaches. Important as they were, none of them alone or in combination could be the basis for psychology as the human science he envisioned it to be in his breakthrough book, *Existential Foundations of Psychology*. His aim would be to develop a systematic, methodological approach that might be acceptable, at least in some circles, to the standards set by the science of psychology as understood to be not only empirical-experimental but also empirical-experiential.

New Research Efforts

When he wrote his dissertation on the experience of really feeling understood by a person, Father van Kaam chose to devise a methodology that would accommodate both the demands for scientific accuracy and the need for experiential precision. He described and analyzed scientifically the psychological structures of a basic human experience and showed by an examination of this happening itself how to provide concepts, constructs, and methods of anthropological psychology to disclose the structures of this or any other experience that manifested itself in the framework of the situation in which one both felt and perceived it.

The experience of feeling understood had to be described by the 360 subjects who were asked to record the relation between what they were feeling and their corresponding life situation. The instruction to the subjects was so formulated that they would recount only those situations of feeling understood that they perceived as personally meaningful. The new method was concerned with incidences that related this experience to our personal and communal formation field. The origin of the data for an anthropological psychology had to be based on the structures of situated experiences as disclosed by a verifiable methodology.

The research done by Father van Kaam starts with the gathering of individual descriptions of a specific experience. From these descriptions emerges a more general positing of a representative experience of the population selected for this research project. After gathering the empirical data in the form of the subjects' written descriptions, the method of analysis developed in the dissertation was applied to them. It later became an effective tool for the preparation of questions used in interviews aimed at examining the structure of those experiences that enabled one to measure more accurately the extent of one's presence and actions in the situation under study. A follow-up body of research would be needed to ascertain the number of people who claim to experience really feeling understood. To devise the right questions for such an interview, one would first have to know what their wording meant for the segment of the population concerned. This empirical-experiential analysis of the structure of feeling understood, as experienced by a significant sample of the population to be interviewed, aimed at helping future researchers formulate proper and provocative questions. The results of this research could be used by psychotherapists and counselors dealing with similar phenomena in their clients and by writers or speakers referring to these ways of thinking and acting in written and oral treatises. Several years later, when Father van Kaam was able to resume the development of the science of human formation he had begun in Holland, he evolved mutually complementary methods of analyzing a formative event, including selection, articulation, elucidation, consultation, translation, transposition, integration, and application.

The phenomenological method used in his dissertation benefitted the work of experts like himself in the field of anthropological psychology. It became the basis of the main method of research used by his colleagues at the university and by their doctoral students. Nuances, refinements, elaborations, and expansions of this methodology have occurred since the years of its inception, which have embellished, though not essentially altered, the fundamental research process laid out originally by Father van Kaam.

The large number of subjects (360) used in the first study of this kind was decreased in other projects—a simplification that was quite understandable. This first study was a demonstration of Father van Kaam's new methodology done in a functionally oriented psychology department. Its faculty had to be convinced by an impressive array of data to allow such an innovation without violating their responsibility to the science of psychology as represented by their university.

Applied Research and Beyond

In the program of psychology as an anthropological or human science at Duquesne University, the sources of the data for this research remained — both for interested faculty members and students — written descriptions such as those Father van Kaam had himself utilized. Others also made use of interviews, observations of human action, and personal reflections. Some used these different sources of data in combination. The method he proposed was intentionally formulated in such a way that it could be expanded in the coming years by colleagues and students through, for example, such refinements as a qualitative content analysis of the data. This example confirms that the methodology designed by him allowed for significant elaborations without one's having to violate its essence. Whatever was added and approved offered students and readers the benefit of an original methodology and its refinements and enhancements by subsequent scholars, who went on to investigate effectively such topics as trust, anxiety, decision-making, privacy, at-homeness, courage, envy, jealousy, anger, loneliness, disappointment, and the experience of being criminally victimized. Most of them collected lingual statements from a sampling of subjects. They focused also on their descriptions of the experiences they were researching, just as he had done for the experience of really feeling understood. Then they examined the descriptions recorded with the assistance of their faculty.

By means of fundamentally the same methodology he had originally employed, they were able to disclose the experiential structure or form of human awareness they had set out to explore. The initiation of this new methodology influenced eventually his development of the articulation method used in formation science on which he had been working since the first days of his research in Holland.

Beginning Shift to Formation

Work on other aspects of the methodology and metalanguage of formation science was inspired paradoxically by the lack of receptivity on the part of some humanistic psychologists to other types of psychology; the relevant contributions of the latter were often neglected. Father van Kaam was especially concerned about a tendency to ignore the impact of religious, ideological, or other prevalent formation traditions on the human psychology of people. Last but not least, in many research data about human experiences a concentration on description and its focalization led at times to a neglect of the exploration of nonfocal dynamics.

In response to this neglect, Father van Kaam went on to develop the method of elucidation of hitherto concealed dynamics of formation. It became one of the cornerstones in his transcendence therapy. In addition, his desire to remain reasonably receptive to the findings of other types of psychology, as well as those of other human and social sciences, would give rise to the method of consultation of their formational data and insights and the methods of transposition and translation of these contributions in formation science. These methods would explicitly include the use of the formationally relevant implications of faith and formation traditions.

During this period of teaching and research in psychology, Father van Kaam expressed his respect for such traditions in his best selling book, *Religion and Personality*. His ongoing concern for distinctively human formation was sustained during these years by work both in the United States and abroad, during weekends and academic recesses. This work was a natural continuation of the practice and study begun by him in the Dutch Life Schools of Formation for Young Adults. During his nine year assignment in psychology (1954-1963), he was able, thanks to these outreach endeavors, to maintain the connection between his current teaching on campus and his original field of academic study, publication, and practice. Some colleagues in the psychology department assisted him in these speaking engagements. A visit from the initiator of the Dutch centers, Ms. Schouwenaars, was most welcome at this time. She came from Belgium to the United States to conduct a series of courses on the distinctively human formation of our everyday life and world.

Return to Full Time Study of Formation

As soon as several factors converged to enable him to start his own graduate institute in 1963, Father van Kaam began to elaborate in more detail the methodology, theory, and content of formation science begun in Holland. His temporary participation in the field of psychology had more than ever confirmed his conviction of the necessity to establish this complementary human science, which would at the same time be both wider and narrower than psychology: *wider* because daily, distinctively human formation is so varied, rich, and complex that it would be impossible to do justice to it by relying exclusively on the data and insights of only the science of functional psychology; *narrower* because formation science can utilize only those insights and data of psychology and other sciences that are formationally relevant. It must bypass and critique numerous other findings and presuppositions that may be fascinating to some in their own right and in relation to other purposes, but that have no direct relevance to the praxis of distinctively human and spiritual formation.

The new human science of formation with its supportive anthropology goes far beyond the project of "psychology as a human science." By virtue of its methods of systematic consultation and integration, it makes available a rich variety of insights and findings from other auxiliary sources. For example, various psychodynamic schools of psychology, such as the Freudian, Adlerian, and Jungian, have dealt with certain psychological aspects of form-reception and donation. Their findings as discerned to be formationally relevant may be useful for the further elaboration of an open-ended, truly holistic view of our human and potentially Christian formation field as a whole.

Formation science is concerned with our life as it unfolds in and through all of our dispositions, dimensions, and dynamics from infancy to the end of life. The psychodynamic patterns dealt with by those auxiliary sciences that are psychological in nature, represent only one facet of the multifaceted flow of an everyday human and spiritual existence. Transposed in the unifying language and vision of formation science, they can be seen as complementing and correcting one another. This science examines such disciplines as pedagogy, andragogy, sociology, philosophical, and cultural anthropology, linguistics, political science, economics, demographics, nutrition, and medicine. The same holds for the dynamics of giving and receiving form disclosed by religious and ideological faith and formation traditions, especially those involving the schools and masters of Eastern and Western spirituality.

However valuable such descriptions may be, they are only the point of departure for more penetrating explorations of our experiential lives as a whole. This is not to deny that many humanistic and other psychologists have to a degree transcended the realm of strict phenomenological description. Some of them excel also in the study and practice of the psychodynamics of human experience. Due to the innate perspectival nature of our empirical intellect, we cannot integrate all such profiles in their totality into one superscience. What we can do is to abstract from them certain implications that refer to the same or similar concerns for what is formationally relevant.

Consider an example from the science of engineering. It abstracts certain practical implications for its own object of research from the sciences of mathematics, chemistry, and architecture. It reformulates their relevant findings in terms of its own object pole of engineering. It presents them to engineers in their own language for use in practical construction projects. Engineering science never aims at integrating these diverse sciences into a superscience; it draws from them what students in engineering need to know about diverse areas of inquiry pertinent to their profession. There is no need for them to gain mastery as specialists in these auxiliary fields.

In a similar vein, formation science commends and fosters the development of scientific perspectives emerging from the arts and sciences as well as from the spiritual-experiential findings of faith and formation traditions. It gathers, integrates, corrects, and complements all such findings and insights on the basis of their compatibility with consonant, distinctively human life formation, understood in the light of its own empirical-experiential research methods. These need to be distinguished from both philosophical-speculative perspectives and empirical-experimental methods of measurement.

Directives from Formation Traditions

Formation science as foundational helps us to disclose the ideal directives at the root of any consonant formation tradition. These form-directives are marked by the following traits:

1. They are in principle common to all consonant human formation.

2. They are ordered hierarchically in consonance with the higher and lower dimensions of our human life form. (For instance, gratification and satisfaction directives should not rule out transcendent appreciation directives.)

3. They are effective in the consonant receiving and giving of form in one's life.

4. They help people to tell the difference between directives that are consonant or dissonant with their own field of formation.

5. Such basic life and field directives endow people and their respective formation traditions with the power to apprehend what appears in their field, to appraise it wisely, and to bring about more effectively the outcomes of this process.

Any formation tradition, insofar as it articulates these basic conditions, can help people to deepen their everyday human and spiritual unfolding. As we intend to show in this book, we need a new way of looking at the events that comprise our search for life's fullest meaning as we attempt to live in fidelity to our mysterious calling in the light of our faith and formation traditions.

In 1963 Father van Kaam was able to start the Institute of Man. I joined him in 1966 as its assistant director. In 1979 it was renamed the Institute of Formative Spirituality to better reflect the numerous books we wrote alone and together, the courses we taught and co-taught, and the seminars we conducted to enrich the original vision of formation begun in the Netherlands. Now this work continues to come to fruition in our co-founded Epiphany Academy, dedicated to the mission and ministry of helping believers and people of good will throughout the world to live to the full their faith and formation traditions.

While acknowledging the basic importance of the theological, administrative, and social differences among the faith groupings to which we belong, we prefer not to dwell unduly on that which sets us apart and to which we ought with wisdom and prudence to remain faithful. Our aim is not to engage in any sort of proselytizing but to encourage one another to be faithful to our personal callings and convictions. We respect the ecumenical attempts professional theologians make to find the precise connections or points of convergence between diverse denominations seeking some source of unity. Our modest mission is not to solve the theological differences among our traditions but to invite sincere seekers to swim together in the great river of spiritual formation that binds and encompasses us as distinctively human or transcendent beings. Our call is to deepen as much as possible the awareness that we are marked not only by basic systems of belief but also by formation traditions. They represent the countless ways in which we try to give form to our faith in the sociohistorical situations we increasingly share on Planet Earth.

The disconcerting disconnections—wars, religious prejudices, genocidal killing fields—that arise over religious and ideological differences are not directly commanded or intended by the foundational truths found in the classical texts of different faith traditions. None of them foster racism or sexism or violence against the innocent. Hostile disconnections are much more the result of the concrete cultural and accretional ways in which we give form to our foundational faith traditions. They do not represent the faith in question itself. Who of us does not regret and feel deep shame in the face of the terrible sufferings that have been imposed on humanity by the ferocious battles people wage against one another in the name of God or Yahweh or Allah or Jesus Christ?

The ravages caused by terrorist claims or genocidal pogroms sicken the heart. They make it imperative that we try to find a way to honor certain aspects of our formation traditions that celebrate diversity while reexamining the deepest ranges of our faith commitments that point to some type of unity among us. We could all benefit by adopting the motto of the Chaplain Corps of the United States Navy, "to cooperate without compromise."

Describing how this comes to pass while criticizing the all too bitter fruits of unnecessary absolutized form-traditional disassociations is the purpose of this co-authored book, the fourth and final text in our series on formation theology. We dedicate it to the laity, clergy, and religious, to the members of various denominational faith groupings, who study with us at the Academy and who facilitate such loving and respectful connections on every level of life. With their help we may find new ways to prevent the devastation of war and to promote the dream of world peace.

Chapter 1

Origin of Formation Traditions

I have decided to listen to what the Lord God wants to say to me.
— Thomas à Kempis

The origin of formation traditions is not hard to find. It coincides with the emergence of human life from the hand of the Divine Forming Mystery of the universe itself. Let's look at the account of The Beginning in the Book of Genesis. After the creation of a marvelous habitat called the earth—once a formless void but filled by the hand of God with light and dry land, with seeds and trees, with waters teeming with life and wild animals of every kind, God saw fit to create humankind "in our image, according to our likeness," giving them "dominion over the fish of the sea, and over the birds of the air..." And so God created them in his image, "male and female he created them," blessing them and telling them to be fruitful and multiply, to "fill the earth and subdue it; and have dominion over the fish of the sea and over the birds of the air and over every living thing that moves upon the earth" (Genesis 1:26-28).

There would be plenty of food to eat and a day to rest. All God asked was that Adam and Eve decide—because they were free to choose—to listen to their Creator, but humankind went the other way. Disobedience allowed sin to enter the world and with it the deformations that threaten to undo the forming, reforming, and transforming traditions set in motion by the Unmoved Mover.

We simplify this ancient account recorded in the Book of Genesis to make the point that our human life form, like all other created forms in the universe, is not a self-sufficient entity. We are made, held, and sustained by an all-embracing formation mystery beyond our understanding but always beside us, especially when we say, "I believe" and "I will obey."

None of us can ever fathom the eons of formation that constitute the beginning of life and its evolutionary unfolding in all the animate and inanimate forms that make up the known world. One way to perceive this dynamism is to compare it to an energy field characterized by a continual rising and falling of forms. Each has been actualized in its particularity in accordance with its own specific constitution from fish to fowl, from mammals to humankind in whom God breathed "the breath of life" (Genesis 2:7).

In this holistic, always mysterious process of creation we share a privileged place as the children of God. This fact of faith is ours to proclaim. The formability granted to us by the mystery that guides us from our earthly habitation to our heavenly home is the distinguishing feature of our humanness. From the Garden of Eden to the gracious ambience of our own backyard, we spend a lifetime responding to our unique yet communal call to formability. This reception and donation of form persist until we breathe our last breath. We are made to assimilate to ourselves whatever preserves and expands our destiny and to resist and refuse what is contrary to the quest for true happiness scripted by God on our soul. While we can and do misuse our free will, it is God's intention that we cooperate with the agapic love that can only will our own good and the good of all with whom we share the benevolent orientation to the Divine that is our destiny.

The principle of formability, its actualization and maintenance, implies another created capacity — that of form-direction or direction-ability. This means that our founding life form emerges and matures in congeniality with our innate direction by the mystery. All that we are and hope to be unfolds in compatibility with our here-and-now situation. Integral to this process is the guiding light emanating from the mystery at the center of our field of presence and action. Minerals, plants, atomic and subatomic particles also evolve in consonance with their preformed direction-ability. The Divine Forming and Preforming Mystery, revealed to believers as the Eternal Trinitarian Formation and Interformation Event, guides our distinctively human development on a time-table none of us can predict. To follow this directive light is to live in the readiness to be formed, reformed, and transformed within the framework of the promise that the Hand that made us is the very same Hand that will save us.

A vast variety of cosmic forms proves to the naked eye that natural creation is the first revelation. Sentient organisms in the plant and animal kingdom are endowed by their Creator with instinctual form directives. They gravitate spontaneously towards those appearances in the environment that provide them with all that they need to exist and survive in a restricted field of unfolding relevant to their emergence or demise. For us humans, these instinctual implants are not enough for survival. We need to assemble a storehouse of faith and formation traditions passed on from one generation to the next. Every custom from food preparation to burial rituals gathers around itself formation traditions that reflect the ethnic groups and cultures of people everywhere in the world.

Directives Bestowed on Us
in Our Human Field of Formation

Our life form emerged on earth with a small but relatively sufficient number of instinctual directives. Devoid of all but a few basic instincts, we had to disclose our own internal guidelines, not alone but in interformative interaction with other human beings over the millennia. In accordance with these self-disclosed and mutually interactive directives, we began to develop frames of reference embodied in formation traditions that would sustain our existence in time and space. The apparent chaos of the universe became over eons of formative evolution a meaningful cosmos, a distinctively human arena in which to follow our calling within the chosen or given community that constituted our family of origin. Among all the life forms in the cosmos, we had to seek direction from those that were disclosed to us as most relevant to our survival and emergence. If the sea was in front of us, we had to devise a worthy vessel to sail across it. If the forest was too thick to build a dwelling, we had to clear it. These increasingly delineated directives made it possible for us to listen to and obey our innate ability to receive form *from* and to give form *to* our field of life and the providential circumstances in which we found ourselves.

Human life gives rise to a continuous movement of receptive and donative form directives and their corresponding fulfillments. In this process, each of us uniquely and together with others develops sets of tightly intertwined and meaningful symbols, customs, artifacts, and traditions to help us in our ongoing pursuit of physical, emotional, and spiritual maturity. Religion has a significant role to play in this process. A belief system handed on from generation to generation provides us with tools, teachings, and traditions pertaining to all the events from birth to death that narrate in full our formation story.

There is no other way for us to survive than to disclose and maintain such transinstinctual directives and their sustaining formation traditions. They set us apart from every other form of life on earth: animal, vegetative, and mineral. In and through them we both internalize and externalize the form directives we receive from our ancestors. Taken together, they comprise our designated culture and its underlying and observable traditions of form-reception and donation.

The fields of meaning in which we humans live always point beyond "raw nature." Our accumulative formation traditions are the best means we have to cope with disaster when the loss of a sense of safety overtakes us often under tragic circumstances beyond our control. We rely on these traditions to see us through many crises of transition as we try to appraise their providential significance. Perennial and changing styles of life are all part of the process of giving and receiving form. Traditions are interwoven with the vicissitudes of our field of life and the meanings we attach to our unique-communal place and purpose on earth.

Telling Our Formation Story

The story of our emergence in a universe alive with symbolic significance has as the centerpiece of every chapter a series of directives each of us has to interiorize. They cover everything from what to wear to the proper words to use in private and public encounters. Each takes into account our gifts and limits. New directives reveal themselves in all phases of our unfolding. We remember, imagine, and anticipate the ways in which we process the countless experiences that together comprise the multi-faceted splendor of our formation field. We search for meaning imaginatively and reflectively, combining and recombining facts and symbols in new associations. We exercise reason and faith in trying to appraise which directives to follow and which to refuse. We structure and restructure all that happens to us personally and in our relationships. We do so at times with focal attention yet this redirecting process also goes on in the pre, intra, infra, inter, and transfocal regions of our consciousness.

In a period of intense mourning, to use but one example, we may be inclined to withdraw into a world of hopeless feelings cut off from the little lights that always shine in everyday reality. So intensely do we miss the person who has died, we disassociate from daily life. This inclination to inwardness deepens when our prospects for the future become too troubling to consider. It seems to us as if we can no longer maintain our own form-potency. Such a threat may be real or imaginary. A momentary strategic withdrawal may be advisable to save our sanity and to prevent our enslavement to unending obsessions about death and the promise of eternal reward or punishment.

Role of Memory, Imagination, and Anticipation

The incarnational sources of memory, imagination, and anticipation play a powerful role in determining the health or sickness of our soul. The word "incarnational" in this context means that these three innate structures can be used to serve the implementation of compatible or incompatible ideals and directives. To remember, to imagine, and to anticipate are ways of facilitating our intra, outer, and interformational decisions and actions.

Functioning wisely in a demanding world compels us to develop independent ways to embody our best choices and to make them concrete in wise and prudent ways to facilitate the betterment of our world. As we mature, we gain in the effectiveness of our own formability. Our potency to decide what to do or not to do sustains fidelity to our calling. We exercise our free will in respect for our own and others' capacity to give and receive form. We engage in reasonable appraisal and apply our conclusions effectively.

Consonant formation demands a balance between our own form-traditional resources and the limits and blessings to be found in our shared fields of life. Nothing we do, say, think or decide is done alone. The Divine Mystery that preforms, creates, and redeems us transcends the limited projects that express our dedication to our own personal, familial, and social life. Thanks to the power of transforming love, the most mundane events take on a deeper meaning.

One main function of formation traditions is to foster appreciation for the perennial truths that carry us to higher planes of wisdom. We express them in the events of our everyday life. Our transcendent imagination devises and articulates traditions associated with the form directives, ideals, and symbols that shed light on the bleakest periods in our history. We see with acute insightfulness what happened and what could have been if other decisions had been made. Our transcendent memory lets these insights live on in our consciousness. It enables us to recall them at appropriate times in relation to corresponding events and our attempts to understand them. Our transcendent anticipation deepens our readiness to be attentive to new pointers that increase our potency to give and receive form in the most challenging situations.

Formative ideals defined by our transcendent imagination ought not to be confused with the functional symbols we use in the daily execution of projects and tasks. The latter draw upon linguistic, artistic, and mechanistic techniques. Transcendent images and symbols, including sacred myths, rituals, and texts, do not have as their first aim the execution of practical plans and projects. As expressions of our holistic spirit, they enable us to unconceal in some small way the mystery of our emergence in cosmos and creation.

Classical formation traditions serve cultures and civilizations in an especially efficacious way. They pass on from one generation to the next a growing treasury of wisdom and truth. The incarnational resource of transcendent memory allows us to bring to light these divine and human direction disclosures, to interpret their meaning for our here-and-now existence, and to heighten our focal awareness of what is lasting or passing. The classical masters of any religious or ideological faith and formation tradition are able to re-articulate the transformative meaning of whatever inspires us as human beings. Their works encourage us to link our unique formative events with the communal bonds that prompt us to seek ways and means to live in peace.

Formative memory also reminds us to participate in supportive rituals that lend dignity to our calling to be givers, not takers of life. As Christians, we may, for example, renew our baptismal promises or our marriage vows, celebrate a special Eucharistic liturgy at Easter Vigil or participate in a solemnity like that of the anointing of the sick. Such rituals sustain the living remembrance of our being the people of God. When we read sacred texts or attend liturgical celebrations, we may experience not only a renewal of our faith but also a rekindling of the memory, imagination, and anticipation of the transcendent they spark. Certain traditions call our attention to the mystery itself, along with its many epiphanic expressions. Songs of praise and thanksgiving contain a tapestry of pneumatic and ecclesial images that invite us to a renewal of faith, hope, and love. These sets of symbolic pointers to the transcendent precede any scientific investigation of them. They belong first of all to our pre-scientific faith and formation traditions and only secondarily to the differential arts and disciplines that strive to analyze and define them.

Disclosures of Form-Traditional Directives

Form-traditional directives and the abundant harvest of disclosures they contain guide many generations-in-formation. Those who have gone before us have appraised and applied them as windows on a world of meaning that makes sense of life's peaks and valleys. They become part of an accepted collection of traditional directives validated by people over the ages who have amassed enough experience, knowledge, and expertise to propose them as foundational and lasting. This generational collaboration gives rise to a style of distinctively human formation that validates the journey taken by past, present, and future seekers of the Sacred.

Such disclosures would be impossible to confirm on the basis of only a few passing generations. Emerging traditions have to be purified of accretional interpretations. Each era spawns a set of candid critics who, over the course of history, are responsible for separating what is accidental to particular situations and what is foundational and conducive to any quest for a whole and holy life. Such universal directives may be concealed within the particular traditions handed over to us by former generations. To trace and disclose these foundationals is an arduous endeavor, but one well worth the effort. The mystery of transforming love charges each of us with the responsibility to heed the call to preserve the dignity of life and to pass on what we have learned of its worth to those who will come after us.

CHAPTER 2

Emergence of Christian Formation Traditions

Whether we regard tradition as the teaching authority of the Church, or the body of teaching itself, or the Church's act of teaching the deposit of faith, all three are mirrored in the history of the authentic transmission of God's revelation of himself to man in the person of the God-Man Jesus Christ.
— *Saint Augustine of Hippo*

Christian formation traditions emerge in tandem with the lived experience of believers committed to putting the revealed knowledge of their faith into practice. The season of Christmas comes readily to mind. The doctrine of the Incarnation tells us that at the appointed time Mary, Virgin and Mother, "gave birth to her first born son and wrapped him in bands of cloth, and laid him in a manger, because there was no place for them in the inn" (Luke 2:7). From this revelation and its luminous disclosures grew the customs, celebrations, and sharings that constitute the way in which nations and individuals remember this event and its confirmation of their faith in the Word made flesh (cf. John 1:14). This foundational faith tradition spawns numerous formation traditions, which become, in effect, the first teachers of the credal truth that "for us men and our salvation/he came down from heaven:/by the power of the Holy Spirit/he was born of the Virgin Mary, and became man." Influencing such traditions are the pluralistic fields of life in which we participate on a daily basis. The combined force of faith-illumined revelations and our diverse sociohistorical situations produces symbols, customs, rituals, and traditions that facilitate our ability to integrate what we believe and how we live these beliefs day by day, so that, in truth, we practice what we preach. We personalize the foundations of our faith every time we try to incorporate our experiences of intimacy with the Trinity into the details of daily life. Formation traditions shrink the distance between God's self-communications in Holy Scripture and our allowing his word to be "living and active, sharper than any two-edged sword...able to judge the thoughts and intentions of the heart" (Hebrews 4:12).

The formative knowledge that keeps our traditions alive can be both pre-systematic and systematic. The latter way involves a first level comprehension of questions pertaining to the "how-to" of effective form donation and reception. Our faith-illumined knowledge functions pre-systematically as a bridge between the information about the Revelation we imbibe as believers and the formation through which it permeates our everyday existence. All that we are and do in, with, and through Christ has to unfold in increasing consonance with the dimensions and dynamics of our human life form and within the ebb and flow of our cultural history. In a more systematic manner, we can look at our Christian formation traditions as somehow analogous to the structures and experiences that link what we know to be foundational for our life of faith and its temporal expressions in each of our maturation phases. Through study and prayer we come to a deeper understanding of the indelible link between our faith and formation traditions. We excel in their experiential adaptation, without undue accommodation, to the pluralistic society in which we find ourselves. To prevent the frenetic dissipation of our formation energy, we try to balance this situational compatibility with the congeniality of our own distinctive call and its lifelong, transforming effects on our obedient heart.

The foundations of our faith and formation traditions are expressed best in Holy Scripture and in the teachings of the classical masters, who have inspired followers of Christ from the first century to the present day. The core of all Christian wisdom and experience consists in our love for Christ as the animating center, the inmost founding form, of all we believe and live. Not only do we excavate the treasures of our tradition age upon age; we also bring this timeless treasury of truth to life in ways that bind us in the present to faithful seekers in the past. At all times, an overemphasis on adaptability at the expense of revealed truth is to be guarded against. In extreme cases it leads to forgetfulness of the formative wisdom and experience that is at the core of our Christian tradition. Its basic catechetical directives must continue to guide and inspire all true believers.

Blind absorption in sociohistorical pulsations may restrict our attention to only contemporary or popular traditions. Too much compromise in the name of cooperation places us at risk of losing our rootedness in the core beliefs we most treasure. The result is a confused and confusing picture of Christian identity that may be hard to distinguish from various shades of moral and social relativism. Without neglecting the development of the current and apparent expressions of our traditions, our actualization of them should be rooted in the timeless teachings upheld by the *ecclesia*. The art and discipline of formative reading of scripture and the masters preserves the nucleus of our faith and its wise and prudent modulations over the course of time.

Formative Reading as Preservative

Formative reading of the recognized classics of our tradition, beginning with the Bible, respects updated exegesis while at the same time being somewhat wary of linguistic and esthetic modes of literary criticism or revisionist historical analysis. Such reading fosters an empathic participation in the text and an adaptive approach to its meaning. These dispositions of docility allow our heart and mind to drink in deeper spiritual inspirations and to pursue their formative applications. Our task is to facilitate and safeguard this appreciative approach to the essentials of our tradition. We regard formative reading as a graced experience in which we witness first-hand the transforming effect of sacred words. They fill our consciousness with confidence. They soften our doubts and draw us with new hope into the life of our faith community. There is on our part neither undue compromise of these traditions nor a too exclusive concern to accommodate them to a few trendy side benefits that may erode the basics. Immersion in the core of our faith and formation traditions provides us with a trustworthy way to find and follow the truth. Like the Prodigal Son we return to the home of our Father (cf. Luke 15:24).

Formation traditions that have passed the test of time are less likely to succumb to the weight of too many accretions. At the same time, they represent particular expressions of our life within the present generation. Lasting traditions facilitate the integration of our basic human anthropology with our Christian formation theology. Some features of this integration, analogous to the way in which grace builds on, enlightens, and expands our nature, include the following:

1. The Eternal Trinitarian Formation and Interformation Event in itself and in its manifestations in all that is constitutes the core of our Christian faith and formation traditions. The Spirit's articulations of this all-embracing mystery are inexhaustible. Whatever we come to understand of the Revelation leaves us with that much more yet to be disclosed.

2. The initial and ongoing formation of our consonant Christian traditions is attributable to the presence of the Risen Lord, who is the animating founding or soul-form of our human life and who empowers us to embody his word in our everyday world.

3. The embodiment of our essence in God in our human existence is another way of saying that we participate in the incarnation

of Christ through the Holy Spirit in the whole of human and cosmic history and in the particulars of our own formation field.

4. Our unconditional, obedient abandonment in faith, hope, and love to the incarnational transforming event of Christ's presence among us, through the gifts and fruits of the Holy Spirit, models the basic abandonment that prepares us for our wholly transcendent passage from this life to the next.

5. The transformation of the spirit of non-Christian traditions, arts, sciences, and practices into possible means of grace by the Holy Spirit enables us to enrich our own faith traditions with insights and findings that are formationally relevant. They complement what we come to know by faith in the Risen Lord at the heart of history. His Spirit elevates and enlightens the ongoing development of these traditions, illuminating in the process the transcendent and pneumatic-ecclesial dimensions of our human life form.

6. The differentiation-integration dynamic that characterizes our phasic unfolding corresponds to the ongoing maturation of our Christian faith and formation traditions as the sustaining source of this growth uniquely and communally over countless generations.

7. Our formative dispositions may, under the impetus of grace, grow into a constellation of virtues inherent in our Christian heart. They uphold in turn the faith and formation traditions that affect the actual emergence of the Christ-form of our soul in the details of daily life. One of the transforming ideals espoused by Christianity—to respect the innate dignity and rights of other—gives rise to a host of directives that uphold in our formation traditions a culture of life over a culture of death.

The differentiation (diversity) and integration (unity) of our Christian traditions benefits from a faith-illumined dialogue with our formative events and the *from-through-to* pattern of change that alters our life for the better. When we begin to live day by day what we believe, our presence always influences our actions. Justice, peace, and mercy become the standard bearers of our life in Christ.

Differentiating and Integrating Structures of Our Christian Traditions

Our traditions differentiate themselves in ways analogous to the five main dimensions of our life form, namely, the sociohistorical, vital, functional, transcendent, and pneumatic as articulated in their respective pulsations, pulsions, ambitions, aspirations, and inspirations. Their formative meanings, dynamics, sources, and historical conditions must be taken into account as we appraise how these traditions are formatively or deformatively disclosed and experienced in both Christian and pre-Christian forms of life.

The initial integration of these five differentiations of our Christian traditions corresponds to the three main structures of our empirical self: the core, current, and apparent. Foundational or core traditions represent the living presence of Christ in the *ecclesia* and in the soul of every believer through the grace of the Holy Spirit. All the dimensions and structures of our faith have to unfold in congeniality with the Christ-form of our soul and its disclosures in our encounters with others. Manifestations of the forming presence of Christ in their varigating splendor are then formulated in the context of our traditions under the guidance of the Spirit and the legitimate guardians of our faith.

Constituting the core of our Christian tradition are its basic tenets, inspirations, and aspirations as rooted in the scriptural and doctrinal foundations of the Revelation. Such tenets coform the enduring heart of our belief system and its living reality as represented in rituals, symbols, and writings of universally acknowledged witnesses to the faith from its inception to the present day.

Current Christian expressions of our traditions reflect the concerns, needs, and interests characteristic of our here-and-now fields of life. They are to be rooted in our faith traditions, seen as the most congenial expressions of the always animating presence of Christ in our daily lives. He is the heart of all that we are and do in the various segments of the population we represent as well as in the historical phases of our Christian maturation.

Our apparent Christian expressions of believing and living affect the way we appear when we witness to Christ in private and public life. This self-representation of our faith and formation traditions has to be as compassionate with individuals abandoned in body and soul as with whole populations suffering unjust persecution. Crimes against humanity call for our help as Christians committed to living the foundations of our faith as courageously as possible. Serving others through its myriad formative articulations enables us to translate Gospel-centered ideals into effective projects that radiate the love of God for all people.

Actualization of Our Christian Traditions

Our actual life form becomes the comprehensive arena in which our Christian traditions are implemented. It integrates the original dimensions, dynamics, and structures that constitute our steadily unfolding life call and its faith-illumined appraisals, affirmations, and applications. Aided by the Holy Spirit, we try to respond to the challenges facing us in the fields of life in which our Christian commitments must come to the fore. This sensitive and responsible accommodation in faith, hope, and love to our own and others' needs remains congenial with the Christ-form of our soul; compatible with the foundations of our faith and formation traditions; compassionate for our own and others' wounded condition; and competent in response to the global quest for wholeness and holiness of life.

Consonance in Christ calls for obedient fidelity to his ongoing incarnation in the core of our being and in all quadrants of our formation field. We become fully Christian to the degree that our lives model the integration of the core, current, and apparent structures of our faith tradition and its actual expression in the decisions and demands we face daily. Nothing matters more to us than what Christ himself would do in this situation. We pray that grace will lead us to new plateaus of spiritual maturity characterized by the courage to live what we believe and the candor to admit when our faith and our everyday formation in family life, church, and society have become either more fully harmonized or more tragically disconnected.

CHAPTER 3

Formation Traditions as Bridges to Human and Christian Living

When my Son was lifted up on the wood of the most holy cross he did not cut off his divinity from the lowly earth of your humanity. So though he was raised so high he was not raised off the earth. In fact, his divinity kneaded into the clay of your humanity like one bread. Nor could anyone walk on that bridge until my Son was raised up.
— *Saint Catherine of Siena*

There is nothing in our human and Christian journey, from our first gasp of air to our dying breath, that has not been influenced by the traditions and customs of formation we have assimilated from our earliest years. The form our life has taken can only be properly understood if we consider the traditions we have imbibed through intimate contacts with our parents, family members, neighborhoods, towns, schools, churches, and places of labor and leisure.

Traditions govern the ways in which we give and receive form in everyday life. They have a direct influence on our dispositions. They complement and ideally comply with the theological truths of our adhered to faith traditions. Their tenets are protected and promulgated by informational theology. In the affairs of daily life, we tend to be guided more immediately by the traditions we deem to be most formative — those that effect for better or worse our decisions and actions. The powerful role they play in our lives must not be overlooked. Neither must we ignore their possible distortions or contaminations by other traditions. Informational theology must stand in the background of the everyday implementation of our faith. It facilitates our understanding of why we ought to respond to Christ's call in the light of our whole credal system. Pastoral guidelines rooted in formation anthropology complement the findings of philosophy and theology. Neither field aims to engage in the detailed art and discipline of dealing with the changes and challenges we face in our becoming more like Christ. Neither can this kind of divine guidance be sought in sciences like sociology and psychology. Many of the ideas we assimilate from therapeutic schools, while helpful, may be contaminated by their own underlying assumptions and popularized formulations. These may neither be conducive to nor compatible with our Judeo-Christian faith and formation traditions. Formation theology provides a frame of reference that prevents the unappraised borrowing of concepts from the human and social sciences without sufficient awareness of their possible contaminations by alien or alienating points of view.

Any distinctively human formation tradition strives to deepen and expand the age old yet ever new teachings that respect life at all stages. Approaches to education, formation counseling, and spiritual direction of groups and individuals must uphold our human dignity under all circumstances. We ought to develop a renewed appreciation for the form-traditional elements that honor all aspects of life and labor. These wisdom traditions complement the contributions of other kinds of arts and disciplines that focus on our vital nature, our functional skills, and our transcendent longings. Every time we hunger and thirst for truth, we attach ourselves to the vast treasury of faith and formation traditions that embody humanity's quest for God.

We cannot live as traditionless creatures. Our human life form differs essentially from those forms of life that are not endowed by our Creator with insight and freedom. We can only survive if we remain reasonably compatible with our surroundings while not being determined by them. The subhuman powers of form reception and donation we witness in animals rely primarily on instinctual directives. We have the burden and blessing laid upon us to appraise which aspects of our surroundings are either beneficial or detrimental to our congenial, compatible, compassionate, and competent unfolding.

An instinctual attunement to subhuman directives that flow forth instantly and automatically produces patterns of behavior that enable a species to adapt to environmental conditions that assure its survival. Due to this instantaneous and instinctual process, subhuman forms of life survive and evolve in environments that enable them to fit smoothly into their surroundings like keys fit into keyholes. Animals do not have to reflect on how to form, reform, or transform their lives into well organized fields of presence and action. We humans have to cope with such questions all the time.

Not being endowed as animals are with regulated instincts, we have to find ways and means to make up for this lack of instinctual attunement to natural and cosmic forces. We do so by means of our spiritual powers of insight and experience, accompanied at times by lightning speed appraisal and reflective pauses. Sentient beings translate whatever is relevant to their survival into predictable actions. Lacking the certainty biological determinism allows, we have to cope with the fact that the cosmos we inhabit appears occasionally as chaotic. Our first striving as free and insightful human beings is to receive and give form to our surroundings. We come to understand that we are a field of formation that is meaningfully ordered and even predictable in some respects while still remaining relatively free and unique to each individual person. Once traditions take the place of instincts, we have the means to search together for ways to increase our awareness of who we are and why we have been placed by providence in this world. We sense the close connection between what is congenial with our human nature and consonant with the Christ-form of our soul.

Horizontal and Vertical Interformation

Our only way to survive and grow as human beings is by interforming with one another in faith, hope, and love, in justice, peace, and mercy. *Horizontal interformation* includes the communications and interactions that take place between us and those individuals and populations with whom we are in contact on a more or less daily basis. Our cordial togetherness encourages us to be more compassionate towards our own and others' vulnerability. We gain in the knowledge of our mutual needs through conversation and encounter. We share in trust our problems and potentials. We may extend our concern to causes like the protection of subhuman species in danger of extinction or ways to address the tragic consequences of world hunger.

Vertical interformation happens between us and the generations that preceded us in their quest for truth. This connection with what occurred before we existed and with what we may anticipate being done after our departure from this earth is part and parcel of our temporal make-up. Together with our predecessors we try to trace the impact of formationally relevant thoughts and actions of the past on our world today. We are not alone in this undertaking. Total isolation from the experience and wisdom of ancestral family members and friends, of the teachers to whom we turned for help, would put our staying power and our progress at risk. All of us profit from the wisdom of countless others who teach us by example. The results of their appraisals and applications constitute the deposit of truth held in common by a rich variety of pre-Christian and Christian faith and formation traditions.

It is from this body of wisdom that we learn how to find our own way to the Divine as the unifying source of universe, humanity, and history. Traditions of this depth sustain and are sustained by various disciplines. Among them would be the comparative study of religions and the history of spirituality. Complementing the data disclosed by these disciplines is a vast treasury of formation wisdom. In it we find illustrated the manner in which people of many diverse times and places have attempted to live their faith compatibly and compassionately in fidelity to their heartfelt convictions and in response to the demands of their religious beliefs and life situations.

Formation traditions are like gathering places for sincere conversations between adherents of the same and different faith traditions. History compels us to discuss and record similar facets of our faith journey. We need to be up front and honest about our points of dissension and consensus; about our tentative integrations and failures, our mutual misunderstandings and moments of respect; about our shared purposes and regrettable prejudices.

Our human life form *is* traditional through and through. The effectiveness of our sojourn in space and time depends on our interformation with others. We must take into account our past and present attempts to give form to life in response to the challenges we face everyday. We cannot shirk the difficult task of exploring alone and with others the remnants of certain traditions that are more accretional than foundational. Cultural directives, symbols, and social institutions are seedbeds of our emergence as acting persons and as followers of Christ. Yet to really understand them in depth, we must dive below their appearances at any given moment of time to explore the form-traditions to which they gave rise. We must not be deterred by the fact that certain accretions have embedded themselves in our non-focal consciousness. It is our task to discern the difference between what constitutes traditions emanating solely from a particular culture and what is of lasting influence on us and others.

Training in the human and social sciences familiarizes us with the standard idea of culture and the role it plays in our individual and common life. It ought not to surprise us that such sciences, because they are relatively recent in the annals of humankind, may not pay sufficient attention to the implicit and explicit power of formation traditions. Cultures in general are only indicators, mirrors, shells or shadows of our life together compared to the all-pervasive power of religious and ideological traditions. The so-called unscientific status of the latter carriers of wisdom ought not to fool us. The concepts of nature and culture may seem more objective in the context, let us say, of the practice of therapy or the analysis of economic trends, but we must not be so mesmerized by these sciences of measurement that we underestimate the power faith and formation traditions exude in everyday life.

Such social sciences as psychology, cultural anthropology, and the study of demographics contribute to our grasp of why certain formation traditions become more significant than their underlying faith foundations, but they cannot exhaust their meaning. Their vision usually restricts itself to the role culture and society play in the formation of our environment. However, it is impossible to grasp the meaning of life only through the window of sociohistorical determinants. We must not neglect our overall transcendent and pneumatic-ecclesial orientation.

Human Nature and Formation Traditions

The attention we pay to culture as an end in itself has been overrated at the expense of our ongoing appraisal of the effects on us of faith-filled or merely secularistic formation traditions. What does such an emphasis do to our understanding of sheer "nature?" Is it not a more powerful influence than traditions? How, then, are nature and formation-by-tradition related to each other? Has our concern for the forming power of traditions simply been added to our natural potency to give form to our life? Or does it in some way change the direction of this potency? What power does nature as such exert in the ongoing emergence of our field of life?

From the beginning of Western civilization, thinkers have been concerned about the part nature plays in our lives. The reason for this fascination may be traceable to the fact that nature in the raw is inseparable from the essence of who we are as existing creatures. Out of this "natural essence" emerges the powers and potentials, the gifts and limits, with which we are basically endowed. Our actualization of them coincides with the providential continuity of our life in one or the other direction for however long we live. The course of our existence seems in this sense to be natural. An almost homogeneous way of understanding life, of growing up and doing our work, seems to happen without much forethought. So natural does our progress feel that for the most part we sense little or no need to ponder the way in which formation traditions influence our lives. They are simply there for us to follow like driftwood meanders down the stream of a river without questioning where these currents may be leading.

Influence of Traditions on Our Nature

The moment we introduce the concept of formation traditions into the forefront of our consciousness, our life becomes more challenging. We are no longer carried on the tide of the unchangeable current set by nature. Doing what is natural is fine to a degree, but in itself it does not offer us a sufficient explanation of how we and others receive and give concrete form to our lives. Formation traditions complicate the easy "going along" mode nature allows; they initiate a tension between our human essence and the way in which we choose to actualize our gifts and limits in the course of our existence.

The more we adhere to certain formation traditions, the more they enable us to move in the directions favored by us in fidelity to our unique-communal life call. Obviously the directions they prompt us to follow should neither deny nor dismiss who we essentially are. In some way we must check to be sure they are in tune with the essence of our life. There must be a consonant flow between the directions given to us by grace and our nature as human beings. Many of the core dispositions we derive from our formation traditions come into our heart by a kind of "symbiotic" process. After a while, they become second nature to us. As such, they are surely not prescribed in concrete detail by our anthropological make-up. However, there is in our nature a dynamic predisposition to go beyond self-centered gain and satisfaction. There is also a potency planted in us by grace for selfless love, dedication, and surrender, even of our life, for a noble cause. How we direct this dynamic, how we dispose ourselves to foster it or to let ourselves be aided by it, depends in great measure on the traditions in which we were formed initially in childhood or with which we later chose to align ourselves in the light of our foundational faith traditions.

Formation traditions are the seedbed of life directives that in their particular details and dynamics are more than what human nature prescribes. By the same token, they are rooted in our nature insofar as they shape and guide the predispositions inherent in them. Such directives are often inspired by the traditions to which we were already exposed in our family of origin. These directives and the formation traditions they serve may or may not be consonant with the ideal distinctive form or essence God intended as ours.

What is typically human is linked to our transcendent aspirations and the ambitions we utilize to embody them. Their actualization can help us to be competent with our gifts and talents while also being congenial with our founding form of life. What is distinctively human is our call to be spiritual beings and servants of the mystery. Guiding us is our human potential for loving appreciation of the beautiful manifestations of a higher benevolence. Connecting our typically human aptitudes and our transcendent longings is the faith formation that gives our life ultimate meaning and purpose.

The question of our beginnings and our endings raises many unanswerable speculations. Our origin is as much a mystery to us as our demise. What do we really know after all? We believe we are preformed by the all-embracing love of Father, Son, and Holy Spirit, but in what way does this mystery of creation, redemption, and sanctification accompany us during our earthly journey? Are we responsible to our mysterious source for the form we give to our life and world? Is that nameless spring of our life and its formation personal or impersonal? Different traditions offer different answers to these ultimate questions. We cannot exist as distinctively human without referring, however implicitly, to our basic nature and its mysterious origins and ends.

Bridging the seeming chasm between our essence in the Godhead, on the one hand, and our empirical existence, on the other, is our foundational or founding life form, which may be described as a bridge between essence and existence, partaking of both in a mysterious manner. Our formation has to manifest a fundamental congeniality with this sacred ground as our inmost reality. Then our existence becomes a gracious expression, a radiant mirror, of the essential destiny the mystery has preformed, created, and redeemed for the sake of our temporal and eternal happiness.

From our essence comes the uniquely transcendent nature of our life and our ultimate calling. From our empirical existence comes our genetic-vital and our sociohistorical-functional make-up. These facets of our formation come together to constitute the fundament on which we build our life in response to God's grace. These socio-vital-functional and transcendent coformants coalesce in intimate interwovenness at the very baseline of our uniquely individual formation from birth to death. They are the basic givens we must respect and obey if we want to attain consonance in the core of our being.

Chapter 4

Traditional Formation in Pluritraditional Settings

Today many who have been formed or deformed—by a sort of pragmatism and a utilitarianism, seem to ask: "When all is said and done, what is the use of believing? Does faith offer something more? Isn't it possible to live an honest upright life without bothering to take the Gospel seriously?
— Pope John Paul II

The story of our life, whether we know it or not, is interlaced with traditions like a weaving that is so tight it cannot be torn apart. Whether familial, professional, social, or spiritual, these traditions guide our "eucharists of everydayness." From childhood on, we feel their influence in our life as much as the air we breathe. We experience our faith long before we receive training in the catechesis behind it. When the adults around us practice what they preach, our chances of remaining faithful increase. When pious words do not embody proper actions, our life of faith is at risk of being deformed temporarily, if not permanently. Our formation traditions bridge the gap between our faith traditions and the pluritraditional settings in which we find ourselves. Perhaps more than at any other time in history we are covered with a multicolored quilt of diverse cultures and traditions threading through our global world. Protestant, Catholic, democratic, capitalistic, individualistic, and functionalistic ways of life characteristic of Western Europe and America influence us not occasionally but all at once.

The formation traditions embedded in this inventory of influences coform our culture and reflect our responses to the realistic demands made upon us by family, church, and society. We learn to modulate the traditions passed on to us by previous generations in accordance with what our current culture prescribes. Sheer observation reveals that Italian, Dutch, Scottish, Mexican, and Asian adherents of the same Catholic or Protestant faith tradition differ in their formative expressions of it. Cross-fertilizations occur continuously between cultures and faith traditions. An implicit process of selectivity also takes place in regard to the lasting and passing formation traditions alive in our own or any other culture. No matter what issue we have to tackle, we bring the knapsack of our formation traditions to the table. We explore both old and new ways of giving form to traditions and then adapting them to our current cultural needs.

We have to find ways of integrating and differentiating between our already existing culture and the formation traditions of others if peaceful dialogue is to prevail. Since culture itself is an adaptive constellation of underlying faith and formation traditions, the nature of these complex selective processes can neither be overlooked nor considered of little consequence. The opposite is true. We must be willing to focus on exactly what constitutes them, on their shifting structures of power, and on the role they play in the rise and fall of a single culture or a whole nation.

Accelerating Emergence of Pluritraditionality

At this moment of history, our world is pluritraditional. We live in a time of critical upheaval. The dynamic history of humanity and Christianity is in the forefront of our consciousness as we cross the threshold to the Third Millennia. We observe on all levels of life an accelerated transition from unitraditional to multitraditional cultures, ranging from the West to the Far East, from North to South America, from India and Africa to the entire Middle East. In past eras, it may have been more possible to let traditions carry us in a non-focal way. A clear understanding and identification of them and their meaning did not seem necessary in a more or less monolithic society. Now we are more vulnerable to the formation directives popularized by so many new traditions, many of which may be incompatible with the basic faith traditions we have freely chosen as our own.

As the pace of development of other past and present traditions accelerates, additional problems arise. Scientific and experiential data, previously unknown, archeological and historical findings, literary and artistic innovations—all multiply daily. Under the impact of popularized media and public education, many sincere seekers wonder what these new life directives may mean in relation to their own more familiar traditions. They may not yet be able to see how they may be compatible with the beliefs they have tightly held onto for so long a time.

Our articulation of this reality becomes more effective when we tackle it from the viewpoint of our understanding of human nature as formational. The way we appraise unfamiliar or totally foreign formation traditions should be complemented by our empirical, experiential, and ecclesial knowledge of who we most deeply are as seen in the light of our adhered to faith and formation traditions. The more our world becomes part of a global internet of nations, the more we must be ready to engage in an analysis of pluritraditional cultures as collections of the significant traditions that give form to them. We usually select prefocally those elements available in a culture that will both conform to and coform with our own traditions. We seek to understand not only our differences but our kinships. The pursuit of Christian unity draws us to claim and proclaim the ways in which we are similar in many respects. From what draws us together we begin to formulate a fund of directives. We do have certain traits in common, but we must not live in the illusion that these generalized characteristics are enough to increase our understanding of other people or their pluritraditional circumstances. It takes much time and effort to come to such clarity.

The prevalence of the human and social sciences—to name but a few, anthropology, sociology, psychology, and education—makes it more possible in the present age to research both cultural determinants and freely chosen form-traditional directives. The latter lend themselves to measurement, definition, control, statistical treatment, and clear-cut comparisons. Focus on the measurable facets of a culture may result in a detailed analysis of the traits its people have in common. We can learn a great deal from this kind of probing into factors in a culture that seem to predetermine its direction, provided they are integrated into a distinctively humane and perhaps Christian frame of reference. The strength of a culture paradoxically often coincides with its unique limitations.

Instead of trying to alter this orientation or change this method of analysis, we have opted to initiate a new, complementary science and anthropology that enable us to focus on the way in which both our human nature and our basic theology of divine grace come to life in our formation traditions. We include in this research an exploration of their transforming effects on both our pretranscendent and our transcendent life. Our intent is neither to rob ourselves of the particular contributions of the positivistic sciences from which we should profit nor to confuse their focus with our own ultimately pretheological and form-theological concerns.

Impact of Traditional Plurality

When we meditate on our journey so far, we realize that we have been formed by a plurality of traditions. To be sure, French, German, Dutch, Italian, Hispanic, Chinese, Indian, Middle and Far Eastern, and African Americans share many life directives. Still within these common cultural traditions, they remain attuned in many ways to their own ethnic vision and lingual articulation of life and world in the United States. Each of us by background and choice falls under the implicit or explicit influence of the faith and formation traditions we call our own. This selection is modified day after day by the directives we imbibe from other traditions unavoidably encountered in the historical circumstances in which we live.

Our world has become a vast internet of multiple, coexisting traditions. Side by side with faith traditions like the Protestant, Catholic, Jewish, Islamic, Hindu, and Buddhist, we are bombarded by the forces of capitalism, socialism, agnosticism, atheism, individualism, aestheticism, hedonism, and functionalism; we recognize distinct lines of division among the upper, middle, and lower classes. The list of these formative and possibly deformative influences seems to be endless.

Add to them others like the academic, the military, the clerical, and the corporate, and we see immediately the inescapable reality of the pluriformity of traditions on our everyday modes of form-reception and donation.

Central to our understanding of a pluritraditional society is the concept we have evolved of the "form-tradition pyramid." It expresses the fact that in pluritraditional cultures and other emerging societal settings undergoing rapid change, we all live by personal and shared "pyramids" of formation traditions. Many directives disclosed in our "pyramid" affect us on different levels of our interiority and in the exteriority characteristic of our daily existence in an increasingly interconnected world.

We can diagram this difference of intensity of form-traditional influences by means of a pyramidical structure. At the base of the pyramid we situate the foundational faith and formation traditions to which we are committed. The levels of influence extending upward from this base comprise congenial and compatible expressions of our chosen belief systems as lived within our here-and-now field of life. For example, if the base of our pyramid is our life in Christ, the line above it may be devotion to our family or community and above that to our professional and ministerial commitments. On the smaller lines extending to the top of the pyramid, we may depict less influential formation traditions like those pertaining to ongoing education and timely recreation. The aim of this pyramidical structure is to integrate over a lifetime all such directive influences as servant sources of our adhered to faith tradition. The point at the top of the pyramid represents the actual penetration of our personal pyramid into our shared field of formation. Taken as a whole, this pyramid depicts a kind of lived synopsis of all our formation traditions as more or less unfolding in fidelity to our foundational faith tradition. It ought to remain the integrative base of our pyramid whereas the top of this structure stands for its actual penetration into our formation field as a whole.

Every person's pyramid is both a here-and-now reflection of their life and a record of the changes that have happened to them. For this reason any pyramid we design should be open to reformations demanded of us by the appraisals we make of the pre- and post-conversion experiences that impact our field of life. For example, a concern for ecology in our society may lead to the emergence of institutionalized ecological formation traditions. We may decide to adapt our own pyramid in such a way that we integrate within it compatible ecological directives that are of more concern to us now than certain educational or entertainment needs used to be. In service of such compatibility we seek to disclose sustaining faith directives that were perhaps less emphasized in our past or less elaborated in previously prevalent formation traditions. For example, those that typified the Industrial Revolution had less concern for the quality of air and water that we do today when everyone is aware of the threat of air pollution and global warming.

Personal and Institutional Aspects of Formation Traditions

Formation traditions that are both personal and institutional may mirror a deeper, more mature adherence to foundational faith traditions and their transpersonal enduring structures. At each successive phase of maturation, we need to initiate, with the help of grace, a new compatibility striving that results in a more committed response to our ever changing field of presence and action. Following the collapse of the Berlin Wall, the world witnessed a cataclysmic upheaval in former adherents of the Leninist-Stalinist regime. The atheistic-materialistic formation traditions that dominated their world collapsed along with the Wall. People had no choice but to alter their economic and political outlook in a radical way that would overturn the previous seventy-five years of communist power and propaganda. Such passionate commitment to freedom sparked life-changing personal and social appraisal. Effected in turn was the conversion of an entire culture and the rise and fall of many new and outworn formation traditions. The former reflected the pyramidical layers of those who were open to these changes; the latter reflected the endurance of old customs that had provided stability for segments of the population not ready to let them go.

Reliance upon a formation tradition ought not to become so rigid that the needs, aspirations, and insights of significant numbers of people crying for change do not gain the ground they deserve. The structures of a tradition must be flexible enough to enable us to personalize them in unique as well as common ways. A truly alive tradition enriches itself by disclosing new avenues for its effective implementation of our faith without severing it from the base of our pyramid.

There are times in history when individuals may be so overwhelmed by the sheer power of a tradition that they subject themselves to its directives uncritically as happened in the Nazi regime. To cite another example of the same, a young lady, wanting to look slender, may refuse to eat a diet balanced enough to nurture her physical and spiritual well being. An anorexic mentality may cancel any sensible affirmations of her vital needs. She may fall into a habit of blind compliance with the directives of a popularized form-tradition promoting a "twiggy" image of the "ideal" feminine figure.

The hold such traditions have on our lives explains why we may think of them as if they were organisms with a life of their own, independent of historical events, but such is not the case. Traditions in and by themselves do not control us. If they make such an impact upon us, we need to reassess what caused us to allow them to gain such power in the first place. One example would be the form-tradition of consumerism. Towards it we followers of the Gospel need to make a freer, less coerced response. Do we want to buy a product because it is being pushed by the media or because we really need it? Our own dispositions and decisions play a part in the power or lack thereof behind a formation tradition. This is not to say that on our own we can halt or redirect the historical course a tradition like consumerism may take. No matter how critical of it we may be, we cannot by ourselves alone effect the continuity of or the change in a formation tradition. Many forces are at work in this process, but formation theology aims to aid our analysis of what role these alterations play in the ongoing emergence of our spiritual and social life. The light it sheds on our fields of presence and action always emanates from our underlying faith tradition.

Connections Within Our Pyramid Structure

The foundation of our form-traditional pyramid is the generally religious or specifically Christian faith tradition to which we pray to be committed for a lifetime. It is the deepest ground of our emergent existence. In its light we acknowledge the place and purpose of the other formation traditions depicted in our pyramid. Their location on successive rungs of this diagram is indicative of the lesser influence they exert on us. Commitment to our basic tradition encourages us to submit each of these traditions to full field appraisal to ascertain to what degree they are compatible with the foundations of our own Christ-centered, Gospel-oriented, and ecclesially directed life as a whole.

Wise appraisal of the compatibility between our own preferred directives and those of other traditions is a complex process. It is perhaps more demanding than the implementation of the results of this process in our everyday life. A first step is to admit that, in spite of our best efforts, the diverse traditions by which we live may not yet be in tune with our basic faith tradition. Our pyramid looks more like a syncretic collection of what "hangs in the air" than a well-ordered plan of life centered in appreciative abandonment to the mystery. Rather than basing our intentions on the Christian ideal of loving service for the sake of others, we may have allowed influences like consumerism, materialism, and careerism to slip into the base of our pyramid. Power, pleasure, and possession may then erode our life of prayer.

If we allow such cultural pulsations alien to the Gospel to dominate our decisions and actions, we may discover that our life has become a shallow assimilation of directives incompatible with our faith. Before sheer ego-desperation overtakes us, we need to examine the strength or weakness of our belief system. To what degree has it been eroded by our adherence to popularized traditions that wittingly or unwittingly have replaced perennial Gospel truths? Lest we lose the chance to change in response to grace, we must address these questions with candor and courage.

Infiltration by New Traditions

A new tradition may begin to infiltrate a society prior to its becoming widely known and accepted by the population. The quest for freedom in formerly tyrannical nations exemplifies that the tradition of liberation can only become a reality when a significant number of people allow it to interform with the common traditions of faith and formation to which they already adhere. We can communicate neither with one another nor with people bound to other traditions without the search for some common ground with which all of us are in agreement. Tradition itself functions as our dialogical frame of reference. It is the setting for that about which we agree to disagree agreeably.

A new tradition cannot be communicated to a sufficient number of people eager for change without being preceded by some interformative dialogue based on traditions already familiar to us. A good example is the convergence of Christianity with Middle and Far Eastern traditions. Any premature ending of dialogue in preference for the imposition of one religion on another will only cause further misunderstanding and may lead to reactive rather than responsive interformation.

Newly introduced traditions must be linked, if possible, to already existing ones. Spreading the Gospel rests on this principle of respectful interformation. It readies us to critique both the old ways to which we have grown accustomed and the new ones that may forecast needed changes in far away places as well as in our own backyard. Out-worn traditions that promote rampant individualism are less likely to last when Christian or other spiritual ideals of self-giving love gain ascendance. Such movements remind us of the need to form and reform our traditions in the face of recognized challenges and calls for renewal.

To achieve this end requires the wise and prudent modulation of our formation traditions without compromising the foundations of our sustaining faith traditions. This open-ended approach also means that our particular traditions have to remain in tune with compatible changes in our shared ways of giving and receiving form and in respect for our dedication to the common good. It is our duty to question facets of any tradition—personal or communal—that run contrary to what we believe by virtue of our baptism and our longing to radiate the light of Christ in every corner of our world.

The faith foundations of the Gospel must find new expressions in our pluritraditional fields of meaning. Potential articulations of the consonant traditions represented in our post-conversion pyramid need to be seen as beneficial to us and others. Our goal as believers is to focus less on what divides us and more on how much we have in common. Whether we are committed Christians or sincere seekers of truth, we must continue to converse in peace, to avoid useless conflicts, and to practice charity.

CHAPTER 5

Formation Theology and Transformational Traditions

Open your compassion to all God's disciples. Don't be put off by appearance or age. Don't fret about those who seem to be penniless, ragged, ugly or feeble and turn away from them. For within their human form dwells hidden the Father and the Son who died for us and rose with us.
  — Saint Clement of Alexandria

As Christians alive at this moment in the history of humanity, we may understandably feel torn between standing on the firm ground of catechetical teachings and being swamped by waves of rapid transition. The time of living in a relatively uniform society under the jurisdiction of believers who helped to shape Western civilization is by all accounts a bygone era. The enclaves of dependable disciples populating medieval Europe have long ago given way to diverse groups of people representing many different humanistic and religious persuasions. All of us have been exposed to a massive diversification of directives and styles of life. Faced as we are by this bewildering number of options and living in a world of increasingly complex traditions touching every aspect of daily life, we may find ourselves at a loss when it comes to knowing how to give form to our true calling in the Lord.

Beguiled as we are by the avalanche of fascinating and seductive products promoted by the media, we may find ourselves being formed according to the dictates of many alien traditions rather than growing as Christ-centered disciples in accordance with the laws of God. We become so adept at adopting new styles of living to be in tune with what is current that we neglect to respond to the ways of the Lord. We define ourselves mainly on the basis of what we earn and on how others assess our worth. We become the secular roles we play to gain the approval of the world. In the process we may betray the image of Christ that should permeate and transform all that we are and do. We take on new patterns of living without appraising whether or not they are in tune with our calling in Christ. We slide along thoughtlessly, bewitched by an unrelenting onslaught of secularistic propaganda.

Propelled by the desire to be "in" with the times, we may soon find ourselves forging along on paths that prove to be at odds with our inner divine direction. Loss of the sense of our life call as unique and communal may cause us to search so desperately for happiness that we end up with substitutes for the transcendent. In our compulsion to be current, we may rush after any fad that offers a quick solution to a quest for meaning already obscured by too many dissonant motifs. An astonishing variety of choices undreamt of in ages past spreads out before us on a smorgasbord of pluralistic traditions. Expressing our true calling within the realistic limits placed upon us becomes exhausting. As we try to find our way through this dense forest of conflicting directives, we may lose our moral compass. Though it may seem as if we have gained more chances to exercise personal decision-making in a climate of pluriformity, it is equally clear that we have lost the stability associated with respect for authority and obedience to basic values.

The time has come to once again celebrate our faith as a source of formative wisdom, which, like leaven, must spread through the dough of a distraught humanity. The words of Christ, the wisdom of the Church, must not fall on deaf ears in the postmodern world. Creative formation of our life and world in the light of doctrine and tradition is a personal responsibility all of us need to take seriously. Secular society is no match for the sacralized formation of a Christian life. The Master calls each of us as members of his "little flock" to hear and heed the message he etches on our heart. He warned us that many would come to lead us astray: "And you will hear of wars and rumors of wars; see that you are not alarmed, for this must take place...nation will rise against nation, and kingdom against kingdom, and there will be famines and earthquakes in various places..." (Matthew 24:5-7). Christ does not predict that the end is near but rather that these are the "beginnings of the birth pangs" (24:8) associated with our being commissioned by him to teach others everything he has commanded us (cf. Matthew 16:20).

Every baptized soul is answerable to him. In prayer and contemplation, we must ponder how to live the Christian life in this new situation in which he predicted we would be. Our task is to so internalize the teachings of our faith that everything we do becomes an epiphany of who we are. We must detach ourselves from the least expectation that we can ever return to a uniform cultural code telling us in minute detail how to incarnate Christ in our life and world. Christian formation and its supportive disciplines guide the search for our destined place in God's eternal plan. Our faith traditions, as rooted in scripture and the teachings of the spiritual masters, inspire the formative dispositions and virtues that enable us to be radiant manifestations of the Christ-form within us. They ready us to do what we can to transform our humble habitations into the house of God.

When spirituality of this depth is put into practice, it heightens our awareness of the socio-vital-functional obstacles that prevent full disclosure of our divine life direction. Our fidelity to the Spirit-illumined guidance we receive is always at risk of faltering. On the pretranscendent level, we may need to avail ourselves of the formationally relevant insights and findings of disciplines like psychology and sociology that may offer us some ways and means of coping with these obstacles. The grace of God may let us see in them a new formation opportunity as we attempt to reformulate what we learn in the light of Christian doctrine. Such a sympathetic understanding of how grace builds on nature to form the life of Christ in us may lead to continual conversion of heart and an ease of spiritual and social presence and action that may surprise us.

A systematic theology of formation also assists us in seeing our human anthropology as a servant source of our becoming a "new creation" in Christ (cf. 2 Corinthians 5:17). The classical and potentially classical wisdom rooted in our adhered to faith and formation traditions provides many points of light for Christian transformation in the fullest sense. The events that move us from a less to a more Christ-centered way of life may prove to be painful, but, as the following account of a dear friend of ours shows, we do grow wise through suffering:

> Last week a surgeon removed the squamous cancer that had recently metastasized just below the big patch on O's face. He was not able to get what they call clean margins and we learned for the first time about the possibility of it moving into the lymph system, for which there is no treatment. This is the next step in our medical journey. The guess is that within two to six months the cancer will have had its way, though it is impossible to be precise...
>
> We have been at the ranch for three weeks. Instead of gaining appetite and energy as the radiation effects diminished, O has become more frail, but his spirit remains strong. We are both slowly absorbing this last turn of events. We are comforted by being home, sitting on the porch swing

observing beaver and moose, watching from our big bed the full moon flood the river, waking up to the mighty protection of the Wind Rivers, seeing sleek black cows wandering through the sage. And, indeed, we feel immensely blessed by our beloved family and friends praying, helping, and supporting us all the way.

As you know, O has been uncomplaining and brave from the start. We shuffled every day four blocks over to Sloan Kettering for eight weeks of radiation and then back. He went down to 122 pounds, lost much of his hearing along with his eyesight, endured all kinds of little indignities, but never once has he asked, "Why me?"

It seems that being at the edge of loss increases our awareness, intensifies our focus. How many times we lay together in these past months silently, floating in a haze of gratitude for our fifty-eight years, for the rich and abundant life we have had.

This long tie of recounting, of caring for each other, has joined us in ways we had not known before. These months, in spite of the downside, have been a true gift—the nursing, the struggling together to live one hour at a time, to be comfortable with uncertainty, to accept unconditionally *what is*.

The saints tell us that ultimately, all that matters is how much we have loved. This little virulent squamous cancer has led the way to deeper love for us. And it has brought forth the beautiful outpouring of your love, prayers, and concern that has sustained us.

Affectionately,
T.C.

The meaning of such life-changing events comes to sudden clarity when we combine our narration of them with the wisdom and truth of our belief in God and one another. What happens to us in the face of suffering love cannot make sense unless we place it against the horizon of unshakeable faith. There, against all odds, we open ourselves to the inspirations filtering from our transfocal into our prefocal and focal consciousness. We no longer give into the temptation to brush off formative events as "cruel fate." We admit in humility that our life is cloaked in mystery. The full meaning of what occurs on these silent levels of our being is in great measure hidden from us. We have only one choice: to believe in our Redeemer's embracing promise of abundant life (cf. John 10:10). Although our understanding of pain and loss slips through our grasp into regions of mystery not readily available to us, we do not give up hope. Paradoxically, our sensitivity to formative events as religious experiences increases by virtue of our personal participation in them. No escape is possible anyway. Adherence to God and one another in faith, hope, and love increases our acceptance of whatever life has in store for us. Events like those described in our friend's letter open us to the Sacred. They bind us heart to heart to our family, friends, and faith groupings. They are the primary bearers, the main guarantors, of the truth of the traditions that sustain our own formation story. They motivate us, amidst the crosses we must carry, to become fully human and to pass on to others the lessons we have learned.

Inexhaustibility of the Mystery

However refined our information about the Revelation may be, we stand in awe before the wonder of the Trinitarian mystery. The love that holds us in being knows no bounds. Its call to intimacy is inexhaustible. The vine of the ecclesial teachings out of which come the branches of our faith reveals layers of meaning none of us can ever fathom in their totality. Both informational and formational theology carry us to the heights and depths of the ultimately ineffable sources of divine wisdom and truth. In the Eternal Trinitarian Formation and Interformation Event, we see mirrored in some limited way the "little trinity" we are in universe and history. We have received our baptism in the name of the Father, the Son, and the Holy Spirit! We are to live in the light of the goodness, truth, and beauty of the infused theological virtues. In faith, hope, and love, our mundane make-up reflects this magnificent mystery. However astute our intellect, memory, and will may be, they can never penetrate to the full the providential plan of God for our salvation:

> ...For I am God, and there is no other;
>   I am God, and there is no one like
>   me,
> declaring the end from the beginning
>   and from ancient times things not
>   yet done,
>   saying, my purpose shall stand,
>   and I will fulfill my intention,
> calling a bird of prey from the east,
>   the man for my purpose from a far
>   country.
> I have spoken, and I will bring it
>   to pass;
>   I have planned, and I will do it (Isaiah 46:9:11).

In the face of this prophecy, we who have received the Holy Spirit beg for the grace to recognize the sins that cause us to deviate from the redemptive path that stretches before us. The hunger in our heart for God becomes an acknowledged need best addressed by faith sharing and formative reading. These practices are no longer seen by us as a luxury for the spiritually elite but as a necessity for our survival as humane and spiritual beings. Such reading reveals form-traditional patterns of comportment that prompt us to make the right moral and ethical choices.

Undoubtedly, as pilgrims on a faith journey, we can lose our way. The *ecclesia* is the Bride of Christ given to us by the Holy Spirit to be the Guide and Guarantor of the pathway on which we must trod to reach the dwelling place prepared for us in our Father's house (cf. John 14:2). To think, study, and teach in submission to our foundational faith tradition and its treasury of doctrinal truths prevent us from taking time-wasting detours. What we long to find are methodical ways to deepen our lives as believers and sincere seekers.

Within this ecclesiastical tradition, that is one, holy, catholic, and apostolic, we are invited by the grace of God to engage in a disciplined reflection on faith formation and its implementation in everyday life. We are tasked as members of our faith community to conserve and expand, update and deepen these resources of wisdom that are as valid for past generations as they are for us in the present age. For example, when we study the works of a medieval master of ascetical and mystical theology like Saint John of the Cross, we touch on foundations of faith deepening that permeate the entire history of the Church. While it is not necessary to identify ourselves exclusively with any one school of spirituality, it is prudent to take into account the contributions of any text or teacher that are perennially relevant to what we believe and how we want to exercise these beliefs all the days of our life.

Articulation of the Historical Humanity of Jesus Christ

The classic of all classics in our Christian faith and formation tradition is Jesus Christ. In his eternal divinity and historical humanity, he is the core of our beliefs. Christ informed the community of disciples about the content of faith in him as their Savior while forming them by word and example. He showed them how to change their hearts and transform the world. Following the descent of the Holy Spirit upon the apostles, what was once a divided gathering of chosen yet fearful disciples became a faith community eager to tell others about the grace and glory of God. The Spirit inspired them and the first believers who listened to them to form their faith in ways that would impress both followers and doubters, converts and persecutors. They verified by their lives the marvel of the Divine Word, who emptied himself for our sake, being like us in all things but sin (cf. Philippians 2:4-10). Because Jesus lived a perfectly consonant life of formation with the Father, he was utterly responsive to divine directives and freed from all the actual and observable limitations that hamper us due to sin. It is because of his redemptive love that we have the chance to grow in more perfect congeniality with our deepest identity in the Eternal Word.

From the time of his birth in Bethlehem to his ascension in glory, our Lord drew us into his own personal and shared field of life. He knew from the start that courageous consent to each disclosure of our call is the key to consonance, the source of peace and joy. Christ's humanity could be conceived as the achievement of perfect congeniality with the love-will of the Father. His life of total fidelity would result in the Paschal Mystery of his suffering, death, and resurrection. It is to Jesus that we must look if we hope to reach our destined goal of happiness on earth in anticipation of our place in God's eternal plan as his children by adoption (cf. Romans 8:15 and 8:23).

Believers in different cultures and cultural periods have responded in many ways to the call to transformation in Christ. Personal devotions like the veneration of the Sacred Heart complement the common ways of liturgy, word, and sacrament. Devotions must not degenerate into mere devotionalism or exercises in popular piety that override adoration of the Eucharist. Ways of prayer helpful to some must in no way be imposed on all people as *the only way* to maturity in Christ. We appreciate how the Son of God has been depicted in familiar images and symbols, in parables and works of art, in poetry and hymns while detaching ourselves from such apparitional forms and means of grace as ends in themselves. Periodically, we need to purify devotions of our own possibly distorting attachments and our tendency to identify as a foundation of our faith what may only be an accretion attributed to a certain style of devotionalism. The danger always exists that certain forms of popular pietism may take the place of true religious worship.

Last but not least, the perfect congeniality of Christ with the Father's will implies that he was also compatible, compassionate, competent, courageous, and candid in his interformation with whomever he encountered along life's way. He healed the sick, fed the hungry, cast out demons, and raised souls from the dead. He did all that he could to open up the divine potency for transformation inherent in our created being. Every time we actualize this potency in interformation with him and in obedience to the foundational faith and formation traditions to which we freely bind our hearts, minds, and wills, we fulfill the divine hope, expressed by Jesus in his Farewell Discourse, when he prayed poignantly to the Father that "they may be one as we are one...that they may have my joy complete in themselves...that they also may be sanctified in truth" (John 17:11-19).

Chapter 6

Integrating Our Christian Faith and Formation Traditions

Lay people's field of Christian service is the vast world of politics, society, and economics, as well as the world of culture, sciences, arts, international affairs and mass media. It also includes human love, the family, the education of children, professional work, and suffering. The more that Gospel-inspired lay people engage in these areas, the more these areas will be at the service of the Kingdom of God.
— Pope Paul VI

The ultimate nature of the formation processes that govern our human life in culture and cosmos are a mystery. No detailed and compelling explanation of their fullest and final meaning has ever been produced. No collection of research satisfies every question we have. The daily formation of our life and world only seems to be possible if we abandon ourselves to this mystery through an affirmation of its wonder in faith, hope, and love. The alternative of feeling abandoned by the mystery is to live as if we were lost in a universe devoid of meaning and indifferent to our fate. To apprehend and ratify a formation process that lacks ultimate direction and beneficence would leave us on the verge of continual dissonance and despair.

Adherence to a faith tradition that gives us hope is both seminal and formative. Its normative sources, notably, the directives available to us in the Bible and the literature of spirituality contain the seeds of those evocative guidelines that secure the overall orientation of our lives in tune with the mystery. Our task is to incarnate them in congenial, compatible, and compassionate ways as individuals and members of a faith community in a manner that forms, reforms, and transforms our lives.

Seminal Messages of the Revelation

Our Christian faith tradition is revealed and communicated definitively in Christ; it unfolds continuously in human history through the Spirit of the Risen Lord. The Revelation of the formation mystery of Father, Son, and Holy Spirit has been handed on from its initial moment of transmission by apostolic testimony to the present time. This ongoing transmission of our Christian faith tradition as formative gave rise to the scriptures that recorded for all ages the early Church's experience of the risen and glorified Lord. The outward or expressive dimension of our faith tradition can be found in the scriptures, creeds, symbols, conciliar decrees, rituals, and customs that bind us together as a community of believers. The inward, experiential dimension of our tradition is that through which we, as the people of God, appropriate the transmitted expressions of our tradition in liturgy, word, and sacrament. The foundational directives, the seminal messages of the Revelation, include ordinary events and extraordinary marvels. In Jesus of Nazareth, the Word made flesh who dwells among us (cf. John 1:14), the Father's definitive truth about himself was spoken forth. In his *Sayings of Light and Love*, Saint John of the Cross says: "The Father spoke one Word, which was his Son, and this Word he speaks always in eternal silence, and in silence must it be heard by the soul."[1]

For us who believe, Jesus Christ is, as he himself declares, "the way, and the truth, and the life" (John 14:6). Following him grants us the grace of entrance into a community of believers, assembled by the power of the Spirit for the sake of going forth to serve others in this world. In attempting to summarize these foundational faith directives, the renowned theologian, Karl Rahner, says:

> [T]he man Jesus...is someone who continually accepts himself from the Father and who in all the dimensions of his existence has always given himself over to the Father totally; in this surrender he is able to accomplish through God's grace what we are not able to accomplish; he is someone whose "basic constitution" as the original unity of being and consciousness is to have his origins in God radically and completely, and to be given over to God radically and completely.[2]

As our faith matures so do the formation traditions that disclose and mediate in concrete ways the meaning of our salvation in Christ. Through his Spirit, we learn how to appropriate and incarnate these faith foundations in all that we are and do. Whereas catechetical theology continues to disclose and interpret the mystery of the Revelation, formation theology offers us general and specific norms for living in consonance with what we believe. These norms deal primarily with the practical effectiveness of customs and communications that have been handed over by generations committed to following Christ in the intricacy of every situation in which we find ourselves.

Because of this orientation towards practical implementation, a formation tradition is more flexible and open to change than the faith tradition in which it is rooted. Every such tradition is always a mixture of lasting or foundational directives and particular accretions that enter the tradition due to passing and contingent sociohistorical conditions and pulsations. A form-tradition embraces the body of formative wisdom developed by its adherents over many ages. This embodiment occurs in the act of receiving and giving form to our life as it unfolds daily. The traditions we pass on receive their form from those aspects of our everyday existence that have proven to be literally and symbolically meaningful in the interconsciousness of many adherents. They move us (receptive formation) and draw forth our creative responses (donative formation) to our field of life and the mystery radiating within it. This creative co-formation preserves and enriches the traditions to which we adhere and the life directives they disclose for present and future generations.

Fertile Ground of Our Faith

In tracing the fertile ground of our Christian faith and formation traditions, we have to return to the scriptural account of the day of Pentecost when, "...suddenly from heaven there came a sound like the rush of a violent wind, and it filled the entire house where they were sitting. Divided tongues, as of fire, appeared among them, and a tongue rested on each of them. All of them were filled with the Holy Spirit and began to speak in other languages, as the Spirit gave them ability" (Acts 2:2-4). This miraculous handing over of the Spirit enabled the followers of Jesus of Nazareth to proclaim him as Lord and Messiah (cf. Acts 2:36). The Holy Spirit instructs the community of believers in everything and reminds them of all that Jesus told them (cf. John 14:26). The gift of the Spirit continually illumines the *ecclesia* in regard to the meaning of the Revelation and the abundant outpouring of faith and form-directives that effect every detail of our lives.

The ongoing experience of the Spirit, handed on from apostolic times to the present age, gives rise to rich religious narratives that proclaim the power of Christ's words and mediate the meaning of his saving deeds. We are the privileged recipients of the originating experience of believers who witnessed the transforming reality of Jesus Christ and his presence among us "to the end of the age" (Matthew 16:20). The form-directives seminally present in his life and teachings reveal the divine intervention of the Trinitarian mystery in human history and trace their dynamism to this accumulated treasury of truth. Further narrations and interpretations of it would come to light over the course of time, but growth in our understanding of the Revelation must occur daily if our life is to unfold, as Christ's did, in accordance with the love-will of the Father.

The traditions initiated by Jesus in the New Testament like prayer, fasting, and almsgiving contain layers of meaning that challenge every generation of disciples. Just as a sponge draws water to itself and expands in the process, so a new formation tradition attracts ideas, insights, and experiences, images and symbols, that have the capacity to expand our knowledge and appreciation of God's ways with us. As water fills the pores of a sponge, so the teachings of Jesus of Nazareth fulfill the longing in our hearts to love him and keep his word (cf. John 14:23) for our own and others' sake.

Complementing the Scriptures is the overwhelming richness of the writings of the spiritual masters, who delved into the in-depth meaning of the life directives Christ gave us. The Fathers of the Church pondered them in defense of the faith in the early eras of the undivided church. The apostolic and patristic tradition gave normative expression to the New Testament writings and witnessed their expansion in the eastern and western members of the Christian community. Most of these original adherents had already been formed in other traditions like the Hebraic, Greek, and Roman. Led by their bishops and teachers, they moved *from* these pre-Christian traditions *through* evangelical dialogue with the revealed propositions of their newly found faith tradition *to* a progressive understanding of the Gospel message for all believers.

This dialogue extended to the evolution in factual knowledge of our human condition in a changing field of formation. The Christian message transformed the cultures in which it emerged. Literature, art, and architecture reveal this interplay between our belief system and the proximate knowledge and practices spawned by a variety of differential sciences and cultural advances in fields like mathematics and music. Insofar as these findings are compatible with the foundations of our Christian faith and formation traditions, we may seek ways to assimilate them creatively and critically. This proximate knowledge and its implementation may then assist us in our efforts to explore the value of these ancient yet ever new traditions in contemporary life.

As we have seen, vertical interformation occurs when we assimilate the foundations of our faith and the classics of formation to which they give rise over many generations. Its complement is horizontal interformation with parents and teachers who practice what they preach and thereby become our greatest source of encouragement. A tradition never seen in action risks losing its plausibility.[3] The classics of Christianity are bound to diminish in relevance if we do not share them with a like-minded faith community. The absence of this encouraging communication may be one of the main reasons for our assimilation of alien traditions that make the link between what we believe and how we live so tenuous it may take only one or two generations to lose it entirely.

Christianity has always stressed the centrality of the ecclesial community as the locus of the living power, the perennial dynamism, of a formation tradition with its invaluable endowment of symbols, images, rituals, and customs. Our faith assures us that where two or three gather in the name of the Risen Lord, he is there among us (cf. Matthew 18:20).

Practice of Christian Formation

The daily formation of our life and world in adherence to the foundations of our faith is only possible when we choose to abandon ourselves to the benevolent embrace of the Trinity whose adopted children we are (cf. Galatians 4:5). Committed to the courageous practice of what we profess, we may become, in cooperation with grace, the humble conduits of the truths Christ taught us. He allows us, frail as we may feel, to mirror the mystery of transforming love. Guided by the vision of life our faith formation validates, we are less likely to lose the sense of our ultimate direction and more likely to experience the peace and joy Christ promises (cf. John 14:27).

Faith never lies fallow. It seeks proximate and effective implementation in our concrete field of existence. True faith moves towards form. The church is in labor until Christ comes alive in all of her members (cf. Galatians 4:19). When the entire universe is brought under the transforming action of Christ's headship (cf. Ephesians 1:10), "when, finally, all has been subjected to the Son, he will then subject himself to the One who made all things subject to him, so that God may be all in all" (1 Corinthians 15:28).

In the light of this prophetic vision of our ultimate destiny, our practice of Christian formation must be anchored in the foundational doctrines of the faith from whence its every expression goes forth. At times of profound, transition, following, for example, the Second Vatican Council, certain forms once thought to be basic to our faith may come into question, due perhaps to their having been influenced by time-bound philosophical or theological assumptions now understood as being in need of reform.

Adherents of the Christian tradition may have mistakenly mixed up certain temporal, non-essential accretions with the foundations of their faith. They may have allowed such time-bound expressions to replace the essence of their inspired adherence to Christ. Such matters must be referred to the teaching office of the Church and its professional theologians. In the meantime, we must do what we can to guarantee that our faith and formation traditions will continue to commingle in a mutually reinforcing interplay so that we may fulfill our mission to be "ambassadors for Christ" (2 Corinthians 5:20) in a broken world seeking reconciliation with God and others.

CHAPTER 7

Symbolic Transmission of a Living Tradition

We know the body's thirst when there is no water; we know the thirst of our passion for life and good fortune. Do we also know the soul's thirst for God? A God who is only an ideal can never still this thirst. Our soul thirsts for the living God, the God and Source of all true life. When will God quench our thirst? When will we come to appear before his presence? To be with God is the goal of all life and is itself eternal life. We are in God's presence with Jesus Christ, the crucified. If we have found God's presence here, then we thirst to
enjoy it completely in eternity.
— *Dietrich Bonhoeffer*

Formation traditions with their underlying directives live on in and through the inter-consciousness of the Christian community, illumined by the Spirit. This interconsciousness is expressed in formative symbols like those of hunger and thirst that exercise a directive influence on our personal and shared history as disciples of Christ. These symbols are essential carriers of our faith.

We draw upon them to preserve, disclose, and elaborate directives of faith deepening in our everyday world. They serve at one and the same time as inward guardians and outward protectors of our tradition as articulated both horizontally and vertically. Verified by our own experience is the fact that horizontal transmission takes place in interformation with the significant others whom we encounter from childhood onward. A mother reverently lights a candle before a sacred image. A family bows their heads and prays before meals. A friend volunteers to drive us to the doctor's office. A colleague dedicates herself to a thankless task in a manner that transcends the achievement model associated with successful service. A group of Christians gathers to read and meditate upon a sacred text. The Word of God comes alive in a homily. The Spirit seems to linger among us during a solemn liturgical celebration. In these and countless other ways, the horizontal, living transmission of form-traditions occurs. Through the efforts of good people acting charitably, we receive directives for the intraformative assimilation of our faith to the degree that we are open to their surplus of meaning and their disclosive dynamics.

Horizontal transmission in the present can only occur because of what has previously been handed on. Vertical transmission is the ground for the possibility of traditions influencing our current life. This vertical passing on allows symbolic form-directives to be transmitted from the past through literature and other sources that comprise the stream of Christian formation experiences, practices, and traditions nourishing each successive generation of believers. The transmitters of a tradition cannot contain the whole of its treasury of wisdom and truth, but they can express it partially. Our quest for truth continues because these symbols are alive with meaning that has to be interiorized in service of the Christian formation of our life and world. What satisfies our thirst for God are not only rational explanations of our faith but a personal understanding of why we believe.

In the midst of passing sociohistorical pulsations, the classics open us to transcendent aspirations and pneumatic inspirations.

They stand firmly behind the ponderings of each sincere seeker, reiterating what is of lasting value in themes traceable from ancient to medieval to modern times. The classics draw us to themselves because they are characterized by an "excess of meaning."[1] A true classic overflows with intelligibility and relevance. It unites the particularity of its origin and expression with disclosures of meaning and truth that are available, in principle, to all humanity. This "excess of meaning" demands constant interpretation; it has about it a kind of *timelessness* due to the *timeliness* of its expression. It is rooted in its own historical time yet it addresses our own historicity.[2] A classic is not timeless in the sense that it calls for mere repetition. It is timeless in that it is always timely; it invites our unique appropriation of it. It calls for interpretation and re-articulation in the light of our own questions and concerns. The two essential notes of any classic are, in summary, excess of meaning and that timeless permanence which is always open to timely appropriation.

Centrality of Christian Classics

Unlike the classical paintings hanging in a museum, explicitly religious classics involve a claim to truth linked to the Divine Forming Mystery. They serve as pointers to the whole and Holy. In the midst of the most ordinary day, we may recognize and be changed by the sacred power that surrounds and sustains a true classic. It meditates the gifted event of the Unlimited breaking into and through the limits of our lives; of the Unbounded piercing through our boundaries; of the Whole entering our world in and through the fragmented partiality of human events and gathering them into a unified meaning. The authority of a religious classic resides in its gratuitous teaching power, in its living communication of faith and reason. We experience it as a revelatory event, an occurrence, a happening, symbolically manifested to our experience rather than being produced in any way by our own ingenuity. Its meaning may radically change our life direction, for in the presence of truth we do not master the mystery; it masters us.

Christian classics include, while infinitely expanding upon, the general characteristics of religious classics, their directives and their depth. In the Christian tradition, there is only one foundational event: the person of Jesus Christ. This event and this person, "normatively judge and inform all other Christian classics...and serve as the classic Christian focus for understanding God, self, others, society, history, nature and the whole of Christianity."[3] The event of Jesus's birth, death, and resurrection is experienced by Christians as coming directly from God and by God's power. It is a transhuman epiphany of the formation mystery, symbolizing the forming whole of all that is.

The event of Jesus Christ means that the present-day experiences of every believer have to be connected in some way to his human and divine personhood. Our immediate personal and shared response to the self-disclosure and self-communication of the Father through the Son in the Holy Spirit puts us in touch with the Christ-event within our own and others' field of formation. Mediating this event are treasure troves of classical symbols, images, rites, and texts, which our faith tradition recognizes as pointers to the classic event and person at their center, Christ the Lord.

The words of the Bible despite their narrative diversity proclaim the unified story of salvation history. In them we find the primordial expression of the self-disclosure of the Father in the redeeming love of the Son through the luminous presence of the Spirit. Scripture is normative for our understanding of formation, reformation, and transformation. It is to its treasury that we Christians turn whenever we want to mine the meaning of our present experiences in the light of the revealed and communicated truth of our faith.

Normative Event of Jesus Christ

The foundation of our Christian tradition and the related classics through which it is disclosed is, in summary, the event of Jesus Christ, recorded in the New Testament; celebrated and represented in the liturgical assembly; formulated in creeds and doctrines; expressed in the arts; reflected upon by the Fathers, Doctors, spiritual masters, and theologians of the Church; and witnessed to by the heroic lives of those who live in the Spirit of Jesus, notably the saints named and unnamed over time. Above all, the event of Jesus Christ is revealed and communicated as the forming and transforming mystery that permeates and transcends the formation fields of each succeeding generation of Christians. Our everyday experiences of faith, hope, and love have as their past, present, and future locus the Christ-event. Together they comprise the faith and formation traditions that are the primary constitutive, and mediating reality of the radical disclosure of the Godhead in Christ, the Saving Event of our lives.

It follows, therefore, that the normative sources of our Christian tradition are found first of all in the Bible, the living Word of God proclaimed most efficaciously in the liturgical assembly. The scriptures inform all other classical expressions of our faith. Scripture and liturgy co-form one another as the "expression of the Church actively living, praising God and bringing about a holy communion with him: the covenant as fulfilled in Christ Jesus, its Lord, Head, and Spouse."[4] Liturgy is the living articulation of the Scriptures. It is a classical expression of our form tradition understood as a dynamic power of ongoing preserving formation:

> Both as a lived action and as a ritualized action, the liturgy preserves and hands on to us elements which are much more numerous than were realized by those who performed and preserved the rites, and actually handed them on to us: many more, even than we ourselves can know the whole Eucharist is given to me in its celebration; I myself possess it in its entirety, although I understand and could express so little of it. The liturgical action is synthetic; its gestures sum up and recapitulate past experience. The whole of our love is expressed in the liturgical kiss, even if we do not really attend sufficiently to what we are doing. The whole of our faith is in the most ordinary sign of the cross, and when we say *Our Father* we already imply all the knowledge which

will be given to us only when we embrace it in the revelation of glory.[5]

Along with the scriptures and the liturgy, we pay special attention to the spiritual masters, who embody in their words and actions the full impact of what it means to believe in Jesus Christ and to carry this belief into every aspect of daily life. Given special prominence in this regard are the formationally relevant texts of the Fathers, Doctors, and saints of the Church, "whose teaching we revere and follow."[6] They have "fathered" us in the way to integrate our beliefs and their practice. They have taught us how to respond in humility and obedience to the revelation and communication of the formation mystery: they have shown us the love of God by the integrity and holiness of their lives. The masters of formation in any era evoke our interest because of the layers of meaning present in their symbolic expressions. We recognize them by their timeless-timeliness; by their ability to hand on their wisdom through the ages without any loss of interest on our part; and by their normative expression of the wisdom and truth of Christian formation. These classical texts connect reflections *about* the event of Jesus Christ with reflections *upon* the obstacles and facilitating conditions that foster our life in him as cordially and effectively as possible.

Wellspring of Classical Wisdom

The number and range of classics in the Christian tradition is immense. In *A Practical Guide to Spiritual Reading* by Susan Muto, we find listed four main classifications of texts from our tradition with examples of those that have achieved major or minor status. These are: essential, secondary, edifying, and recreative.[7]

1. *Essential* texts include the writings of the Fathers, Doctors, and saints of the Christian tradition as presented in books like *The Art of Prayer: An Orthodox Anthology* and *Writings from The Philokalia on Prayer of the Heart.* For example, among the Apostolic Fathers, Ignatius of Antioch and Clement of Rome address key virtues of the Christian life like purity of heart, simplicity, docility, and other dispositions that prepare us for

the gift of knowing in love and humility the mystery of the Most Holy Trinity. Clement of Alexandria and Origen speak of the reality of the soul's marriage with the Logos in likeness to God and the conditions for this union, such as *ascesis* that readies the soul to resist the onslaught of the demonic and *apatheia* that leads to inner peace. The Cappadocian Father, Gregory of Nyssa, explains the nature of Christian transformation with his theory of *epectasis* or perpetual ascent to God. He examines the compenetration of the divine and human powers of formation in his original reflections on *synergy*, in which the *eros* of humanity is so changed by the *agape* of God that we are drawn by grace into union of likeness with the Trinitarian mystery. *The Sayings of the Desert Fathers*, along with the *Praktikos* of Evagrius Ponticus, the *Institutes* and *Conferences* of John Cassian, the *Rule of the Master*, and the *Rule of Saint Benedict*, disclose and transmit proximate conditions for and obstacles to Christian discipleship within an eremitical and cenobitic form of monastic life. These writings uncover foundational directives applicable to Christian practice and the search for ultimate meaning that engages believers and all others who sincerely seek to know, love, and serve God.

Among the writings of the Doctors of the Church, who give expression to the essence of faith formation, we find those of Saint Bernard of Clairvaux on humility, charity, and union with the Word in detachment and obedience, lasting dispositions of the heart that facilitate our growth in the image and likeness of God. Complementing these essentials would be Aelred of Rievaulx's presentation of spiritual friendship as a mirror for our union with God and others; John of the Cross and Teresa of Avila's intensive explorations of what facilitates and obstructs our spiritual ascent to transforming union and mystical prayer; and Francis de Sales' description of how to live the "devout life" as Christians involved in worldly services without being of the world.

Included also in the category of essential texts are autobiographical writings that inform the mind and uplift the heart. Prime examples would be Saint Augustine's *Confessions*; Thérèse of Lisieux's *Story of a Soul*; and Thomas Merton's *The Sign of Jonas*. Added to them are contemporary treatments of virtues and vices that bless or block our intentions to live the Christian mystery under the most mundane circumstances. One example would be Carlo Carretto's *Letters from the Desert*, which brings the ancient tradition of the desert experience to bear on a modern brother's account of his complete commitment to Christ in the solitude and silence of the Sahara. Another would be Adrian van Kaam's *Spirituality and the Gentle Life*, which describes in detail the dispositions of gentleness and firmness as prerequisites for spiritual emergence and intimacy with the Trinity.

According to the classification from *A Practical Guide*, *secondary* texts comprehend biographical expressions of our form-tradition that depict and explain the lives of the saints and spiritual masters whose history bears witness to the Christ-event in the form of focused and concrete testimony. Examples would be: G. K. Chesterton's *Saint Thomas Aquinas – "The Dumb Ox"* and Johannes Jorgensen's *Saint Francis of Assisi*. Listed also in this category are texts that articulate the faith presuppositions that are most relevant to Christian formation, including such works in spiritual theology as Louis Bouyer's *Introduction to Spirituality* and C. S. Lewis' *Miracles*. Texts in this classification that have themselves become servant sources of formation would be, among others, Martin Buber's *I and Thou*, a powerful exposition of the dynamics of interformation between us and God; Dietrich von Hildebrand's *Transformation in Christ* on the attitudes that signify our striving for Christian perfection; and Susan Muto's experiential reflections on silence, formative reading, meditation, journal-keeping, contemplative prayer and action in *Pathways of Spiritual Living*. Finally, these secondary texts also trace the historical development of the Christian formation tradition as represented by Dom Cuthbert Butler in *Western Mysticism*; Ronald A. Knox in *Enthusiasm*; and Dom Jean Leclercq in *The Love of Learning and the Desire for God*.

In the category of *edifying* reading, *A Practical Guide* lists texts written in the style of personal witness that inspire us to live the foundations of our faith in ordinary reality, understood as the arena in which lasting transformation takes place. One thinks of treasured books like Anthony Bloom's *Beginning to Pray*; John Donne's *Devotions Upon Emergent Occasions*; Søren Kierkegaard's *Purity of Heart Is to Will One Thing,* and Thomas R. Kelly's *A Testament of Devotion.*

The final category is that of *recreative* texts, including fiction, essays, plays, and poetry, that tell the story of a person's search for meaning from an implicit or explicit religious perspective. Some favorite works would be the novels and shorter narratives of Fyodor Dostoyevsky, Leo Tolstoy, Georges Bernanos, Francois Mauriac, Graham Greene, Chaim Potok, and, more recently, Walker Percy and Flannery O'Connor; the seventeenth-century metaphysical poetry of John Donne, George Herbert, Richard Crashaw, and Thomas Traherne; and the nineteenth and twentieth century poems of Gerard Manley Hopkins, Emily Dickinson, T. S. Eliot, and Rainer Maria Rilke.

This classification of major and minor classics from both Western and Eastern Spirituality demonstrates, with several examples from each category, the width and breadth of our formation traditions and their fidelity to our human and Christian experiences. Complementing them are the doctrinal elaborations of our faith tradition in creeds, conciliar teachings, philosophical and theological treatises, and catechetical texts, characterized by a more informational way of thinking about the revealed word of God. The literature of spirituality focuses more fully on everyday directives for the formation of our life and world in the light of our adhered to system of beliefs. Classical transmissions of its tenets may also utilize creative resources in Christian art and music—from stained glass windows to hymnology. These symbolic expressions disclose a potentially inexhaustible treasury of proximate directives that serve to deepen our presence to Christ through the gifts of his Spirit revealed in the scriptures; celebrated in the liturgy; and reflected upon in the essential, secondary, edifying, and recreative texts of the masters preserved in the *ecclesia* to sustain and enhance Christian formation from the earliest times to the present age.

Chapter 8

Traditions and Transformation

Without God there can be no order anywhere. How long, then, shall we continue to concern ourselves with our own liberty or our own capacity to suffer the trials and tribulations of the present moment? When will God be all in all to us? Let us see things in their true light and rise above them to live purely in God himself.
— Jean-Pierre de Caussade

The threefold path of purifying formation, illuminating reformation, and unifying transformation is central to our pledge of fidelity to Christ. It reflects our concept of the Father as the Formator, the Son as the Reformator, and the Holy Spirit as the Transformator of our personal and communal life in this world. To live as "other Christ's" means to apprehend appreciatively the ways in which we give and receive form in the "eucharists of everydayness." From the viewpoint of our final deification of soul in, with, and through Christ, now and in the life to come, all that pertains to the forming, reforming, and transforming plan of God for our salvation is meant at some point to be actualized by us.

Only if these efforts of ours are permeated by the grace of God can they bear fruit in daily life and become signs pointing to the destiny decreed for us by the Trinity. As we read in the Letter of Paul to the Romans:

> I appeal to you therefore, brothers and sisters, by the mercies of God, to present your bodies as a living sacrifice, holy and acceptable to God which is your spiritual worship. Do not be conformed to this world, but be transformed by the renewing of your minds, so that you may discern what is the will of God—what is good and acceptable and perfect (Romans 12:1-2).

Behind all particular expressions of faith formation in Christ stands the exquisite Trinitarian presence that interforms with our life since baptism. Christ offers us a chance to attain the grace of true congeniality with the Father's will in and through the power of his Spirit. The gift of our uniqueness is inseparable from the hidden, holy ground form of our life in Christ. Our essence in him is the sacred root of our empirical existence. Our transcendent identity and its origin in our founding life form is the harbor from whence we sail and the port to which we return on our life's journey.

The congenial direction willed for us by God concretizes itself in the compatible situations and compassionate relations that enable us to live in fidelity to our deepest calling. During the particular history of our maturation in Christ, many directives conducive to the unfolding of our life call may be disclosed to us, if not focally, then surely transfocally since our Divine Caller never ceases to call us. The fullest meaning of our life in Christ may take time to discover, but if we are open to these stirrings in the transfocal region of our consciousness, we may catch glimpses of our direction in the day-to-day routines that occupy us. The art and discipline of reverential listening fosters heightened awareness of the invitations, challenges, and appeals Christ issues to us through the most ordinary channels as well as in the privileged places of revelation in scripture and tradition. The more we come to know Christ, the more we long to love and serve him.

The Father granted to his Son as the Incarnate Word the singular privilege to be wholly with us in his humanity yet wholly beyond us in his divinity. At the core of our faith tradition is the decision made by the Second Person of the Blessed Trinity to relinquish any divine prerogative that would have made it possible for him to escape his destiny as the Divine Redeemer who chose to suffer out of love for our sake. This ultimate facet of his identity is so mysterious and glorious that no articulation of its meaning is adequate. The New Testament at once reveals and conceals the way in which the Risen Lord sent his Spirit to inspire us to search for our own deepest identity and to obey the direction that allows us to fulfill our destiny.

To meet Christ at any time is a transforming event that changes us forever and especially so amidst a crisis of transcendence. Intimated to our focal consciousness by the transfocal inspiration of the Spirit is a sometimes shocking sense of what we must do to move *from* an old current form of life *through* a transition crisis *to* a new phase of maturation in the Lord.

This quest for consonance with the Christ-form of our soul enables us to grow in fidelity to the will of the Father. We realize that on our own we could never achieve this sense of communion. Without his abiding presence, we might not have survived this crisis nor benefitted so fully from it. Through Christ we come to experience more congeniality with the transformed self we are called to be. We are at peace with our situation and much kinder to all whom we encounter, ourselves included. Lifted from our shoulders is the burden of self-scrutiny and the aching tension of perfectionism. As humble recipients of the gifts of divine mercy and forgiveness, we know who it is on whom we can rely.

Unparalleled Achievement of Christ's Life

In line with the foundational teachings of our faith tradition, we seek to mirror Christ's Paschal Mystery. Through his life, death, and resurrection, he released for our benefit a hidden power of interformation that links all people together as members of his Mystical Body. He inaugurated such a change in the formation story of humanity that time itself is dated before and after his coming among us. His life could be conceived as having opened for all who believe a divine potency for transformation that will continue to be actualized until the end of time.

It is Christ's saving compassion for our fallen condition that enables us, mundane creatures that we are, to affirm the divine core of our identity as eternally preformed, created, and redeemed souls who have been adopted into the family of the Trinity and who are destined for eternal glory in a deified state no mortal words can describe. Indeed eye has not seen, ear has not heard, human hearts have not conceived, what God has prepared for us who love him (cf. 1 Corinthians 2:9). It is our duty and our privilege, in response to the mind of Christ, to "speak of these things in words not taught by human wisdom but taught by the Spirit, interpreting spiritual things to those who are spiritual" (1 Corinthians 2:13).

Womanly Words of Wisdom

An outstanding Doctor of the Church, Saint Catherine of Siena (1347-1380), addresses in her masterpiece *The Dialogue* the foundations of Christian formation through which we encounter truths of timeless value that deepen our faith, sustain our hope, and strengthen our love for God, self, and neighbor.

At the base of Catherine's teaching are the locutions she received concerning the central dogma of Christianity: the union of divinity and humanity in Jesus Christ. She met her Master with a rare intimacy many times during her life.[1] His revelations pertaining to her unique-communal call were unambiguously clear. He told her in words reminiscent of the Great Commandment:

> ...it is your duty to love your neighbors as your own self. In love you ought to help them spiritually with prayer and counsel, and assist them spiritually and materially in their need–at least with your good will if you have nothing else. If you do not love me you do not love your neighbors, nor will

you help those you do not love. But it is yourself you harm most, because you deprive yourself of grace. And you harm your neighbors by depriving them of the prayer and loving desires you should be offering me on their behalf. Every help you give them ought to come from the affections you bear them for love of me.[2]

In Catherine's life and in her writings, we detect many foundations of spiritual formation. One concerns the integration of solitude and solidarity, of discovering who we are before God and then showing others the depth of divine compassion we have undeservedly received. In their dialogue, the Father assured her that "to attain charity you must dwell constantly in the cell of self-knowledge. For in knowing yourself you will come to know my mercy in the blood of my only-begotten Son, thus drawing my divine charity to yourself with your love."[3] At the core of her Christocentric spirituality Catherine proclaimed the mystery of God Incarnate. The saint could not contain her intimacy with this mystery of her own interiority; she had to share this wondrous revelation with her friends and disciples, with the people of Siena and with the whole Church.

Another foundation of Christian formation, reiterated in *The Dialogue*, is that of centering our lives on Christ, who declared himself to be *the* Way, *the* Truth, *the* Life (cf. John 14:6): the *Way* because he shed his blood to redeem souls deadened by sin; the *Truth* because in his presence we see the whole Trinity; the *Life* because his Spirit renews the face of the earth, transforms his Body, the Church, and draws us into the fiery furnace of Trinitarian love.

Jesus describes himself to Catherine as the bridge, the mediator, between us and God. He makes it possible for us to cross over the chasm of sin and selfish sensuality and meet him as prodigal children, who return to the Father:

> So first I made a bridge of my Son as he lived in your company. And though this living bridge has been taken from your sight, there remains the bridgeway of his teaching,

which as I told you, is held together by my power and my Son's wisdom and the mercy of the Holy Spirit. My power gives the virtue of courage to those who follow this way. Wisdom gives light to know the truth along the way. And the Holy Spirit gives them a love that uproots all sensual love from the soul and leaves only virtuous love. So now as much as before, through his teaching as much as when he was among you, he is the way and truth and life — the way that is the bridge leading to the very height of heaven.[4]

Following the Threefold Path

Saint Catherine compares the traditional threefold path of purgation, illumination, and union, to Christ's wounded feet, pierced heart, and tender mouth. On the purgative way, our motivation for obedience often remains fear of punishment rather than purity of love. Though the illuminative way signifies a deepening of conversion of heart, our love for Christ and our following of his truth is still mingled with selfishness. Though we may lack a lived understanding of what our Lord has done for us, we still want to make progress on the path to spiritual maturity, no longer acting as fearful slaves but as faithful servants.

If the first step sparks our desire for God and the second enlightens our mind, then the third leads to unitive love and profound transformation of heart, imaged by Catherine as the mouth of Christ. He himself claims the soul with a mystical kiss and instills as a permanent disposition of our core form the grace of filial love, granting us a taste of true peace.

Catherine adds to this threefold path a fourth stage, symbolized by the fire of charity towards our neighbor. She emphasizes our obligation not only to hear the word of God in our heart, but to proclaim it to the world. An excellent summary of these three ways can be found in one of Catherine's letters to the Abbess and nuns of an Augustinian Monastery near Florence:

> ...to enable the soul to attain this perfection, Christ has made his body into a staircase, with great steps. See, his feet are

nailed fast to the cross; they constitute the first step because, to begin with, the soul's desire has to be stripped of self-will, for as the feet carry the body, so desire carries the soul. Reflect that no soul will ever acquire virtue without climbing this first step. Once you have done that, you come to real, deep humility. Climb the next step without delay and you reach the open side of God's Son. Within, you will find the fathomless furnace of divine charity. Yes, on this second step of the open side, there is a little shop, full of fragrant spices. Therein you will find the God-Man; therein, too the soul becomes so satiated and inebriated as to become oblivious of self for, like a man intoxicated with wine, it will have eyes only for the Blood spilt with such burning love. With eager longing it presses on upwards and reaches the last step, the mouth, where it reposes in peace and quiet, savoring the [serenity] of obedience. Like a man who falls asleep after drinking heavily and so is oblivious of both pain and pleasure, the bride of Christ, brimming over with love, sleeps in the peace of her Bridegroom. Her own feelings are so deeply asleep that she remains unruffled when assailed by tribulation and rises above undue delight in worldly prosperity; for she stripped herself of all desire of that kind back on the first step. Here [on the third] she is conformed to Christ crucified and made one with him.[5]

Crossing the Bridge

According to Catherine, the only way to cross the bridge that leads to union with the Bridegroom of our soul is to remember the abyss of selfish sensuality that lies beneath it. The gifts of memory, intellect, and will are the dowry left to us by Christ to aid us in this crossing.

The function of memory as formative is not to catalogue faults and failings but to recall God's faithfulness to us. His giving and forgiving love is everlasting. Deformed memory wallows in its own misery, causing us to forget the boundless depths of Christ's mercy. Our Savior wants us to use our intellect to apprehend and affirm the truth of his love and to acknowledge in humility that we are dependent wholly on him. If self-love is the source of all deformation, so love of God and willing the good are the sources of all transformation. Deformed will forces us to attach our affections in an inordinate way to that which is infinitely less than God, resulting in avarice, gluttony, and lust. Catherine highlights her teachings on these three powers of the soul in a letter to the Abbot of a nearby monastery to whom she writes:

> When the understanding has received the light from the fire…it is transformed into it so that the two become one: thus, the memory becomes one with Christ crucified, retaining nothing, delighting in nothing, thinking of nothing but the Beloved, for the memory is flooded in an instant with the ineffable love it sees poured out on itself and on all mankind, and the person becomes so great a lover of both God and his neighbor that he would give his life for him a hundred thousand times over…the three powers of the soul are at one in this fire: the memory treasuring all God's benefits; the understanding knowing his goodness and his will…and the will so expanding with love that it cannot love or even desire anything apart from God. All the soul's movements are centered on God, and it has eyes only for him; its one concern is to do what is most pleasing to its Creator…[6]

Walking in the Truth

Catherine's love of truth draws her with passionate affection to the Cross that brought light to a world overshadowed by deception. It made her seek the deepest knowledge of herself and God. This intermingling of cognition and affection led her to the discovery that, as disciples of Christ, we share in three degrees of light. The first is ordinary. The light of reason reveals that we cannot find our true selves unless we compliment our understanding of who we are by the light of faith. In Catherine's words, if we "exercise this faith by virtue of the light of reason, reason will in turn be enlightened by faith, and such faith will give [us] life and lead [us] in the way of truth."[7] With this light we will reach Christ, the true light; without it we will remain in the darkness.

To this first light, Christ adds two others. Both are bestowed on us in the hope that we will choose to become mature Christians, who follow the lead of grace to mystical union and intimacy with the Trinity. A "more perfect" light enables us to sense the transitory nature of this world. It stimulates our hunger and thirst for God and for the more disciplined life that supports this desire. We engage in sacrifices of self not for their own sake but for the sake of slaying our selfish will.

"Glorious light" is for Catherine what we are granted by God when we are able to recognize his will in all that is, was, and will be. No matter what God sends our way, we try to bow our heads in reverence and receptivity. The pain may not go away but neither does the joy of living in the light of God's providential care. We accept suffering in a spirit of Christ-like surrender until we enter, with Christ's arms around us, the "sea of peace."

> When the soul...has come to taste this light after so delightfully seeing and knowing it, she runs to the table of holy desire, in love as she is and eager with a lover's restlessness. She has no eyes for herself, for seeking her own spiritual or material comfort. Rather, as one who has completely drowned her own will in this light and knowledge, she shuns no burden, from whatever source it may come. She even endures the pain of shame and vexations from the devil and other people's grumbling, feasting at the table of the most holy cross of honor for me, God eternal, and salvation for others.[8]

Catherine further connects these three lights to the situation of one-on-one spiritual direction between a master of formation and a disciple. If, as seekers of truth, we are to attain purity of heart, three facilitating conditions need to be cultivated. First, we must be united with God in loving affection, remembering with gratitude the blessings bestowed upon us. Secondly, with the eye of our understanding, we must come to see how much God loves us and awaits our lasting union. As long as we consider God's will as our primary goal, we can set aside our own selfish intentions and, thirdly, seek the good of others in charitable service.

From the side of the master or director, perception of the light of Christ's truth demands that we be non-judgmental. Catherine is adamant on this matter. She says that we must never pass ultimate judgment on others. Even if we have to make practical and just decisions, we must refrain from condemning anyone, for no one can see a person's hidden heart and mind but God. Our attitude of compassionate concern pleases God because, as the Lord tells Catherine, "You would think you were judging rightly when in fact you were judging wrongly by following what you saw, for often the devil would make you see too much of the truth in order to lead you into falsehood. He would do this to make you set yourself up as judge of other people's spirits and intentions, something of which, as I told you, I alone am judge."[9]

In compassion for the souls under her care Catherine explains how judgment, a formation issue, should be qualified by what our faith tradition teaches us. In a word, we are to shun the sin but love the sinner, complementing the vices we behold in others by virtues we ourselves strive to cultivate. The rule of gentleness balanced by firmness must prevail. At times, admonition has to be added to admiration for the basic dignity of ourselves and others. Moreover, we are to feel the weight of the vices of sinners on our own shoulders and empathize with them compassionately. Rather than focus on our own or their wrongdoings, we ought to hold fast to the knowledge of God's generosity. In short, "Compassion is what you must have, you and the others, and leave the judging to me."[10]

Another formative area of Catherine's teaching takes us into her original analysis of the experiences of extraordinary phenomena like visions or locutions. When are these experiences God's dispensations and when are they delusional? The Lord answers Catherine: "...when my servants love me imperfectly, they love [their own consolation] more than they love me."[11] Catherine herself is distrustful of such phenomena because our general inclination is to pay more attention to these gifts than to their Giver. We become so desirous of spiritual consolations that we either do not see or we refuse to help a neighbor in need. This hindrance happens when:

> Under pretense of virtue they say, "It would make me lose my spiritual peace and quiet, and I would not be able to say my Hours at the proper time." Then if they do not enjoy consolation they think they have offended me. But they are deceived by their own spiritual pleasure, and they offend me more by not coming to the help of their neighbors' need than if they had abandoned all their consolations. For I have ordained every exercise of vocal and mental prayer to bring souls to perfect love for me and their neighbors, and to keep them in this love.[12]

To test our faith, to see if we love the God who consoles more than the consolations we receive, God may withdraw them for longer or shorter periods of time with the intention of bringing us to greater perfection, of humbling us and helping us to identify with Christ crucified that we may know the steady flow of his love whether we feel it or not. This time of testing reminds us that we have no choice but to rely on faith alone in life's midnight moments. We pray for the grace not to fall into the hands of the Evil One, who no sooner spots our gluttonous desires for consolations than he feeds us with false visions. The Lord assures Catherine that the devil can present himself to our mind and imagination under the appearance of light:

> He does this in different ways: now as an angel, now under the guise of my Truth, now as one or the other of my saints. And this he does to catch the soul with the hook of that very spiritual pleasure she has sought in visions and spiritual delights. And unless she rouses herself with true humility, scorning all pleasure, she will be caught on this hook in the devil's hands. But let her humbly disdain pleasure and cling to love not for the gift but for me, the giver. For the Devil for all his pride cannot tolerate a humble spirit.[13]

Is there a sign by which we can tell if a visitation is of God or of the devil? Catherine offers this one:

> If it is the devil who has come to visit the mind under the guise of light, the soul experiences gladness at his coming. But the longer he stays, the more gladness gives way to weariness and darkness and pricking as the imagination becomes clouded over by his presence within. But when the soul is truly visited by me, eternal Truth, she experiences holy fear at the first encounter. And with this fear comes gladness and security, along with a gentle prudence that does not doubt even while it doubts but through self-knowledge considers itself unworthy.[14]

God's visitation brings fear at the beginning, but this anxious feeling gives way to gladness and a hunger for virtue that remains in our soul long after the visitation subsides. We especially hunger for the virtues of humility and charity, which are for Catherine the main foundations of faith. We must not cling to any consolation as an end in itself but test its authenticity by the love that flows from it.

Becoming Living Prayer

The Dialogue is a masterpiece among the classics of our faith and formation tradition in great measure because of its teachings on the life of prayer. Already in the Prologue, Catherine prays for self-understanding, for the Church, for the whole world, and for God's providential care. She insists on the absolute necessity of crafting in our soul an interior cell into which we can go to be alone with God and attend to his Word before we venture into the world. We seek in prayer the inspiration that makes our actions effective. With heads bowed and voices raised in praise, we face the disedifying fact of our sin. This felt sense of compunction, far from being discouraging, increases our hope of obtaining God's mercy. For Catherine, unceasing prayer is possible as long as we maintain a holy desire for God, who thirsts for souls as much as they run to the wellspring of divine and endless love.

Catherine minces no words in her denunciation of those clergy in her time whose neglect of abandoned souls caused many to doubt the unconditional love and mercy of God. An inner locution from Christ assures her that their sins do not render the sacraments less efficacious, although their actions may be a source of scandal among the faithful. Catherine beseeches the Good Shepherd to reform these shepherds of the Sacred and remind them of the obligation placed upon them to feed his lambs and tend his sheep.

She returns to her central theme that the root of deformation is self-centeredness or selfish sensuality. It breeds pride, indiscretion, and a passion for worldly power. Such confused ministers provide for their own needs first and neglect the poor. They shun just admonitions from their superiors and jeer at those who obey their rule of life. In place of fraternal love, they choose the fleshpots of gluttony and lust, even to the point of parading with their lovers in public. So bad is the dissonance she observes that Catherine asks the Lord point blank if anything can be done about it. He replies:

> My daughter, let your respite be in glorifying and praising my name, in offering me the incense of constant prayer for these poor wretches who have sunk so low and made themselves deserving of divine judgment for their sins. And let your place of refuge be my only-begotten Son, Christ crucified. Make your home and hiding place in the cavern of his open side. There, in his humanity, you will enjoy my divinity with loving affection. In that open heart you will find charity for me and for your neighbors...Once you see and taste this love you will follow his teaching and find your nourishment at the table of the cross. In other words, charity will make you put up with your neighbors with true patience by enduring pain, torment and weariness no matter what their source. In this way you will flee and escape the leprosy.[15]

The Lord does not offer Catherine an easy solution to Church reform. He counsels mainly a return to the foundations of faith and the rooting of our life in constant prayer. Thanks to the witness of such faithful souls as she, Christ will accomplish over time the ecclesial renewal for which she prays. Against the three pillars of vice (impurity, avarice, and pride), he will plant in the souls of his friends purity of heart, generosity, and humility, sustained by the efficacy of unceasing prayer:

> To you, eternal Father everything is possible. Though you created us without our help, it is not your will to save us without your help...I ask this of your infinite mercy. You created us out of nothing. So, now, that we exist, be merciful and remake the vessels you created and formed in your image and likeness; reform them to grace in the mercy and blood of your son.[16]

God cares lovingly for the whole world and for each person called uniquely by name. In the light of this love, Catherine is not blind-sided by the deformative experiences she describes. For her both trials and consolations are means of grace used by God to advance our salvation. Our place is to be patient. The Lord asks Catherine not to forget the simple fact that no matter where his faithful ones turn, they will not be satisfied until they embrace his burning charity, his perfect providence.

God treats each of us as we are with our diverse needs and desires. He wakes up worldly souls with a "pricking of conscience." The weariness they feel in trying to find happiness on their own becomes the catalyst that encourages them to fall more deeply in love with his mystery. As we begin to bring our disordered memory, understanding, and will into consonance with the heart of Christ, he orchestrates our spiritual unfolding just as a conductor encourages the players of each instrument to form a symphony. The more we engage in intimate conversation with Christ, the more we experience harmony between our inner and outer life, between solitary adoration of God and generous service of our neighbors.

On the basis of these revelations, Catherine concludes that all of us are being sent by God into the vineyard of life to play our part in the ongoing processes of purifying formation, illuminating reformation, and unifying transformation. Because she trusted totally that God would not fail to hear her prayers, Catherine asked for four things. Each of these petitions was answered in full. God explained to her how to attain knowledge of the truth through knowing herself and his mystery in the light of faith. He heard her plea for mercy and explained that it had been granted to her and the whole world through the entrance into history of his only begotten Son. He showed how this Bridge is to be mounted by the soul's powers of intellect, memory, and will and only to be crossed when pride ceases to rule us and we operate from the center of our humility.[17] Lastly, the Father revealed to her the glory of his providence and the inclusivity of his love and care for every facet of creation. Catherine's task was twofold: to pray always and to show mercy to others until that day when the grace of final consummation would be hers and she would lose herself in the abyss of the Godhead, singing:

> O eternal Trinity, fire and abyss of charity, dissolve this very day the cloud of my body! I am driven to desire, in the knowledge of yourself that you have given me in your truth, to leave behind the weight of this body of mine and give my life for the glory and praise of your name. For by the light of understanding within your light I have tasted and seen your depth, eternal Trinity, and the beauty of your creation. Then, when I considered myself in you, I saw that I am your image. You have gifted me with power from yourself, eternal Father, and my understanding with your wisdom—such wisdom as is proper to your only-begotten Son; and the Holy Spirit, who proceeds from you and from your Son, has given me a will, and so I am able to love.
>
> You, eternal Trinity, are the craftsman; and I your handiwork have come to know that you are in love with the beauty of what you have made, since you made of me a new creation in the blood of your Son.
>
> O abyss! O eternal Godhead! O deep sea! What more could you have given me than the gift of your very self?[18]

Chapter 9

Foundations of Our Faith and Formation Traditions

...every moment of our life has a purpose...every action of ours, no matter how dull or routine or trivial it may seem in itself, has a dignity and a worth beyond human understanding...yet what a terrible responsibility is here. For it means that no moment can be wasted, no opportunity missed, since each has a purpose in man's life, each has a purpose in God's plan. Think of your day, today or yesterday. Think of the work you did, the people you met, moment by moment. What did it mean to you — and what might it have meant for God? Is this question too simple to answer, or are we just afraid to ask it for fear of the answer we must give?
— Father Walter J. Ciszek, S.J.

God's word is the bridge between human trial and error and divine direction disclosures. Without the lights of a faith and formation tradition to guide us, we risk losing our way on roads paved not with awe but with arrogance. We can hardly control our anger when projects of self-salvation implode before our eyes. Like the poor man, Job, we have to cease listening to puny attempts to justify God's ways and attend again to the voice that thunders out of the whirlwind, reminding us who laid "the foundations of the earth" (Job 38:4). Job's humility enabled him to acknowledge before God that no purpose of his providence "can be thwarted" (Job 42:2).

Such appreciative modes of sensing and responding stand in stark contrast to depreciative tactics that debunk God's plan with empty boasts that we have all the answers. Faith tells another story. We believe that God is nearer to us than we are to ourselves. Cosmic, human, and transcosmic epiphanies of the mystery evoke our wonder. We revere the self-communications of the Divine. We receive and accept them on faith. We allow their mystery to startle and expand our narrow mind-sets. We admit to what we will never know and, in dust and ashes, we repent (cf. Job 42:6).

Appeal to the Heart

The Word of God appeals to our heart. In the core form of our character, abstract knowledge finds its best complement in the luminosity of revealed truth. The Holy Spirit grants this light of knowing to us amidst the darkness of not knowing. Our Divine Formator addresses us through the channels of mundane appearances. We accept the challenge to find their deeper meaning. We appraise in appreciative presence to the Divine what is most conducive to this phase of our formation in Christ. With the passage of time, we sense that there is something different about us. It is the graced emergence in our whole being of a new depth of discipleship. In dialogue with our classical teachings and traditions, we grow in the humble and sincere awareness of how indebted we are to the people, events, and things the mystery allows in our life. The one directive to which we cling is that we must do unto others what Christ has done for us. In cooperation with grace, we do all that we can to keep our experiential formation traditions connected to the beliefs that undergird them. We want our worship and our work to reflect as faithfully as possible this compenetration of belief and practice. Our sensitivity to our profile of sin sharpens. On a regular basis, we seek reconciliation with God. We pray to find the inner certitude that our thoughts and actions coincide with the Commandments and the Beatitudes Christ asks us to ponder in our heart.

Given the rapidity and proliferation of the mass media, we may be exposed prematurely to speculative teachings and interpretations of the faith not ratified by the legitimate authority of the Church and certainly not accepted into the body of catechetical truths espoused by our faith community. Whether or not such speculations are compatible with already promulgated doctrines and dogmas only time will tell. Discretion prompts us to remain obedient and to wait upon the guidance of the Spirit. We pray that our hearts and minds will be properly formed and informed by timeless ecclesial truths that enable us to see the difference between passing pulsations and revealed wisdom. The rhythm of contemplation and action preserves us from a superficial reliance on subjectivistic interpretations about our faith that preclude rational reflection and humble obedience. We choose instead to base our appraisals on the formative directives emanating from the Gospel that sustain our call to live within the framework of a foundational Christian spirituality. We resist any tendency to impose on others our own unexamined conclusions about what constitutes faith deepening. Catechetical doctrine, not controversial declarations, is the ground on which we stand.

Appraising Formation Events as Providential

One perennial appeal of our tradition can be found in the invitation to detect the always traceable thread of Divine Providence in all that we are and do. This thread works its way through joyful blessings like the birth of a child and devastating events like the accidental death of a loved one. In the first case it is clear, in the second more obscure, but faith assures us it is there in minor moments like driving to work or preparing a meal as well as in major happenings like losing a job or changing a career. Personal appraisal of the meaning of providence is often bypassed because we do not pause in the process to praise the Lord and appraise if our interpretations are in tune with the cumulative wisdom of our ecclesial traditions. What new lights may be shed on this thread if we see it in the light of scripture and the classics? If we do detect a divine direction disclosure, have we the courage to listen to it? Are we willing to probe more deeply into the concepts of formative spirituality that can illuminate these providential occurrences?

Such ponderings not only shed light on the present; they take us on a journey through formative remembrance to our past. Reflecting on the significance of his own upbringing, Father Adrian van Kaam recalls what it was like to be born and raised in a family struggling to keep the flame of faith alive in difficult times:

> Most of my uncles and aunts were not practicing Catholics. My cousins had not even been baptized. Their ethical ideals were high. They were committed to the cause of peace and justice. We got along fabulously well, learning much from one another. This experience instilled in me a love for both ecumenism and transecumenism. My best lay friends had similar experiences. We all looked for links between our formation history and that of others. Our concern deepened as rumors of war and the beginnings of the anti-Jewish horrors in Nazi Germany were brought to light. We hoped for the opportunity to build bridges between battling formation traditions.
>
> One condition for such meetings of the mind and heart would be the avoidance of any betrayal of the basic beliefs to which each of us were committed. Forthright sharing of formation traditions caused us to respect the differences between us and adherents of other belief systems. Our lives had to include moments of praying together for a world desperately in need of finding some peace by fostering mutual compassion and interformative appreciation. Prayerful encounters could open the way to more consonant

dialogues among religions, cultures, and nations. Together we might be able to hear and support the voices calling for reconciliation. At least we could try to uncover possible paths towards the diminishment of the deformative forces of depreciation, intolerance, and extremism.

Our most important decision at that time was that interformational dialogue should be guided by reverence for the unique-communal call of each person. Proselytizing had to be avoided. We hoped to promote shared charitable services in solidarity with one another. While this hope was music to our ears, we had to face the sober truth that the time was not yet ripe in religion and society for our ecumenical and transecumenical ideals to become a reality. Religious prejudice, fueled by an anti-Semitic Nazi ideology, is difficult to uproot. Relief would only happen later in our providential history.

The life span of any individual, to say nothing of a few generations, is simply too short to disclose experientially the full range of the workings of providence in the life of each person. It takes time to test out if the dimensions and dynamics that constitute our experiential existence are consonant with the mystery. The basic truths embedded in classical formation traditions enrich and deepen our grasp of the past, present, and future. We are challenged by faith to accept God's promises and to adapt them to our here-and-now situation. We are obliged to hand these truths on to those who follow us. We cannot understand the hallmarks of our own or others' complex journey towards a transcendent-immanent existence unless we resource ourselves in the formation wisdom culled from our ecclesial-experiential appraisals of events that shake us loose from the corridors of complacency and become life changing. Our goal as Christians is to appraise appreciatively what has been granted to us providentially.

God's Ongoing Creation and Coformation of Our Life

Another foundation of our faith and formation tradition is the distinction (not separation) between God's initial and ongoing creation and the divine coformation of our life. We believe, in accordance with the first Revelation in creation, that God made all that is out of nothingness. Cosmos and humanity are held in being by a love that is everlasting. Our Creator has endowed us with dynamic powers of relatively free choice and consent. We are from the beginning oriented to transcendence. To humans God granted an option for free cooperation with his ongoing coformation of our existence. In awe and adoration, we revere God as the mystery sustaining all that is and as the Beloved who calls us personally by name. God's initial act of creation continues in his benevolent guidance of our ongoing formation. In one and the same outflow of unending love, our being was made in God's image and likeness (cf. Genesis 1:26-27). Despite the fact that our soul was wounded and weakened by original sin and its heinous consequences, we have been found worthy of redemption through the saving love and mercy of God's only begotten Son.

We can observe both a simultaneity and a distinction between initial creation and the coformation of our lives by God. Our Creator endows our human personhood with the radical potency of freedom to coform our lives in his light and to cooperate with his grace. This divine ongoing donation of the form of our being can be seen as an extension and fulfillment of our primary receptive potency, moving us from our essence in God to our existence in time and space. This potency to be and become who we most deeply are in the grand design of God is granted to all creatures, but, once again, that of coformation with God in relative freedom is reserved only for us humans.

God endows us with a dignity that lifts us beyond the realms of instinctual preservation and reproduction granted to prehuman life forms. Our greatest gift from God is this unique endowment, this gratuitous bestowal of an ultimate potency for redemptive transformation. Our actualization of this gift has been severely compromised by the disobedient deformation of our fallen condition. The story of salvation is itself still unfolding insofar as Christ lifts our defective powers of coformation to the astonishing reformation of his redemptive mercy. This restoration of our wounded potential by his presence in our heart humbles us. In silent awe, we accept that God has elevated us to a potency for transformation in Christ as adopted children of the Trinity.

This Christ-formed potency for transformation purifies, elevates, and strengthens our cooperation with the grace of coformation. We become partners in the mystery of redemption as the secret of our deepest identity hidden in the Godhead is disclosed to us over a lifetime in response to our unique-communal call. As partners with Christ in this divine process, we find ourselves immersed in a relationship of intimacy with the Trinity that carries us through time to eternity.

Centrality of Traditional Ecclesial Appraisals

These events of creation and redemption have been communicated to us by ecclesial traditions over two millennia of inspired wisdom. As members of Christ's Mystical Body, we bear the awesome responsibility to pass these revealed truths on to other believers and pilgrims on the way, who hunger and thirst for their disclosures but who have had to proceed on their life's journey not yet knowing that they are not alone.

Countless providential events shape our life from day to day. Rather than letting either subtle or overt directives stream by thoughtlessly, we ought to resolve, with the help of grace, to unpack their meaning for us personally and for the companions we meet. Our formative reading of scripture and the literature of spirituality helps us to compare our faith journey with the exemplary directives that have enabled obedient disciples to follow Christ with joy despite the crosses they had to carry. Tracing their story and comparing it to our own enhances our preconscious and conscious awareness of deformed dispositions that despoil our call to discipleship. Their spiritualization, through grace is a goal worth pursuing. The likelihood of our succumbing to fickle mood swings lessens while our listening to the inspirations and aspirations of the Holy Spirit increases.

Appraisal in the light of traditional ecclesial teachings encourages us to submit these patterns of disobedience to the reforming dispositions of repentance and forgiveness. The teachings and truths found in the classics caution us not to let falsehoods pulsating through our culture prevent us from surrendering freely and joyfully to the veracity of our faith. Cultivating the disposition of appraisal boosts our appreciation of the timeless and timely validity of the classics. We respect the humane contributions of pretranscendent arts and sciences that do not conflict with the foundations of our faith and formation traditions. They encourage us to trace the links between our knowledge of human anthropology and the credal truths put into practice by formation theology. The complementarity of these two fields allows for whatever correction, elucidation, and reformulation of these pretheological findings may be necessary. We also learn to test the consonance of formation theology in the light of Holy Scripture and the essential ecclesial traditions and doctrines that illumine our everyday existence.

The insights gained by these comparative appraisals widen our understanding of the way in which each event we experience is an epiphany of the transforming mystery. Grace guides the unfolding of our unique-communal call in the span of life allotted to us by the Providence of God. We implement this call in our heart and its matching character and in the dispositions and virtues that coform the pneumatic-ecclesial unfolding of our whole personhood. In loving obedience to the Father, the Son, and the Holy Spirit, we proclaim with the Apostle Paul:

> Blessed be the God and Father of our Lord Jesus Christ, who has blessed us in Christ with every spiritual blessing in the heavenly places, just as he chose us in Christ before the foundation of the world to be holy and blameless before him in love. He destined us for adoption as his children through Jesus Christ, according to the good pleasure of his will, to the praise of his glorious grace that he freely bestowed on us in

the Beloved. In him we have redemption through his blood, the forgiveness of our trespasses, according to the riches of his grace that he lavished on us. With all wisdom and insight he has made known to us the mystery of his will, according to his good pleasure that he set forth in Christ, as a plan for the fullness of time, to gather up all things in him, things in heaven and things on earth. In Christ we have also obtained an inheritance, having been destined according to the purpose of him who accomplishes all things according to his counsel and will, so that we, who were the first to set our hope on Christ, might live for the praise of his glory. In him you also, when you had heard the word of truth, the gospel of your salvation, and had believed in him, were marked with the seal of the promised Holy Spirit; this is the pledge of our inheritance toward redemption as God's own people, to the praise of his glory (Ephesians 1:3-14).

CHAPTER 10

Traditions Enhancing Christian Formation

The whole of a person's life consists in a series of balanced responses to this Transcendent-Immanent Reality. Because we live under two orders, we are at once a citizen of Eternity and of Time. Like a pendulum, our consciousness moves perpetually – or should move if it is healthy – between God and our neighbor, between this world and that.

The wholeness, sanity, and balance of our existence depend entirely upon the perfection of our adjustment to this double situation; on the steady alternating beat of our outward adoration, and our homeward-turning swing of charity.
— *Evelyn Underhill*

The frames that wrap around the pictures depicting our formation story and its ceaseless emergence are our foundational religious and ideological faith traditions. Their timeless and timely directives become the basis of our character and personality formation in Christ. Once faithfully lived, they can soften our stubborn hearts and illumine our clouded minds. Like people waking up from a long sleep, we see the connection between our ordinary concerns and the providential decrees of God. We cease losing our peace under the pressure of an endless litany of stressful questions. We practice more intentionally appreciative abandonment to the mystery.

We may read a Christian classic like Saint Thérèse of Lisieux's *Story of a Soul* and start to follow the "little way" of waiting upon God's will in everyday events rather than waiting for dramatic disclosures. Soon we become aware of "just noticeable improvements" in our spiritual life. We defer to the Holy Spirit to monitor our moment by moment movements towards consonance with the mystery. We reorder our reflections and actions in compassionate ways that motivate us to grow in self-knowledge and service of others. We see the link between the goodness we seek personally and the quest for universal peace all people of good will want to foster.

The dream of world-wide harmony begins to be realized the moment we witness to ways of life that respect human dignity and facilitate the outflow of justice, peace, and mercy. This respectful approach to form-reception and form-donation makes our lives more joyful and effective. It becomes second nature to us to maintain loving concern for others whether or not they share the fruits that accompany our personal profession of faith. Our goal is to radiate the epiphany of God's love and mercy with friends and foes alike. This is the motivation that has changed our heart, and we are not tempted to forfeit it.

These natural and supernatural motivations, bestowed by grace, stir us not only in the core of our being; they also stimulate dispositions like trust and risk-taking that enable us to be more open to the leading of the Spirit. The questions we ask about becoming more Christ-like are not merely academic; they compel us to consider our decisions and deeds from a formational as well as an informational perspective. Two kinds of auxiliary sciences are especially helpful in trying to attain this balance: the speculative-practical that are remotely directive and the empirical-experiential that are more proximately applicative.

Examples of speculative-practical sciences would be philosophy and psychology, both of which shed light on our basic anthropology. Examples of the empirical-experiential sciences would be cultural anthropology, sociology, medicine and medical ethics, demographics and economics, which in many instances may serve the implementation of the faith commitments we have made.

Insights provided by both frames of reference, with their respective methods of research and their metalingual expressions, can be appraised from the perspective of what is formationally relevant in them. Guiding our appraisal at all times is our awe-filled abiding with the Trinity that is the centerpiece of our field of life. Our apprehension of the mystery of God's infinite benevolence frames our interpretation of the formative events we experience day after day in the inner and outer spheres of our existence. In the light of the infused virtues of faith, hope, and love, we recognize and reject those egocentric deformations that deflate our longings for wholeness and holiness. Our counterfeit pride-form resists our efforts to find and follow God's will. It is an act of divine mercy to plunge us into a transcendence crises that shatters our illusion of control and confronts us with the challenge to go beyond the patterns of deflating dissonance that entrap us. Detachment from our narrow, self-centered expectations grants us a deeper awareness of what awaits us if we dare to cooperate with divine grace.

The mystery of God's word manifests itself more often than not in the ordinary ups and downs of daily life. Still special moments of disclosure may come to us when we least expect them. Interrupting the sleepy order of our routinized existence are events that seem at first glance to threaten what we define as our wellbeing. If we choose to dwell on them under the sign of this cross and not to reject them out of hand, we may find ourselves at a new level of awareness of our supernatural call. The transformation Christ invites us to undergo elevates our human condition to heights of faith deepening previously unknown.

Our Traditional View of the World

From the moment we are born into a particular culture, we inherit its consonant and dissonant traditions. The familial, social, and ecclesial community to which we belong by virtue of our birth is as much a part of us as the silent mystery of formation at the center of our being. Our perception of who we are is inseparable from the ways of life handed over to us by our parents and significant others representative of the faith and formation traditions in which we were raised.

It is the task of a lifetime to attune ourselves to our true transcendent identity. In the process we may learn to perceive the world more appreciatively than some of our relatives and friends may have done. Our struggle to grow reflects the necessity of our rising above blind submission to the malformation we may have imbibed from infancy onward. We know we are "more than" our sociohistorical dimension, our vital limits, our functional talents, or their lack thereof. The transcendent mystery always beckons us to go beyond where our circumstances say we are or must stay.

Our Christian world-as-transformative is the new creation that has become the house of God (cf. Galatians 6:15). By virtue of our baptism, we received through the power of the Holy Spirit the capacity to align our world with the covenant bond of love given to us by Jesus Christ. Our history alone and as a people is not a useless suffering but a saving event. Nature is not a raw power but a proclamation of the glory of God. Transmitting these revealed truths from one generation to the next is not a boring duty but a blessed source of renewal. We know from experience that a formation tradition cut off from its faith foundations can be the parent of terrorism, hatred, and war. The message of Christ taken in its purity does not contain one hint of religious prejudice.

He invites us to grow into a community of friends unified by love. Our supernatural understanding of the life of the Spirit is rooted in one Lord, one faith, and one baptism. These are the rocks on which our entire credal system is built (cf. Ephesians 4:5). The more we link our events and experiences to the epiphany of Christ's presence, the more meaning we find in every phase of our formation story.

Principle of Pneumatic Formability

Pneumatic formability could be defined as our capacity to hear and heed the inspirations of the Holy Spirit. Thanks to this gift of grace, we are freed in principle to follow the path of transcendence initiated in us through baptism. The Spirit invites us to be faithful to the divine direction disclosures we perceive. Every instance of their actualization represents our prior receptivity to the already given potency to live in their light. The Spirit does not coerce us to act upon any inspiration granted to us. We are free to accept or refuse it. No matter what we decide to do, God's love for us remains the same. Freely given, it is meant to be freely received. Our aspirations for the transcendent are met by the inspirations of the Holy Spirit.

This supernatural relationship elevates our natural transcendence-ability to a higher state of pneumatic formability. This gift is God's to give, not ours to control; it is the answer to our call to place ourselves under the tutelage of the Eternal Trinitarian Formation and Interformation Event. Our life has been endowed by the Trinity with a pneumatic capacity to incarnate in everyday tasks our truest form in God. Through the mediation of our faith and formation traditions, we become more receptive to this undeserved pneumatic-ecclesial invitation to both accept and fulfill our calling in Christ.

Pneumatic formability readies us, however weak and sinful we may be, to receive the self-communications of God in liturgy, word, and sacrament. We have done nothing to deserve this grace; it is granted to us solely by the merits of Jesus Christ. In, with, and through him, we receive all that we need naturally and supernaturally to assure our salvation (cf. Romans 5:1).

Pre-Revealed and Revealed Foundations of Formation

The revealed foundations of formation build upon the pre-revealed gifts embedded in our nature as created by God. We are essentially formable. God has endowed us with the potency to hear his word and believe it, for "without faith it is impossible to please God, for whoever would approach him must believe that he exists and that he rewards those who seek him" (Hebrews 11:6). This potentiality for transcendent transformation is directed upward to God by the natural light of our human spirit, stretching towards the supernatural luminosity of the Holy Spirit.

This interaction between pre-revealed and revealed formation confirms our need to respect the human anthropology on which grace builds. Our theological reflections on the Revelation never cancel our deep appreciation for the pre-revealed foundations of our humanity as created by God. Briefly, the revealed foundations of our faith illumine, elevate, and enhance with our pre-revealed make-up. Their spontaneous interaction is unavoidable because of the forming and preforming mystery of love that makes us be: "See what love the Father has given us, that we should be called children of God; and that is what we are" (1 John 3:1).

Our formation traditions affect and are affected by what we now know revelationally through the divine directives our life in Christ discloses. Prior to our becoming the undeserved recipients of what Divine Revelation teaches us about the true meaning of our being, we are endowed with a pre-revelational potency to embody what our lived knowledge of the mystery has communicated to us. We integrate at times spontaneously, at other times intentionally, what it means: 1) to be human and Christian; 2) to maintain our potency to give and receive form; 3) to put our gifts and talents to use as Christ commissions; and 4) to appreciate who we are in him and who he wants us to become: "We know love by this, that he laid down his life for us — and we ought to lay down our lives for one another" (1 John 3:16).

The necessity of this integration of love and service cannot be over-estimated. We are exposed in today's world to a bewildering variety of form traditions and directives that appeal in isolation to our pretranscendent ego strivings and their selfish consequences as if our life had no higher purpose, no supernatural meaning. We may imbibe indiscriminately socio-vital-functional influences that inundate our conscience and consciousness. Countless peer pressures and other cultural pulsations produce a confusing array of information that obscures our ability to pay attention to the Spirit-inspired foundations of our faith. Our attempts to pull these bits and pieces of revealed and pre-revealed knowledge together in a superficial, uncritical manner may only result in further fragmentation.

Sadly, we often lack the capacity to engage in a more systematic style of reflection that might prevent such an unfulfilling outcome. Experts in the field of foundational formative spirituality can assist us in our struggle to connect the experiential data we have assembled from many pre-revealed sources with the ecclesial truths that reveal the divine directives we ought to pursue. Such an approach enables us to correct, complement, and unify the pre-revealed foundations that sustain the infrastructure of our revealed Christian faith and formation traditions. This integration yields in turn trustworthy applications of the foundations of formation to the particular situations in which we live and labor as disciples of the Lord.

It is never enough to rely exclusively on pre-revealed experiential, psychological, educational, or philosophical sources of knowledge. Neither ought we to neglect the insights and data of these sciences. To do so would be to limit the concrete possibility of our being able to incarnate the revealed foundations we do receive into our already ongoing processes of formation, reformation, and transformation. Were this to happen, we would risk isolating the revealed principles underlying our traditions from the concrete questions, problems, obstacles, and conditions we encounter daily. Revealed foundations of formation would still be edifying and inspiring in their eternal wisdom and truth, but their radiation into our fields of presence and action would be seriously impaired and insufficiently related to the art and discipline of daily Christian living in a pluralistic world.

Foundational faith formation is by necessity bound to the revealed sources that are its deepest ground. Our respect for their pre-revealed disclosures in human life shows us the indelible link between nature and grace. The principles of application disclosed by our human experiences and the insights we derive from the arts and sciences enrich our treasury of traditions and offer ample proof of their validity. They prove to the doubters among us that Christ, unlike a thief in the night who comes only to steal, kill, and destroy, "came that [we] may have life, and have it abundantly" (John 10:10).

CHAPTER 11

Tradition and Our Communal Life as Christians

'See how these Christians love one another' might well have been a spontaneous exclamation in the days of the apostles. The Holy Fellowship, the Blessed Community, has always astonished those who stood without it. The sharing of physical goods in the primitive church is only an outcropping of a profoundly deeper sharing of a Life, the base and center of which is obscured, to those who are still oriented about self, rather than about God.
– *Thomas R. Kelly*

Every phase of our life in Christ occurs under the influence of our faith tradition. Baptism, Confirmation, Eucharist--the sacraments of initiation–seal our relationship to the Trinitarian mystery. Our response to Christ's call to discipleship is not merely an individual matter. It engages us in the salvation history of humanity. It challenges us to use the gifts and talents granted to us to fulfill our part in the communal mission and ministry of the *ecclesia* from the environs of our immediate neighborhood to the farthest reaches of the globe.

Disciples of Christ experience life-changing turns to spiritual maturity the moment they surrender to his saving power. From converts like Saint Augustine to new Christians accepted into the Church at Easter vigil, one common trait can be identified. All allow his plan to guide their lives. All exercise the gifts bestowed on them uniquely for the good of their faith community.

Many formation traditions facilitate our becoming cultural participants in Christ's name. They cover a vast variety of fields and endeavors from the service professions to the arts. Whatever task we undertake, we realize that we do not operate on our own but in obedience to a higher authority. We submit to the guidance we need—catechetically and personally—to follow Christ in our respective life calls as laity, clergy, and religious.

Responding to Transformative Direction

Thanks to his glorious risen lordship over all of creation, Jesus Christ invites us into an intimate partnership in the mystery of redemption. He shows us the way to replace our old life by one that is new and continually to be renewed:

> You were taught to put away your former way of life, your old self, corrupt and deluded by its lusts, and to be renewed in the spirit of your minds, and to clothe yourselves with the new self, created according to the likeness of God in true righteousness and holiness (Ephesians 4:22-24).

This dramatic change, inspired by Christ, takes place under the direction of the Holy Spirit. Our joy rests in our becoming, in accordance with the graces we receive, servants of the Suffering Servant. We know in our heart the Divine Person we most want to emulate. We try to incorporate the sacred truths in which we believe into the secular worlds of presence and action over which Christ has made us his stewards. By attending to all that he taught us, we come to a deeper understanding of scripture, doctrine, and tradition. We chart a steady course from the uplifting experience of first conversion to the sober reality of accepting the Cross. Our style of participation avoids jumpstarts with no follow-through and becomes one of perseverance and promise-keeping. We do not pick and choose what to believe; we live in fidelity to the beliefs we have been taught. Our lives become radiant epiphanies of the saving presence of Christ himself, humble signs of his glory. As competent and compassionate workers in the vineyard, we hold nothing of ourselves in reserve. Christ gave his all to us, emptying himself for our sake (cf. Philippians 2:7), and we must have the courage to do the same.

No matter how faithfully we try to live our Christian formation traditions, we will experience the pushes and pulls of temptations to compromise the Commandments. We pledge to uphold the dignity of life and are put to the test in nurturing a newborn or caring for an aging parent. We seek paths of peace but find ourselves at war over issues concerning injustice and discrimination. We want to forgive others as we have been forgiven by God but find it impossible to forget the hurt inflicted upon us. A Christian faith ideal, valid as it is, may be more difficult to translate into a real formation practice than we would like to admit.

Our deviation from these ideals reminds us that we are still sinners in need of redemption. There is a tug of war raging on the battlefield of our heart. We know from experience what the Apostle Paul means when he says, "I do not understand my own actions. For I do not do what I want, but I do the very thing I hate" (Romans 7:15) because, as he adds, "evil lies close at hand" (Romans 7:17). While the apostle delights in God's law in his inmost self, he recognizes in his members "another law at war with the law of [my] mind." It makes him "captive to the law of sin that dwells in [his] members." Paul's self-accusation sears our own heart. We know the wretchedness of which he speaks. We, too, cry out in pain like him, "Who will rescue me from this body of death?" The response of Paul to his own question is as simple as it is true: "Thanks be to God through Jesus Christ our Lord!" (Romans 7:21-25).

The assurance given to us of new life in Christ does not remove the stain of the sinful state of our fallen condition. The path to integrative unity of heart and mind, of body and spirit, though delayed in its actualization, still opens before us because "the law of the Spirit of life in Christ Jesus has set [us] free from the law of sin and of death" (Romans 8:2). True liberation is meant to be activated on every level of our form-tradition pyramid. The good news is that Christ asks us, weak as we are, to repair the breach between faith and formation, belief and action. In small but significant ways, our presence will make a difference in this world. Crushed as we are by the law of sin and death, Christ hears our secret longing for release from bondage into a new and abundant life.

In trying to embody the directives flowing from his Holy Spirit into our human spirit, we must be prepared to confront formation traditions like racism that are contrary to the message preached and lived by Christ, a message that was as clear as it was radical in the climate of his times: "There is no longer Jew or Greek...slave or free...all of you are one in Christ Jesus" (Galatians 3:28). Christ's transformative vision shatters the destructive assumption that faith will always be in conflict with formation. He is the mediator who brings us peace (John 14:27). He assures us in tones of shepherding love, "I will not leave you orphaned" (John 14:18). So powerful is the bridging role of Christ that he changes the course of human history through his Cross. Suffering love overcomes death itself and gives us a new lease on life stretching through time to eternity.

Remembering Our Mission and Ministry

The general mission we share as baptized Christians is to bring the fullness of Christ's message of love to a world waiting in doubt and hope to receive it. Whenever we integrate what we believe with the way we live, we become part of the healing ministry initiated by our Lord. Doing his will in accordance with the Father's design for our lives is the only sure way of binding together our faith and formation traditions. Grace nudges us to pass through these doors of obedience but fear of what God may ask of us can pose an obstacle to our final entrance. Our hesitation may diminish if we close our ears to compromising voices and listen anew to Christ's liberating call. A change of heart may already be in the offing whether we perceive it on the level of focal consciousness or not. The peace of an integrative heart may radiate into our formation field and become a source of attraction to others.

Once activated, this disposition causes us to flow with rather than to resist the call to ongoing conversion. It is as if we feel a sudden burst of energy to do what we were not previously able to accomplish. We remember the deepest meaning of our mission and ministry. Works of mercy renew their appeal not as a result of our own efforts but because this outreach to the least of these is what Christ asks of us (cf. Matthew 25:31-46). It does not rely on our feelings or moods but on our love-will, which responds to the commandment to love one another as Christ has loved us (cf. 1 John 4:19-21).

Grace actualizes the transformative potency already implanted in us by God. Its efficacy is twofold: we respond to his demands and we grow in the knowledge of his design for our lives. At first vaguely, then more noticeably, we sense that we are being released from the "unfreedom" of a fragmented, deformed existence separated from God to the "freedom" of a life of union and communion with God. Deepened day by day is our unique-communal commitment to love and serve others for Christ's sake. This inspiration flows first into our transfocal consciousness through the power of the Holy Spirit and then becomes more focal. Listening to God's word causes us to take a second look at the rich traditions of wisdom and truth it embodies. This reflective stance towards our mission and ministry directs us to further explorations of our faith. Acts of simple obedience translate into corresponding directives that enable our formation conscience to mature in Christ. We meet in a more gracious manner the practical concerns that arise in the situations where we find ourselves.

Traditions we once took for granted take on greater significance as we draw more consciously upon their treasures. What a difference there is between mere worldly directives that leave us feeling empty even if they are fulfilled, and trans-worldly pointers to a truly hope-filled future with the Gospel in the vanguard of our concern. Christ himself is our light. Our plans may at times go astray, but his do not. He fulfills the prophecy confirmed of old and in our own experience:

> I bring near my deliverance, it is not
>   far off,
> and my salvation will not tarry:
> I will put salvation in Zion,
>   for Israel my glory
>   (Isaiah 46:12-13).

God's redeeming love and forgiveness restores our fall from grace. Thanks to the lasting truths found in our faith and formation traditions, our life lights up with new meaning. The Spirit invites us to relinquish our illusions of control and to make a fresh start.

Our cooperation with grace lessens our sadness about what has been and quells our fears of what is to come. Alone and together with our faith community, we celebrate every sign of transformation of heart. Although the way to integrative unity in Christ is a gradual one, we accept the truth that the vision will have its time (cf. Habakkuk 2:2-4). All that Christ asks of us is that we be faithful to our mission and ministry in the beauty of the moment.

There are three steps that make the attainment of this Christian formation ideal a more likely reality. First, we must be mature enough in our faith to detach ourselves from any self-centered quest for power, pleasure and possession as ends in themselves. Secondly, we must find ways to pour the transformative love we have received from Christ into whole-hearted involvements in service projects that spread the message of the Gospel in our homes, in the marketplace, and in the wider world.

Thirdly, we must operate from a transcendent plane of meaning that puts functional gain in its proper place and refuses to posit a false separation between the sacred and the secular.

Functionalism is the one formation tradition, perhaps more than any other, that erodes our faith. With ears poised to listen (cf. Matthew 11:14), we may be able to make the turn to a transcendent-functional existence that takes into account our foundational faith traditions. They are the only reliable basis on which to balance our ambitions to do good with our aspirations to be friends of Christ, committed to live in obedience to his word, with or without visible signs of worldly success.

Chapter 12

Fruits of Transformative Participation in Our Traditions

Sugar sweetens green fruit and in ripe fruit corrects whatever is crude and unwholesome. Now devotion is true spiritual sugar for it removes bitterness from discipline and anything harmful from our consolations. From the poor it takes away discontent, care from the rich, grief from the oppressed, pride from the exalted, melancholy from the solitary...

It serves with equal benefit as fire in winter and dew in summer. It knows how to use prosperity and how to endure want. It makes both honor and contempt useful to us. It accepts pleasure and pain with a heart that is nearly always the same, and it fills us with a marvelous sweetness.
— *Saint Francis de Sales*

A pastor with whom we meet on a regular basis for our direction-in-common sessions at the Epiphany Academy confessed a source of recurrent regret in his long life of ministry: "If the people leave the sanctuary with the same turn of heart as when they entered it, I have failed them as a pastor; I will be answerable to God for why I did not do more to assure their return to the world as transformed Christians. To cross the threshold of the house of God and to walk away unchanged is a contradiction in terms! Religion becomes as routine as going to the grocery store. When we come into the presence of the living God, we ought to leave the church singing for joy."

This pastor points to a meaning of church-going we ought never to forget. The fruits of transformative participation in the rich legacy of our faith and formation traditions are not there for occasional picking but for steady nourishment. They must never be allowed to rot on the vine. It is our duty and our delight as faithful Christians to change routine religiosity into an encounter with the Radical Mystery, into an intimate conversation with the One who loves us. We pray to meet God at such a depth of intensity that our everyday life—not occasionally but as a rule—becomes an epiphany of his presence. The mystery we adore invites us to behold this same presence in each person who crosses our path. In due time, we may begin to apprehend, in response to grace, the transformative horizon against which the most ordinary happenings occur. As our friend said so well, "On Sunday we sink into the comfort of our favorite pew, not realizing that God intends to set us on fire. On that altar is a burning bush, capable of searing our safety nets. We walk and pray on holy ground."

The grace of redemptive transformation in Christ floods our formation field with a luminescence no shadow of sin or death can destroy. The Lord binds together our bodily make-up, our mental and emotional state of mind, and our integrative heart. He asks us to accept the humbling fact that we will never fathom the width and breadth of the mystery of transforming love. Embedded in the pneumatic-ecclesial dimension of our baptized being, amidst the darkest moments of doubt and despair, we may suddenly see the hidden splendor of the Father, the redemptive love of the Son, and the abiding presence of the Holy Spirit.

This liberating experience affects every phase of our formation. Touched by the same light are the inner and outer spheres of our existence as well as our interformative relationships. In dialogue with like-minded believers, we accept the challenge to apprehend, appraise, and affirm the divine meanings inherent in the mundane routines we must follow. Necessary as they are, they could stifle our receptivity to the undeserved gift of transformative participation in our faith traditions. Boredom leaves us when we bore more deeply into the meaning of any chore, no matter how matter-of-fact it seems. We must believe that it has already been taken up into the ultimately meaningful, saving mission of our Lord.

God does not delay our redemptive spiritualization until the end of time. It is a here-and-now happening in humanity and history. It is embedded in the everydayness of our particular calling. We participate in the coming of God's reign on earth as in heaven. This truth may not be manifest at first glance, but it resides, as it were, behind the scenes, nourishing and renewing our attempts to cooperate with grace and to pursue Christian excellence in all facets of our cosmic and human formation.

From Formative to Transformative Presence

The word *formative* has many connotations in relation to tradition; it influences the shape and style our life takes at every moment. It also emphasizes the fact that our spiritual life cannot be reduced to our inner or intraspheric existence only. Neither can it be confined to our prayerful intentions, motivations, and feelings. The life of the Spirit expresses itself in our whole field of presence and action from its most subtle to its most overt expressions.

This notion of spirituality as *transformative* encompasses our attempts, under the guidance of grace, to embody our faith in the form-traditions that surround and sustain us. The specificity of this potency comes into play spontaneously when we integrate worship and work, contemplation and action, prayer and participation. The transforming effect of this integrative approach prevents the reduction of our spiritual life to excessive devotionalism or non-contemplative activism that truncates our transcendent orientation.

Living behind a walled off prison of intraspheric pietism is as contrary to Christian spirituality as fostering a purely activistic interpretation of its incarnational intentionality. The tendency to entrap ourselves in our interiority paralyzes the ultimate transformative mission Christ gave us to "Go into all the world and proclaim the good news to the whole creation" (Mark 16:15). The holistic flow of contemplative action and active contemplation is our preferred path to personal and communal maturation in obedience to the Incarnate Word.

In psalms and hymns, in poetry and dance, in painting and sculpture, we thank the Father for having shown in his Son the way to actualize our gifts of reception and donation. We bow in humility before the Lord for having made us part of his plan over the millennia to form, reform, and transform our lives until we reach our final destiny as his chosen, called, and commissioned disciples. We thank God for allowing us to share personally in the story of transformative love that holds in being the works for which we are responsible. As good stewards, we honor the mystery of the Most High wherever it discloses itself, be it in a mustard seed or a moment of mystical union. Nothing that we do ought to become so absorbing in itself that we close ourselves off from an at least implicit, prefocal presence to the mystery at the center of our field of unfolding. We pray that the Spirit will enable us to "lay aside the works of darkness and put on the armor of light" (Romans 13:12). Amidst the opaqueness of increasing secularity, we seek to become signs of God's unconditional care for every creature on earth.

From Transformative Love to the Life of Prayer

When we pray, we enter into a bond of love that brings the Divine Presence into the particularity of our formation field. Each task we perform becomes part of a tradition of transformation that keeps us fully alive. Amidst affliction and adversity we aspire to be little lights shining in the secular world, who reflect the light of Christ and the tender compassion of his Sacred Heart. Finding the deeper meaning in what we do purifies the motives behind our service; it keeps us from sinking into self-pity when worldly success eludes us. Trust in God illumines these shadows of doubt. We believe that God's plan for our life cannot fail, however many times he chooses to rewrite it.

The traditions of faith deepening we have inherited take on new meaning in every crisis we face. They are like ancient rock formations that have withstood the fiercest storms. They reinvigorate our beliefs in the circumstances that threaten to erode them. Every time we rise to the challenge of implementing transformative directives, we pass on the faith of our own spiritual fathers and mothers. Despite the adaptations we must make to accommodate the signs of the times, we do not ever arbitrarily alter the foundations of our faith traditions. The ways in which we express our adherence to them may lead to new forms of ritual practice like celebrating the Eucharist in the vernacular, but these modulations do not affect the basics of our faith.

Our affirmation of acceptable changes, our apprehension of new directives, and our application of them, are fruits of a sound appraisal process conscious of the need to reform any disposition that threatens to block the light of transformative love. In the words of the Apostle Paul, we receive the assurance that "neither death, nor life, nor angels, nor rulers, nor things present, nor things to come, nor powers, nor height, nor depth, nor anything else in all creation, will be able to separate us from the love of God in Christ Jesus our Lord" (Romans 8:38-39).

Facilitating this turn to transformative participation are the following twelve suggestions. They may be implemented as part of our practice of spiritual self-direction or become part of a small faith sharing group. Whatever the case may be, it is never too late to ask Christ for the grace to change our lives for the better. Any or all of these directives are good starting points:

1. Stay in touch with your calling in Christ through cultivation of the dispositions of praise and thanksgiving. Shun the burdens of self-scrutiny and perfectionism and place yourself in the presence of the saving love and mercy of God.

2. Cultivate stillness in the midst of service. Practice meditation in motion. Do not give in to the deception that there is never enough time in the day to read, meditate, and pray. Be present to God wherever you are and in whatever you do.

3. Listen attentively in awe-filled abiding to every moment of every day. Find sacred meanings in what might otherwise remain mundane appearances. All is a gift if you live in gratitude.

4. Step off the speeding train of mere activism and assess in prayer the direction in which you are being led by God.

5. Allow even the minor events that happen on your journey through life, to say nothing of the major ones, to open your eyes to the workings of Holy Providence.

6. Ask yourself morning and evening if your heart—who you are—is truly in what you do. Strive to integrate transcendent inspirations and aspirations with functional ambitions, lest work override worship and labor cancel leisure.

7. Attune the ear of your heart to spiritual readings by boring below their surface significance to seek the pearl of providential meaning. Keep in mind favorite texts from scripture and the masters that help you to reflect on God's will and ask for help from the Holy Spirit.

8. Develop the custom of ordering the seeming disorder of your day around the divine guidance you have received in prayers of intercession and petition.

9. Take time in quiet presence to process with candor and courage the timid whispers of the Holy Spirit addressing you in your here-and-now situation. Develop your graced potential for contemplative presence in a world of action. Be guided by the wisdom and experience of ongoing faith formation.

10. Remain true to God's call amidst the opaqueness and ambiguity caused by your disobedient proneness to "miss the mark."

11. Become aware of the many openings to prayer provided by the everyday richness of reality and rejoice in them.

12. Enter into the presence of the Divine Presence inviting you to be a carrier of compassion in empathy for your own and others' wounded condition.

CHAPTER 13

Tradition and Transfiguration of the People of God

For when we hold up the life of another before God, when we expose it to God's love, when we pray for its release from drowsiness, for the quickening of its inner health, for the power to throw off a destructive habit, for the restoration of its free and vital relationship with its fellows, for its strength to resist temptation, for its courage to continue against sharp opposition — only then do we sense what it means to share in God's work, in his concern; only then do the walls that separate us from others go down and we sense that we are at bottom all knit together in a great and intimate family.
— *Douglas V. Steere*

Our tradition teaches us that the Divine took a disgruntled group of disobedient idol-worshipers and remade them into the people of God. Many prophets in the Old Testament articulate this mysterious intention and none more poignantly than Hosea:

> When Israel was a child, I loved him, and out of Egypt I called my son. The more I called them, the more they went from me; they kept sacrificing to the Baals, and offering incense to idols. Yet it was I who taught Ephraim to walk, I took them up in my arms; but they did not know that I healed them. I led them with cords of human kindness, with bands of love. I was to them like those who lift infants to their cheeks. I bent down to them and fed them (Hosea 11:1-4).

> The more the people turned away from God, the more God turned towards them, saying: "I will not execute my fierce anger; I will not again destroy Ephraim; for I am God and no mortal, the Holy One in your midst, and I will not come in wrath" (Hosea 11:9).

Such mercy transcends the range of human predictability. In it lodges the essence of our faith tradition. The ways of transfiguration granted to us as the people of God compel us to turn away from every form of transgression. They strengthen our resistance to the idolatrous temptations lodged in all pseudo-spiritual movements. God, not self, must be the center of our existence. Proofs may satisfy our reason, but they cannot replace the efficacy of pure faith. Submission is the first step to transforming union. God wants our whole anthropological and theological makeup to undergo transfiguration. No part of us is to be left out of this change. God refuses to retreat to the silence of infinite spaces. The Bible is a record of one long dialogue between him and us. The result is an increasingly integrated understanding of the divinely initiated commitment to reform our lives in this world in accordance with his plan:

> Come, let us return to the LORD; for it is he who has torn, and he will heal us; he has struck down, and he will bind us up. After two days he will revive us; on the third day he will raise us up, that we may live before him. Let us know, let us press on to know the LORD; his appearing is as sure as the

dawn; he will come to us like the showers, like the spring rains that water the earth (Hosea 6:1-3).

This prophecy confirms the doctrine of redemption that underpins our faith and formation tradition. In its light we see more clearly how God uses our very transgressions to enable our return to him. His unsparing forgiveness bolsters our belief that what he says is true: "For I desire steadfast love and sacrifice, the knowledge of God rather than burnt-offerings" (Hosea 6:6). Our place is not to question this favor but to accept it in humility. This and many other divine favors that reverse our expectations of God's ways with us strengthen our faith and cause us to ponder the God-initiated direction of our lives as believers. Thanks to such clear revelations, we have a better understanding of the mystery of love that chooses, in the face of corruption, to restore the bonds of covenant love (cf. Hosea 6:11).

Here we find the living arena in which we are called to move from loss and defeat to renewal and hope. The fruits of this convergence of faith and formation can best be seen when we stand on the razor's edge of what it means to defend or forsake dedication to our life call. Our pride testifies against us and blocks our return to the Lord; our humility seeks his nearness and reminds us that without him we can do nothing (cf. Hosea 7:10).

Retelling Our Story

We are inclined to tell and retell the story of salvation history because so much in it defies explanation and becomes an epiphany of mystery. No matter how sophisticated our attempts to move from confusion to clarity may be, it is not possible to grasp at a glance the ways of God with us nor to comprehend their reshaping power on the dimensions and dynamics of all that occurs in our field of life. From the selective powers of our neuroform to the inspirations entering our transfocal consciousness, we come to believe that nothing stands outside of the embrace of the Eternal. We do not take credit for any effort at transfiguration. Grace does it with our cooperation. Every emerging attempt at clarification proceeds in awe and wonder. With sufficient discretion, we can risk delving into any developmental discipline that may be of help to us in the analysis of our pretranscendent "I" with its tendency to digress from the transcendent. We try to discern whether or not these insights are compatible with our own traditional view of spiritual formation. It is necessary to ask if certain traditions alien to our faith have slipped unnoticed into the set of directives by which we now live. How extensive is their influence? Can we reverse it before the "golden calf" idolatry swallows the little candle of faith God wants us to light?

Spiritual masters are the chief instruments chosen by God to oversee the proper spread of our faith and formation traditions; they also articulate their own scripture-based concerns about what it is that preserves or weakens our trust in God. In their works we hear constant pleas to guard our imagination and to purify our intellect, memory, and will. Saint Teresa of Avila warns us that many "vipers" will distract us from entering the interior castle and experiencing the joy of intimacy with the Trinity. Saint Ignatius of Loyola examines the good and bad spirits that are at work in us as we enter the portals of transfiguration. At any price the demonic does not want us to go there. The master of Saverne, the Venerable Francis Libermann, cautions anyone assigned to serve those abandoned in soul not to engage in arrogant shows of erratic heroism but to practice moderation and to remember—as he told his early missionaries in Africa and the Amazon—that they were fragile instruments used by God to do his will, not super heroes automatically immune to new diseases!

Masters of this depth pay attention to the formational, not merely the informational, facets of spirituality. They base their teachings on scripture, tradition, and a wealth of personal observation. The insights they have made available to us have been complemented in our day by a more systematic body of knowledge. It integrates these fragments of wisdom into a methodical view of the sociohistorical, vital, functional, and transcendent formation of people in many states of life and stages of prayer. By developing our own theoretical-integrational methodology and metalanguage, we are better able to articulate, elucidate, and translate the experiential dynamics of human and Christian formation across a wide sweep of cultures and religious traditions. We trace foundational themes of faith deepening in general as well as their application to the specific situations in which we may be asked by grace to embody them.

This holistic approach prevents us from being absorbed in our own naively overlooked and unvoiced assumptions about life or from forcing ourselves to imitate the calling of others, especially when it proves to be incompatible with the transcendent nature of human life. The popularization of functional-vital formulas for guaranteed happiness or functional-transcendent projects purported to result in spiritual growth abound in our culture. In such a climate this basic link between spiritual formation and theology is an absolute necessity. Adherents of ideological and religious traditions are at risk of assimilating principles of pretranscendent living that might smother or kill their faith altogether. This loss of integration between faith foundationals and their embodiment in everyday life creates a vacuum into which pour secular trends by the media and educational methods that promote self-esteem at the expense of serving others. Forces of indifferentism and narcissism may undermine, after one or more generations, our adherence to traditions once thought to be ageless but now blithely swept aside.

Retelling our story is an essential part of the formational approach to life. It puts our prior understanding of human and Christian maturation to the test of reality. One recurrent theme of this retelling is the need to make the commitment to living our faith tradition not a side issue but a central concern. Rather than run the risk of having nothing substantial to pass on to the next generation, we seek to restore the rich tapestry of transscientific symbols, texts, and rituals related to the life of the Spirit. By making them a primary focus of our reflective and practical endeavors, we resurrect interest in the art and discipline of transformative spirituality as well as in the formationally relevant information we derive from arts, sciences, and disciplines on the cutting edge of new knowledge.

We do not undermine in any way our faith and formation traditions when we engage in these explanations. Our decision to examine the formational facets of human and Christian living has been made in the hope of disclosing the common ground of all transcendent traditions. Their core meaning cannot be comprehended by methods of measurement only. This attention to specific formation traditions sheds light on why we act the way we do. Within each of these traditions, we find particular expressions of spirituality that facilitate interformative dialogues and cultural exchanges pertinent to the aim of transforming our lives in Christ.

Restoration of Traditional Meaning

A lament heard among young and old today is like the refrain of a song we cannot shake from our mind: "It feels as if we have lost our center. Life seems so fragmented. Frantic schedules pull us apart and make the pursuit of Christian excellence in the marketplace or any ministry almost impossible." Holistic traditions attentive to body, mind, and spirit fall by the wayside as people move faster through life's paces while reporting a loss of peace. These forsaken words from the Book of Lamentations could have been written for us today:

> The joy of our hearts has ceased;
>   our dancing has been turned
>   to mourning.
> The crown has fallen from our head;
>   woe to us, for we have sinned!
> Because of this our hearts are sick,
>   because of these things our eyes
>   have grown dim:
> because of Mount Zion, which
>   lies desolate;
>   jackals prowl over it
>   (Lamentations 5:15-18).

This death knell of meaningless will either erode and delete our reason for living or be the catalyst that propels us to restore traditional meaning. To identify what is detrimental to the trans-scientific nature of our human life, we need to reclaim the holistic directives offered by our faith and formation traditions. In their light, we are less likely to be swept up on a tide of pretranscendent reductionistic, materialistic, deterministic, or secularistic counsels, to name but a few of the obstacles to living our faith. They must be faced directly and overcome if we are to transfigure our lives in imitation of Christ.

We may try for a while to live by the dictates of fragmented concepts incompatible with the truth of our traditions, but such efforts come to a crashing halt in the face of our own inadequacy. That is when we have no choice but to plea for mercy:

> But you, O Lord, reign forever;
> your throne endures to all
> generations.
> Why have you forgotten us
> completely?
> Why have you forsaken us these
> many days?
> Restore us to yourself, O Lord, that
> we may be restored;
> renew our days as of old—
> unless you have utterly rejected us,
> and are angry with us beyond
> measure.
> (Lamentations 5:19-22).

Having made such a mess of our lives, it may seem to be the end of the line but for God it marks the beginning of a new era of honesty and a restoration of our reliance on him alone. The fact that the "joy of our hearts has ceased" (Lamentations 5:15) is music to our Master's ears. When our haughty self-assurance turns to abject humility, when the crown of selfish sensuality falls from our heads, when we say, "Woe to us, for we have sinned" (Lamentations 5:16), we are ready to start again.

A person, a segment of the population, an entire nation can fall into the grip of demeaning directives that mock human dignity. It is only when we have been brought so low that starting again seems to be a real possibility. God sends laborers into the vineyard of transcendent formation to initiate our renewal and to assure us that we have not labored in vain (cf. 1 Corinthians 15:58). We went wrong, but his love was there to set everything right again. With renewed vigor we proclaim the true story of redemption in a way that respects our human nature as existentially flawed by sin but as essentially graced by God. With the psalmist we sing: "The Lord is gracious and merciful, slow to anger and abounding in steadfast love. The Lord is good to all, and his compassion is over all that he has made" (Psalm 145:8-9).

CHAPTER 14

Aids to Articulating Our Christian Traditions

It is impossible to avoid the dangers and hazards which life is full of without God's actual, constant help; let us ask him for it continually. We cannot ask him for it unless we are with him. We cannot be with him unless we habitually practice this holy exercise. You will tell me that I always say the same thing. It is true. I know no other means more appropriate or easier than that! And since I practice no other, I recommend it to everyone. We must know before we can love. To know God we must think of him often. And when our love is strong we will think of him very often for our heart will be where our treasure is. Think about this often and think about this carefully!
— *Brother Lawrence of the Resurrection*

Restoration of our community of faith by the Spirit increases our responsibility to share this era of renewal with others. We must not hide our light under a bushel (Matthew 5:15), but proclaim from the housetops what we believe (cf. Matthew 10:27). The Good Shepherd whom we are to emulate invites us to love and serve others in opposition to the selfish ways of the world. His Spirit guides our passage from the bondage of sin to the free offering of forgiveness. Sustaining our commitment to follow Christ are the directives for wholesome living found in scripture, doctrine, and the classics of Christian spirituality. In the light of these counsels, we come to see what it means to imprint our faith so deeply on our heart that we are able to pass it on spontaneously to all those suffering from the bane of abandonment in body and soul.

Traditions as Formative

Our Christian faith and formation traditions are a remarkable blend of unity and diversity. Their foundational form is contained in the revealed information recorded in Holy Scripture. Their core form consists of their expression in Christian doctrine and in our reflection on and practice of these revealed teachings and their directives in daily life. Their thematic current forms are articulated over the ages in the already acknowledged and potential classics of our various traditions that record and clarify the scriptural and doctrinal wisdom cherished by generations of believers.

Accompanying these three coformants are three corresponding modes of articulation, including: 1) their transscientific expressions in Holy Scripture; 2) their informational/formational expansion in doctrinally sound liturgical customs, rituals, and symbols; and 3) their recurrent themes as traceable in the classical texts that exemplify the fruits of formative reading of the scriptural, doctrinal, and liturgical expressions of our faith. These are brought to life age after age in the arts and disciplines that may contribute to our personal and shared experiences of prayer and presence to the tasks through which we exemplify Christ's teachings.

Scripture is the soil out of which the fruits of our tradition come into full bloom. Doctrinal and liturgical expressions function as the main servants of this foundational form of biblical revelation. These named coformants and their articulations interform with one another as we strive, under the guiding power of the Spirit, to apply concretely in everyday life what we profess to believe.

Classical Articulations

This applied spirituality demonstrates itself most impressively in the Christian classics. The link between the classics and the scriptures is analogous to the strongest of marriage bonds. The compositions of the masters range from explicit commentary to experiential reflections on the Bible. We identify in them recurrent themes like mirroring the Paschal Mystery of dying and rising to new life in our own crucifixion and resurrection events.

The classics reveal in hidden and manifest ways the ultimately benevolent plan of Holy Providence for our lives. In them we find testimony to the truth of God's goodness. Formative reading of the classics, along with other devotional practices and celebrations of word and worship, offer us an abundant harvest of ultimate and proximate directives applicable to the Christian ideal of faithful discipleship. These directives flow from and return to the doctrinal core of our traditions. They interform with the foundational facets of our faith. Their divinely guided interpretation, elaboration, and expansion give birth to rituals and customs that exemplify how we, as the people of God, learn our faith and live it in fidelity to our unique-communal life call.

Because that to which we adhere originates in and returns to its deepest ground in the word of God, we know that our faith carries us in spirit across vast expanses of time. Its universality catechetically confirms its uniqueness formatively. One faith encompasses a large family of believers. Our shared ecclesial traditions give rise to countless form-traditional articulations. Their impact on our lives is not a matter of mere subjectivistic interpretation; it has to be validated by the legitimate authority invested in our faith grouping. In this way, succeeding generations draw upon the same treasury of directives for living in conformity to Christ. Transformational truths found in the classics become familiar territory. The underlying doctrines they uphold give rest to our wandering souls.

Texts like *The Confessions of Saint Augustine*, *The Dialogue of Saint Catherine of Siena*, *The Imitation of Christ* by Thomas à Kempis, *The Cost of Discipleship* by Dietrich Bonhoeffer, to offer a few examples, enable us, as formative readers, to become the fortunate recipients of perennial counsels and applicative reflections on the life-changing nature of encounters with Christ. Many texts of Holy Scripture light up with meanings not noticed by us prior to this confirming experience, reminding us that we never make the journey to God alone. Such reading prevents our life from racing by so quickly that we miss the messages meant for us by the mystery. With the help we derive from the writings of the spiritual masters, we may see with renewed clarity the track our journey ought to take. We may listen to our heart and follow the Spirit's leading from one phase of Christian maturation to the next.

The recurrence of foundational themes makes them powerful indicators of the link between doctrinal truths and daily life. These themes weave together like a symphonic composition, revealing recurrent motifs and latent sources of formative wisdom and truth explored and confirmed by both formational and informational theology. They enrich our credal systems and the formative teachings upon which we rely for personal and communal guidance. There seems to be a direct correlation between our spiritual growth and our knowledge of the classics.

Attention to Articulation

Two modes of understanding strengthen our attention to the treasures of our tradition: the one is scriptural-ecclesial; the other is classical-experiential. The former concerns the attention we must pay to catechetical theology and its direct influence on our knowledge of how to live our faith in the midst of whatever demands our sociohistorical fields of endeavor ask of us. This mode of guidance does not necessitate our having mastered all the linguistic, exegetical, and archeological knowledge related to the scriptures or accumulated by us and other experts. Neither do we need to engage in speculative interpretations of the word of God that move afield from the guardianship of ecclesiastical authority. The articulation that accompanies our reading of the classics respects the foundational teachings of the faith grouping to which we adhere. To its body of catechetical wisdom we offer our full and free consent.

Our knowledge of Christian formation as classical-experiential indicates our adherence to timely and timeless themes of faith deepening that still effect our here-and-now arenas of presence and action. Our interest is not to consider the processes of formation in piecemeal fashion but from the perspective of a full field theory of articulation that demands a thorough understanding of our distinctively human nature as always tradition-bound. Our whole field of meaning as immersed in the classics becomes a dialogue between our created existence and the uncreated essence of who we most deeply are. This experiential understanding of formation avoids the sway of passing "best sellers" because it rests on a holistic paradigm of human and Christian life that respects its structures, conditions, and phases. It provides a basis for faith formation that benefits from a comprehensive articulation of classical and classics-compatible wisdom and truth.

This two-pronged mode of attention to our tradition enables the continuity of respectful dialogue with the human and social sciences without any loss of faith or fervor. We learn how to respond to people who may not adhere to our ways of honoring the mystery but who share similar commitments to worldwide justice, peace, and mercy. The solidity of the foundations of Christian formation enables us to hold our ground as we ponder our faith-based ideals in the light of every person's experience of seeking words of wisdom that do not pass away (cf. Matthew 24:35).

Continuity of the Classics

As servant sources of our foundational faith traditions, our Christian formation traditions find continuity in the classics. The writings of acknowledged spiritual masters contain perennial wisdom pertaining to the life of the Spirit. They are not as such issue-oriented or of interest only to one segment of the population. These and other time-bound concerns would detract from their timeless significance. The classics appeal to believers and sincere seekers, who value the fact that these renderings of spiritual experience offer insights into the ascetical and mystical life that transcend any single period in the history of Christianity. What was relevant in the ancient or medieval era still speaks to us in these times. When, for instance, we read the works of Saint John of the Cross and John Wesley in dialogue with one another, we appreciate their shared love for the Lord and notice more sharply what it is that makes our formation tradition an integrated whole. We begin to see how its foundational message transcends any epoch, community, commitment, or special school of spirituality.

The recurring and diversifying themes of Christian maturation proceed in a flowing stream from one classical writer to the next. Shared themes of faith deepening are less likely to be lost if they have been recorded in a Christian classic. Such texts represent sensible responses to the challenges we face in trying to keep our faith traditions fully alive and influential on each succeeding generation. Mastery of the essentials introduces us to the main doctrines that root our life in Christ. We begin to feel more at home in the formational meanings of scripture and doctrine traceable in the classics, beginning with the literature of the undivided church and extending to the writings of pre- and post-reformation spiritual masters. All have been gifted by grace with an ability to show us how God "in-forms" the soul with a supernatural wisdom that becomes the basis of our giving and receiving of form in daily life in the most humane and Christian manner possible.

This classical articulation lays bare, as it were, the fundamental structures of the cathedral of Christian formation built from the beginning of Christ's coming into this world. For this reason alone, it cannot be reduced to any one period of history or body of work. Each contributes its own fragment of truth so that one perspective may be balanced by another.

At the same time, in the light of biblical revelation, each tradition gathers to itself an historical succession of mutually complementary texts pertaining to the in-depth formation of our Christian heart and its matching character. One author's attempt to live in the light of his or her own received scriptural and spiritual directives goes deep enough to allow anyone pursuing a similar path to continue with courage. All such works, taken together, exercise a decisive influence on the entire course of our human and Christian journey through life. What we learn on our own and with other pilgrims along the way is a more enlightened approach to integrating what we believe and how we live in the light of these beliefs.

By contrast, exclusion of the classics undermines and contributes to the loss of the cumulative body of spiritual, doctrinal, and liturgical wisdom that is the mainstay of our faith. The classics, re-appreciated in this manner, validate our contention that a view of human life as formational leads us to a keener understanding of revealed Christian directives as transformational. Classical articulation through the art and discipline of formative reading adds a new dimension to our capacity as disciples of Christ to embody our adhered to beliefs not in abstraction but in the concrete reality of a world often devoid of such basic Christian ideals as courtesy and respect.

Classical Articulation and the History of Spirituality

We must not confuse our approach to the articulation of classical formation with the study of the history of spirituality, which focuses on such interest areas as the times, places, and periods in which an author wrote. These texts provide secondary knowledge of the essential traits to which we turn as formative readers. A mainly informational, textual critical or literary analytical approach serves its own academic aims. When we articulate the form-traditional facets of the classics, we take into account this background information while tracing those themes that are more directly relevant to our everyday formation in Christ.

What draws our attention to the essentials moves us beyond the historical circumstances that surround these writings. We look for their trans-historical relevance to what increases our own and others' growth in spirituality and its implementation in agapic love and service of our neighbor. We extrapolate from the text and its time-bound setting insights and findings that are both universal and unique. We do not focus our attention on one special school of spirituality only but on how many different schools provide fragments of knowledge, which taken as a whole, facilitate our understanding of foundational formation together with its basic directives and practices. We lean towards those themes that manifest common ecclesial validity and contribute to our form-effectiveness. We note the link between transcendent transformation and pretranscendent development and between distinctively human formation and those theistic and non-theistic traditions that exert an influence on us. We also examine the doctrinal truths that undergird these classical texts insofar as they shed light on the conditions that help and the obstacles that hinder our capacity for joyful living in the Lord. Now is the time to pay less attention to informational data and more to the lights that can only be obtained by faith in the Christian Revelation. It is not our intention to neglect historical, textual, critical, and literary information; we simply bracket it for the moment to consider the classics in a manner that serves our emergence in Christ in a timely and formative fashion.

Such articulation coforms our character and personality. It adds a new dimension to our reading skills. We learn how to access the relevance of works written in earlier eras. We begin to comprehend the resplendent differentiation and complementarity of our traditions. Above all, we see what a difference it makes in our life when we assimilate their expanding richness. We appreciate anew the link between the foundations of our Christian formation traditions and their underlying faith traditions. In fulfillment of this aim, we try to articulate the classical wisdom we have gained in the everyday language of those segments of the population we serve, from beginners in the study and practice of formation theology to those more proficient in this approach.

Thanks to our openness to the masters of formation, we may come to understand the distinction between formative and deformative modes of asceticism. We may be able to help others implement the directives disclosed by the mystery in their formation field. We may encourage novices to deepen and diversify what they read to such a degree that they are not caught in the net of pop-spirituality and passing fads, of superficial cultural influences or struggles for dominance among groups vying for their market share of people hungering for meaning. Beyond functionalism, beyond modes of functional-transcendence that drift away from the classics, beyond a futile search for only the side benefits of spirituality, is the opening to the land of likeness to Christ we now enter in gratitude to grace. As the Apostle Paul instructed the Colossians, so he instructs us in the essence of our faith:

> As God's chosen ones, holy and beloved, clothe yourselves with compassion, kindness, humility, meekness, and patience. Bear with one another and, if anyone has a complaint against another, forgive each other; just as the Lord has forgiven you, so you also must forgive. Above all, clothe yourselves with love, which binds everything together in perfect harmony. And let the peace of Christ rule in your hearts, to which indeed you were called in the one body. And be thankful. Let the word of Christ dwell in you richly; teach and admonish one another in all wisdom; and with gratitude in your hearts sing psalms, hymns, and spiritual songs to God. And whatever you do, in word or deed, do everything in the name of the Lord Jesus, giving thanks to God the Father through him (Colossians 3:12-17).

CHAPTER 15

Integrative Field of Our Faith and Formation Traditions

And so I struggled on with worship and teaching that had ceased to be real. Until one drizzly raw afternoon when just enough light came through the window to read by, I came to Paul's account of his "thorn in the flesh." Three times, he said, he had begged God to take away his weakness, whatever it was. And each time God had said, "Rely on me." At last Paul concluded — the words seemed to leap from the page — that his very weakness was something to give thanks for. Because now Paul knew that none of the wonders and miracles which followed his ministry could be due to his own virtues. It was all Christ's strength, never Paul's.
— *Corrie Ten Boom*

As the representative masters of our tradition show us, integrating our faith and formation traditions is the task of a lifetime.

For one reason or another, many assumptions that are neither Gospel-directed nor Christ-centered tend to interrupt the unified life we long to pursue. Schools of education, the media, and society at large, movements like new age spirituality, neo-gnosticism, cultic paganism, and transpersonal psychologism, become for many ideological, if not quasi-religious, traditions. Their adherents are at times more defensive about their beliefs than we tend to be about ours. Resistance to the distorting influence these movements might have on the way we understand and live our faith and formation traditions is a responsibility we cannot pawn off to people in higher authority. We all need to defend our faith. Such distortions may result in a progressive, albeit often muted, alienation from our own ecclesial community. By the same token, critical yet respectful dialogue with all such traditions is necessary if we are to identify what may be compatible in them without compromising what we ourselves believe.

Center of Our Formation Field

Our concept of life as a dynamic field of formation locates at its center not a "higher" or a "cosmic self" but the "Radical Formation Mystery." It is not possible, in accordance with our scientific, anthropological, and theological findings, to reduce our field of existence to *only* a field of consciousness that offers mainly subjectivistic interpretations of traditional formation. Our approach to formative thinking counteracts the purely humanistic assumption that life is a collection of causes and effects that determine our every decision and act over which we exercise little or no control. To counteract this truncated view, we hold in faith that ours is a relatively free formation field in which we celebrate the beauty and dignity of our biological givens without any illusion of our being determined by an impersonal "life force." One dimension of our field of being is vitalistically grounded, but we are not *only* a vital field. We are also responsible and sensible, freely formed and forming persons endowed by the mystery with a distinctively human transcendence dynamic.

By locating the Divine Forming and Preforming Mystery at the center of our field, we resist the tendency to make our ego or "lower self" in any way the exclusive center of our presence and action. We oppose the notion of a "cosmically enclosed self" capable of realizing itself by autonomous modes of actualization based on the assumption that nothing, not even ourselves, is ultimate. This position is incompatible with monotheistic faith and formation traditions like Judaism and Islam and certainly intolerable to a Trinitarian tradition like Christianity. The word "mystery," as used in pretheological formation science, is accurate yet open-ended; it leaves room for the way in which different traditions define and describe it. Formative reflection presupposes in this regard that we can agree in principle on the impenetrable mysteriousness of our human and cosmic condition, no matter how much knowledge we may have amassed about it.

Spheres and Dimensions of Our Formation Field

Replacing the common assumptions held by the human sciences of successive levels of life from infancy to old age is our concept of the spheres, dimensions, and phases of maturation present in any human field of life from the start to the finish of our sojourn on earth. It is not tenable to us that all higher forms of development can be attributed to a kind of sublimated unfolding of predetermined biological needs on the vital level only. Such an assumption undermines faith in the fullness of our human and Christian personhood and of our life as centered in the love-will of the Trinity. This absolutely free will of the mystery that loves us into being may activate at any time the preformed higher dynamics of our transcendent and pneumatic personhood. Serving their emergence are the sociohistorical, vital, and functional dimensions of our pretranscendent make-up. Such an holistic sculpting of our personality can be contrasted, among others, to a Freudian libidinal viewpoint that where *id* is *ego* must be or to the contention held by a humanistic thinker like Abraham Maslow that any fulfillment of a higher need in our so-called "hierarchy of needs" is only possible *after* our lower needs have first been fulfilled.

All the spheres and dimensions of our field, whether potential or actual, radiate from the Radical Mystery at the center. Our field with its regions, ranges, and horizons makes possible an existential (not existentialistic) embodiment of our founding life form or, dynamically speaking, our unique-communal life call preformed by the Radical Mystery to whom we bow in reverence and awe. Such a belief counters completely the humanistic assumptions of atheistic, agnostic, or psychologistic existentialism. The self as an enclosed entity can never replace the epiphanic radiation of the Radical Mystery nor its eternal preformation of countless manifestations of its radiant light in the cosmos. Our preformed, created, and redeemed human essence comes into existence thanks to the bountiful love of God, who called us to participate in his unique plan before we came to be. Our existence cannot be loosened from its moorings in our essence in God and ultimately in the eternal preforming ground of all essences and existences: the Radical Mystery of Formation.

Our Interformational Sphere

Our social and personal sphere of interformation flows from and returns to our mysterious center as much as does our intrasphere. Effective interformation, engaged in communally and personally, depends on the connections we maintain with others past and present in the light of our mutual consonance with the mystery. All spheres and dimensions of our field of life (inner, situational, and mondial) interform as a dynamic whole. We are no more determined by our social history than we are by any other action isolated from the freedom the mystery gives us to find the meaning behind our relationships, be they traumatic or tender. Transcendent aspirations influence and deepen our functional ambitions, social pulsations, and vital pulsions as do the pneumatic-ecclesial inspirations flowing into our baptized soul. None of these dynamics can be relegated to our inner dreams and desires only. All interform in the context of our whole field and in service of our faith and formation traditions.

Another facet of our personal and shared interformation concerns the influence on us of both the horizontal and vertical coformants of our relationships from childhood encounters to freely chosen friendships. Interformation with contemporary and classical traditions provides sources of wisdom and experience that influence us for a lifetime. Their fruits show up in what we say and do and in the hierarchical pyramids of formation that depict our way of living our faith in a pluritraditional world. It is our responsibility to appraise to what degree our tradition pyramid is consonant with our quest for justice, peace, and mercy in the context of an often demanding arena of sociohistorical interformation.

We must be especially alert to the influence of socio-cultural pulsations strong enough to give rise to formation traditions alien to our faith. For example, we witness in the western world such a push for wealth, in some cases such an embarrassment of riches, that this pulsation has given rise to the form tradition of consumerism for its own sake. Many people cannot control their spending habits. They live under the burden of almost hopeless debt yet they feel compelled to buy the latest products the media claim they must have. A pulsation that drives one to pursue pleasure for its own sake can give rise to a hedonistic formation tradition as contrary to the dictates of the Gospel as pure narcissism that cares nothing for the poor.

There is perhaps no more powerful force playing upon that emergence of our human and Christian character and personality than this kaleidoscope of pulsations under which we have to live as the beloved children of God. The decisions we make, the traditions by which we choose to live, determine in great measure whether we can or cannot pass on to the next generation the truths the Gospel teaches.

Danger of Denying the Power of Traditions

Certain social, clinical, psychological, and educational disciplines seem to underestimate, ignore, or deny the all permeating and coforming power of traditions. A simple depiction of our pyramids of faith and formation proves their influence on who we are and on why we act as we do. This fact of life reminds us that not all pulsations are problematic. Cultural forces in the free world can combine at a certain point in history to eradicate heinous sins like sexism and racism and can influence other cultures that condone, for example, the slave trade of young children or the despisal of people of color, to change their ways. Once a tradition attaches itself to a pulsation it is difficult to disentangle ourselves from its tenacious hold. We may cite a variety of historical accounts to prove the military defeat of the Nazi regime under Adolf Hitler, but we cannot claim to have erased the Nazi ideology, which collects around itself hate groups, racist fanatics, and neo-Nazi gangs in places as surprising as modern day Europe and America. All of this goes to say that without a detailed understanding of tradition and its binding power in the life of every person on earth, we would not be able to grasp what makes us "tick" whether we are conscious of it or not.

The forces pressing upon us may be so confusing, especially those concerning the sanctity of life and the proper direction of our sexuality, that we may need to avail ourselves of personal or group counseling. The aid we receive in a crisis situation may complement the Christian values we already hold or it may be infected by transpersonal, merely humanistic formation traditions tinged by various forms of gnosticism or false irenicism. Their promulgation, often in the popular media, may undermine or simply push aside the formative power of our own adhered to faith traditions, thus severing us from what truly comprises the solid basis of our character formation. Without even offering us the opportunity to reconsider the perennial worth of our faith-based creeds and moral codes, we may be swept up in the tide of alienating cultural pulsations. Their effect on our core form or heart and its matching character may not be detected all at once, but its corrosive result is sadly all too predictable. Under such circumstances, our formation in Christ is bound to be handicapped and a time of falling away from the faith may be inevitable.

Our stress on the power of socio-cultural pulsations and their effect on our faith traditions sharpens our ability to appraise forces that may either support us in living what we believe or cause a split between what we profess in the silence of our heart and how we act in the public square. The consequences of our decisions shape for better or worse our character and personality formation and the good or bad example we set for future generations. The integration of faithful commitments and daily actions is a lifelong struggle. In our times pretranscendent counseling may not be enough; we may have to seek a complementary transcendence therapy, respectful of our creeds and doctrines, followed perhaps by formal spiritual direction and reception of the sacrament of reconciliation. The harm caused by a naive underestimation of deformative splits between "what everyone does" and "what we as Christian ought to do" must not be taken lightly; it can infect our moral consciousness, allowing us to rationalize away even serious aberrations like disobedience of legitimate authority, lying, cheating or sexual abuse. Although some modes of pretranscendent counseling or therapy may serve to overcome the pain of a divided existence, they cannot heal us totally.

Secular humanistic and relativistic opinions and behaviors, incompatible with Christian teaching and tradition, seem to dominate much of society today. While the findings of contemporary human and social arts and sciences illumine our pretranscendent dimensions—from the biogenetic to the functional-transcendent—we must guard against uncritical absorption of their usually unvoiced assumptions, many of which are neither conducive to nor compatible with the Revelation. No ideological faith and formation tradition in and by itself alone—neither humanism nor positivism, neither conservatism nor liberalism—can sufficiently disclose or fulfill the transcendent orientation of life that is ours from the moment we are born.

Sheer observation proves that we humans are *more than* what any ideology may attempt to reduce us to. World views dismissive of the Sacred cannot satisfy our inmost longings. They need to be complemented, corrected, and reformulated in the light of formation theology and the great care it takes to draw forth the formationally relevant insights of any credible research effort while seeing where it fits in relation to our fully human and Christian character formation.

The subsequent articulation of our adhered to faith and formation traditions benefits from a complementary relationship between the fields of philosophy and theology. In the pursuit of ultimate meaning, theology identifies philosophy as its "handmaiden" in the same manner as faith respects reason. Yet in the order of a teaching sequence, philosophical training may precede theological reflection, as is the case in many seminary programs. Similarly, in an attempt to understand the transformational effects of traditions, we may first need to study the pretheological science of formation, followed by studious attention to the scriptural and doctrinal articulation of these anthropological underpinnings in service of a comprehensive formation theology. This dual aim is best fulfilled in dialogue with everyday life as formational. This holistic approach both precedes and accompanies the disclosure of related Christian and Christian-compatible formation directives.

A Crucial Problem

It should come as no surprise to any of us that absolutized humanistic perspectives loosened from the mystery of creation and redemption increasingly permeate the lives of elementary, high school, and college students. Therapy and counseling groups, individual clients, readers of self-help books and articles, internet communications—none escape the long tentacles of sheer secularism. The Judeo-Christian basis of our character and personality formation may be hollowed out before we so much as suspect what is happening to us. Whole generations may be incapable of pursuing not only a strong work ethic but also a wise and balanced integration of what in their religious heritage best guarantees their spiritual survival today and for years to come. In a world where "anything goes," it is increasingly necessary to seek the guidance of our age-old catechetical treasury of wisdom and truth. The educational-formational mindset we foster does not rest on the shaky foundations of our own willfulness but on the love-will of the mystery in which we participate as the children of God. This mystical grounding of our own transcendent will to grow beyond sheer erotic strivings to agapic love is the basis of our spiritual life and its blessed unfolding in the Eternal Trinitarian Event that embraces us from birth to death.

Expressions of Our Love-Will

The human potency to express agapic love represents the highest actualization of our need for pretranscendent expressions of erotic desires and passions. Eros, as initially preformed in us by the Forming Mystery, is by the same token predisposed to higher expressions of self-giving love and transcendent transformation. Our distinctively human love-will elevates and deepens the meaning of bio-erotic passion. The desire to love and be loved dwells in us from the beginning of our creation in the womb. It is latent in everything we are and do. It is not the fruit of sublimation but a source of transformation of our pretranscendent passions, which long for infinite fulfillment despite the fact that eros has been wounded by original sin.[1]

As children we are not yet awakened to the beauty and power of this inmost gift. We live mainly in the throes of vital eros. We feel animated by our need for felt love and appreciation. Our sheer survival depends on these expressions of care. We crave sympathy and empathy from the significant others around us. We need the comfort of familiar surroundings at home and in our neighborhood to feel safe. We have no choice but to trust others because our vital eros cannot survive or thrive alone. This fact of life is what makes the heinous sin of child abuse so devastating.

In early childhood we are not yet able to distinguish between the selfish or selfless needs of those who care for us. We welcome from the start of life being the center of everyone's attention, but we are bound sooner or later to be put in our place. Disappointed by the limits of what we now enjoy so vivaciously, we may find our boundless passions bumping into unyielding walls that awaken us, through the disillusions of eros, to the possibility of a transcendent fulfillment that addresses and nourishes the deeper hungers to which our pretranscendent passions point.

In a mistaken understanding of human sexuality, these boundless passions of childhood are considered by some to be ends in themselves. Their ultimate goal—their transcendent fulfillment—is overlooked in favor of satisfying these childhood passions in various ways of pseudo self-fulfillment that may last for the rest of one's life. Consequently, erotic needs stagnate at the vital level and never offer us an opportunity to go beyond the self-centered eros of childhood. Neglected are the deeper hungers to which our pretranscendent passions point.

What we thought would fulfill our desires vitally proves incapable of doing so. This realization may give way to certain experiences characterized by transformed eros or the gift of agapic love in the depths of our being. This God-given gift renews and purifies the aberrations caused by our blunted passions, our illicit sexual drives, and our inability to foster responsible celibate or marital love. Initially, selfish sensuality may confine us to the prison walls of wounded eros. We may try to harness our transcendent longings to suit our own self-centered purposes, but such efforts prove to be futile. Nothing our dominating ego can attain can substitute for the Other-centered orientation sustained by classical transcendent traditions, which uphold the self-sacrificing worth of reformed eros and its redemption by Jesus Christ. The divine command to love one another as God has loved us (cf. 1 John 4:19) is the sublime goal that awaits us when we let go of our self-centered desires and try to see in every person we meet the countenance of Christ. In the words of Pope Benedict XVI in his first encyclical on the power and beauty of agapic love, we understand what constitutes true self-fulfillment in relation to God and others:

> Faith, hope, and charity go together. Hope is practiced through the virtue of patience, which continues to do good even in the face of apparent failure, and through the virtue of

humility, which accepts God's mystery and trusts him even at times of darkness. Faith tells us that God has given his Son for our sakes and gives us the victorious certainty that it is really true: God is love! It thus transforms our impatience and our doubts into the sure hope that God holds the world in his hands and that, as the dramatic imagery of the end of the Book of Revelation points out, in spite of all darkness he ultimately triumphs in glory. Faith, which sees the love of God revealed in the pierced heart of Jesus on the Cross, gives rise to love. Love is the light—and in the end, the only light—that can always illuminate a world grown dim and give us the courage needed to keep living and working. Love is possible, and we are able to practice it because we are created in the image of God.[2]

Chapter 16

Teaching the Classics in Service of Our Traditions

It was necessary for our salvation that there be a knowledge revealed by God, besides philosophical science built up by human reason. Firstly, indeed, because the human being is directed to God, as to an end that surpasses the grasp of his reason.
— *Saint Thomas Aquinas*

From the viewpoint of foundational Christian formation, we cannot restrict the teaching of the classics to only one or a few epochs or masters. The widest and fullest knowledge of our tradition is our best protection against over-attachment to passing accretions that become substitutes for the ageless foundations of our faith. If we want to access and assimilate our classical traditions as an integrated whole, we must resist the temptation to let our personal reading of a text obscure other layers of meaning still to be disclosed. In small groups where participants feel free to express the resistances or resonances that may have formed in their minds, more directives for faith deepening found in these writings may come to the forefront of our attention.

Teachers of the classics need to respond to such points of contact with expert knowledge of the texts under consideration. They also ought to acquire a comprehensive view of other writings that serve to balance any possible one-sidedness in their own interest or interpretation. The best option is to be thoroughly at home in the formational texts of each epoch and culture by studying and teaching them over regular cycles of courses. In this way, one may offer continual enlightenment to many different students. Another option is to relate the forms of asceticism and mysticism proposed by the classics theologically to the pretheological insights of formation anthropology. In this way we can appraise more wisely what is pertinent to our daily experience as disciples of the Lord.

A contemporary text may be appreciated as potentially classical: 1) if it deals with the foundations of Christian formation; 2) if it is linked with one or more already acknowledged collection of the classics; 3) if it is consonant with the doctrinal theology underlying its formational expositions, even if some of them may be innovative in their formulations; 4) if its scope, depth, and expression are of such a quality that it seems probable to various experts in the field of Christian articulation that it may be identified in the future as an integral part of the historical stream of major or minor classics; and 5) if it lends itself to a critical articulation by experts in proto-theological anthropology as a servant source of ongoing form-theological reflection.

Such classical Christian approaches are not geared primarily to analysis of the historical development of a particular school or system of spirituality but to the identification of foundational formative themes, directives, and practices that manifest a universal or common validity, appraised from the viewpoint of their form-effectiveness. Highlighted as well are possible links to distinctively human formation and to other non-adhered to faith and formation traditions. Important in this teaching process is an investigation of the possible relevance of these classics to the expansion or correction of the propositions offered by formation science. This goal can only be achieved if we do not suggest in any way that an empirical-experiential science can articulate insights obtainable only by faith in the Christian Revelation. Last, but not least, teachers in this field may provide students with a selective list of non-Christian classics they deem to be relevant to issues raised by their Christian counterparts as read and reflected upon in courses that cover the ancient, medieval, and contemporary literature of spirituality. These texts may be mainly edifying or listed as potentially classical according to the mature appraisal of experienced teachers, who appreciate first and foremost those contributions to faith deepening that have passed the test of time and influenced generations of believers representing a variety of faith groupings.

Teachings from an Ancient Master

Pseudo-Dionysius (c. 500) is an enigmatic yet profoundly influential spiritual figure, possibly a Syrian monk of the sixth century, who wrote under the pseudonym of Dionysius or Denys the Areopagite, whom Paul the Apostle refers to as one of his converts (cf. Acts 17:34). His writings, which first appear at the beginning of the sixth century, reveal a unique preference for the *via negativa* or "apophatic theology" that stresses the utter inability of the human heart and mind to penetrate the impenetrable abyss of the mystery of God. The spiritual power of his works touched many subsequent masters, among them the anonymous author of *The Cloud of Unknowing* and Saint John of the Cross, both of whom mention Denys by name.

The surviving body of Dionysius' work consists of four books: *The Divine Names; The Mystical Theology; The Celestial Hierarchy;* and *The Ecclesiastical Hierarchy;* added to these are *The Letters,* numbered One to Ten.[1] Pervading all of these works is the author's belief in the union of the whole creation with its Creator, a union in which the created order will attain perfection or, to use the word preferred by the Eastern masters, "deification."

Dionysius' most seminal book is *The Mystical Theology*. Here he formulates in terms that will be retained in Christian classics for ages hence the threefold path of purgation, illumination, and union. The Dionysian tradition also distinguishes three types of Christians: 1) the beginners are those introduced to or approaching contemplation, whose main concern is the practice of virtue (*praxis*); 2) the proficients are those in the middle way to whom contemplation (*theoria*) and the suppression of passions (*apatheia*) are particularly suitable; and finally 3) the perfect are those to whom God reveals in an experiential way knowledge of himself (*theologia*). These various stages are understood to interpenetrate one another. They demarcate movements in the human soul responsive to divine transformation.

Though he writes of the names by which we address the Divine, Dionysius held to the belief that God is above any and all attempts to actually name him. He is a Being beyond being itself, residing in the dark reality of the super-essential nature of the Godhead that always and forever defies definition. Awe grips the soul as one passes beyond anything one can perceive or know into the darkness where God is; one is reduced to "complete speechlessness" and united in one's highest part in utter receptivity to him who is completely unknowable; one "knows beyond the mind by knowing nothing."[2]

Dionysius never fails to stress the impotence of every human attempt to penetrate the veil that stands between us and God. This is the divine darkness, the "cloud of unknowing." God draws us in an upward movement from purification to deification.[3] In the context of the *via negativa*, the soul learns to relinquish its own knowledge about God and to submit to God, who himself takes the initiative to lead the one who seeks him through love into the intimacy of union with the Trinity. Our soul goes out of itself and into "the ray of the divine shadow which is above everything that is."[4] There we bow in humility before the allness of God and acknowledge our nothingness. In this prayer of petition from *The Mystical Theology*, "Denys" summarizes his longing to be led by the ultimately unknowable Trinity to new depths of knowing in unknowing:

> Trinity! Higher than any being,
> any divinity, any goodness!
> Guide of Christians
> in the wisdom of heaven!
> Lead us up beyond unknowing and light,
> up to the farthest, highest peak
> of the mystic scripture,
> where the mysteries of God's Word
> lie simple, absolute and unchangeable
> in the brilliant darkness of a hidden silence.
> Amid the deepest shadow
> they pour overwhelming light
> on what is most manifest.
> Amid the whole unsensed and unseen
> they completely fill our sightless minds
> with treasures beyond all beauty.[5]

Influence of Dionysius

Early glosses by Maximus the Confessor (d. 662) attempted to bring the works of Dionysius "into conformity with Orthodox spirituality and dogma,"[6] making them not only acceptable to the Church but rendering him one of the best-loved and most read writers among the Fathers and Doctors of the Church. Translation of his writings came into the West around 827 when a copy of them was sent from Byzantium to Paris. Subsequently, the translation by John Scotus Eriugena in 862 popularized Dionysius for Latin Christendom and extended his influence by the twelfth century to the works of Cistercian masters like Saint Bernard of Clairvaux and William of Saint Thierry.[7]

The medieval traditions of both mysticism and scholasticism honored his principles as we see in a text like Saint Bonaventure's *The Journey of the Soul to God* and in the treatise written by Saint

Thomas Aquinas on *The Divine Name*. The Rhineland school of spirituality was especially influenced by Dionysius, as is evident in the works of Blessed John Ruysbroeck, Henry Suso, John Tauler, and Meister Eckhart.[8] His influence on the English school of spirituality through the work of the anonymous author of *The Cloud of Unknowing* is undeniable. Other authors indebted to Dionysius include Nicholas of Cusa (d. 1464) and Denis the Carthusian (d. 1471). These and many other lines of interest in the Dionysian teachings culminate in the writings of Spanish mystics of the sixteenth century, most notably those of Saint John of the Cross.

In the Reformation, the Dionysian spirit played only a marginal role, due perhaps to the suspicion surrounding such neoplatonic terms as "ecstasy" and "divine darkness."[9] Interest in the *apophatic way* has been revived in our day because contemplative teachings and practices have gained new ground. As we grow more disillusioned with scientism, functionalism, and pragmatism, with the general de-constructionist tendency of the postmodern era, we seem ready once again to hear the voice of Dionysius declaring that we must plunge into the abyss of not knowing if we want to meet God in love. In short, we need to remember that reason is only one wing of truth; the other is faith in a mystery that surpasses all knowledge and beckons us to "leave behind...everything perceived and understood, everything perceptible and understandable, all that is not and all that is...."[10]

Ways of Knowing God

In the literature of spirituality we find references to two main ways of approaching the mystery. The first is *cataphatic* or the way of affirmation of what we can see and know of God through reason aided by faith. The second is *apophatic* or the way of negation of all that we know *about* God so that we can come in love to know God while never fully understanding who God essentially is. According to Dionysius, it is only by unknowing that we may know him whom we can never comprehend intellectually.

Knowledge of created things always carries with it a temptation to "learned arrogance" which may destroy "learned ignorance," the only way by which we can attain to God in himself. It is precisely this quality of incomprehensibility which, in Dionysius' mind, is the one definition proper to God. There will always remain about the Godhead an "irrational residue" which escapes analysis and which cannot be expressed in concepts; it is the unknowable depth of things that constitutes their true, indefinable essence. It is impossible to define God in words. Awe seizes the soul when we contemplate the mystery in and beyond all that is. Although cataphatic theology celebrates the manifestations of God in creation, of which the supreme epiphany of God in the world is the Incarnation, it, too, retains its apophatic character since:

> The Cause of all is above all and is not inexistent, lifeless, speechless, mindless. It is not a material body, and hence has neither shape nor form, quality, quantity, or weight. It is not in any place and can neither be seen nor be touched. It is neither perceived nor is it perceptible. It suffers neither disorder nor disturbance and is overwhelmed by no earthly passion. It is not powerless and subject to the disturbances caused by sense perception. It endures no deprivation of light. It passes through no change, decay, division, loss, no ebb and flow, nothing of which the senses may be aware. None of all this can either be identified with it nor attributed to it.[11]

Negative theology is an expression of that foundational attitude which transforms the whole of our spiritual life into a contemplation of the mysterious depth of the revealing and concealing truth of the Trinity. The apophatic view of mysticism forbids us to follow representational, projective, and calculative ways of thought or to form concepts that would usurp the ultimate ground of truth in a mystery beyond our ability to comprehend it.

The word chosen by Dionysian to designate an interior experience of "knowing in unknowing" is *mystical*. Reason and feeling may be part of this interior experience, but neither mode of knowing can explain how we discover the presence of the Divine within us as well as beyond us. The apophatic way does not lead to an absence of encounter or to an utter emptiness inside us, because the *Unknowable God* we love is not an impersonal deity. Dionysius commends himself to the Holy Trinity when entering upon the way of not knowing that is to bring one to the fullness of loving knowledge. In this ecstatic experience of the "More Than," we are caught up in the love of God for us. We live, no longer for ourselves, but for the Beloved who lives in us (cf. Galatians 2:21).

The effort of intellectual reasoning allows us to know ourselves and our interior experiences as participating in the Divine, but our powers of analysis can only take us far. At a certain point, reason comes up against a barrier beyond which it cannot go. Behind this wall, this cloud of unknowing, resides the Godhead in his essence. The only gift which grasps the being of God, beyond feeling and beyond reasoning, is pure faith.

Dionysius holds that nothing in creation can impede our union with God since we are free to choose or contest the course of action that leads us to consuming union. Evil, he concludes, is a "lack of being." Purification means drawing our soul away from multiple distractions to God alone, who is the object of our faith and the agent of our transformation. This radical asceticism supplants our natural way of knowing by a divine way of understanding that includes the redemption of our anthropological makeup as a whole.

To let go of what may be known by sense or understanding is to attain in divine ignorance to union with God, who transcends all being and all knowledge. Renunciation is a disposition first directed towards the world of created things so that we may gain access to the *un*created. Renunciation is the key to liberation, which, at least in part, is characterized by being freed from what our senses alone disclose to us. While they offer us hints of the Infinite, we must resist the temptation not to go beyond them if we hope to enter a realm of knowing that is not the product of our limited reasoning processes but an understanding given to us without understanding.

> But now as we climb from the last things up to the most primary we deny all things so that we may unhiddenly know that unknowing which itself is hidden from all those possessed of knowing amid all beings so that we may see above being that darkness concealed from all the light among beings.[12]

Here Dionysius advises us to abandon freely and willingly all that impedes our way to God (that which is impure) and to scale at God's bidding the supreme heights of sanctity. The word "impure" does not refer only to obstacles to bodily chastity. Its wider meaning points to pride, arrogance, and paralyzing fear. "Impure" can be the reasons or the proofs we try to attach to the Divine. It is only through the purifying of our heart of all useless words and modes of egocentric mastery that our soul can be readied by grace to penetrate the darkness wherein God who is beyond all created things makes his dwelling.

> But my argument now rises from what is below up to the transcendent [apophatic], and the more it climbs, the more language falters, and when it has passed up and beyond the ascent, it will turn silent completely, since it will finally be at one with him who is indescribable.[13]

God became like us in his Son Jesus Christ, who was fully human without loss of his essential incomprehensibility as fully divine. God is the hidden God of the psalms, who made darkness his secret place (cf. Psalm 32:7). In this humble acknowledgment of God's infinite transcendence, we experience an up-drawing and in-drawing of consciousness; we pass from particulars to universals. God is not any thing we can comprehend and, therefore, by abstraction, we arrive at the super-essential darkness which outshines and obliterates the limited light of our sense perception.

The way of negation does not lead to the false conclusion that God is a supreme, uncaring force, but to the revelation of God as our Creator, Redeemer, and Lover, who being "beyond every limitation...is also beyond every denial."[14] At the end of *The Mystical Theology*, Dionysius brings us to a presence and a fullness without measure. He introduces us to a Person, to Jesus Christ, who transcends our understanding of his essence while bringing us to intimacy with the mystery of the Trinity.

CHAPTER 17

Teachings from a Medieval Master

Accordingly, if we want to reach the highest summit of humility, if we desire to attain speedily that exaltation in heaven to which we climb by the humility of this present life, then by our ascending actions we must set up that ladder on which Jacob in a dream saw "angels descending and ascending" (Genesis 28:12). Without doubt, this descent and ascent can signify only that we descend by exaltation and ascend by humility. Now the ladder erected is our life on earth, and if we humble our hearts God will raise it to heaven. We may call our body and soul the sides of this ladder, into which our divine vocation has fitted the various steps of humility and discipline as we ascend.
— *Saint Benedict of Nursia*

Though Julian of Norwich (1342-c. 1423) is a medieval contributor to the treasury of our faith and formation tradition, she echoes Dionysius' love for the mystery. She herself is an extraordinarily gifted fourteenth century English mystic and solitary "anchoress" whose entire life was devoted to prayer and contemplation. She lived simply yet comfortably in her "cell" attached to the Church of Saint Julian in Norwich, England. She was around thirty years old and in the throes of a near-fatal illness when she experienced a series of sixteen revelations or "showings," which included the recollection of Christ's passion in vivid, even frightening detail; the meaning of suffering and bodily sickness, beheld in the light of God's fatherly and motherly goodness; and the sight of three wounds that imprint the passion of Christ on our soul, these being contrition, compassion, and longing for God.

For the rest of her life, Julian pondered the meaning of these visions, both their apophatic depth and their cataphatic applications. In the short and the long form of her book, she affirms the goodness of creation, the friendship of Christ, and the tender solicitude of the Trinity. She knows with the certitude of one who has seen her Redeemer that he wants to be united with us. She also introduces the notion of Jesus as our true Mother. In celebrating the tenderness of his humanity and the saving grace of his divinity, Julian was convinced that love, not sin, is the ultimate determinant of our existence. No words are more characteristic of this spiritual master than her oft quoted conviction: "All shall be well...and all manner of things shall be well."

Though little is known of Julian biographically, it is certain that she wrote her famous *Showings* or *Revelations of Divine Love* in a turbulent era, riddled with catastrophic events like the Black Plague, the Hundred Years' War, religious persecution, and a papal schism centered in Avignon from 1305-1378. Women were largely unrecognized in intellectual circles, but Julian's contributions were taken seriously, since the cloistered life gave her a voice commanding respect. Her incredible optimism has contributed to her reputation as one of the holiest and wisest of the English spiritual writers. Her work is lauded not only by scholars but also by the same common folk she loved and guided. Like us, they were people who questioned the meaning of life in the light of their always fast approaching death.

Despite the chaotic times in which Julian lived and wrote, she never failed to see the presence of God everywhere, even in something no bigger than a hazelnut. When she held this tiny bit of creation in the palm of her hand, Julian saw something of the nature of God, who made it, loves it, and preserves it as he does all of us, his children. As far as she is concerned, prayer makes the soul like God:

> Prayer unites the soul to God, for although the soul may always be like God in nature and substance, it is often unlike him in condition, through human sin. Prayer makes the soul like God when the soul wills as God wills; then it is like God in condition, as it is in nature. And so he teaches us to pray and to have firm trust that we shall have what we pray for, because everything which is done would be done, even though we had never prayed for it. But God's love is so great that he regards us as partners in his good work; and so he moves us to pray for what it pleases him to do, for whatever prayer or good desire comes to us by his gift he will repay us for, and give us eternal reward.[1]

Julian offers our tradition a feminine-intuitive approach to the highest reality and in this her work is comparable to that of Saint Catherine of Siena and Saint Teresa of Avila. Out of her spiritual experience emerged her doctrine and her formative counsel to other seekers. There is in the *Showings* a movement from experience to expression; from God's grace to our response; from an acceptance of illness to a vision of its meaning; and from the waning of bodily powers to the release of transcendental reflection. In infirmity, Julian finds opportunity; in human weakness, divine strength; in spiritual poverty, dependence on God for everything; and in misery, the mystery of outflowing mercy. She understands above all that a revelation is an operation of divine love. It offers insights into what might otherwise be unknown; it is a gift freely given. When the time of the showings is past, when what was seen has receded, its fruits are reflected upon, savored, and preserved by the grace of the Holy Spirit to the end of the visionary's life.

Influence of Julian

Though Julian describes herself as a simple, unlettered creature, she is the first English woman of letters. Her knowledge of our faith tradition included, among other sources, the Cistercian writings of William of Saint Thierry and Saint Bernard of Clairvaux that influenced her thinking on the motherhood of God and texts from the Franciscan tradition focusing on popular devotion to the Passion of Christ.[2] She herself became part of the now famous school of English mystical writers, including Richard Rolle, the anonymous author of *The Cloud of Unknowing,* and Walter Hilton.

Despite her maidenly modesty, Julian had a powerful mind which enabled her to thread her way through the labyrinths of metaphysical thought and speculation. Her force of will gave her heroic fortitude so that in the midst of her suffering, which brought her to the point of death, she was able to laugh heartily. Her special genius, as elevated, illumined, and coformed by grace, carried her to the highest summits of contemplative life and vision. In addition, she had a rare gift for literary expression that makes her book a devotional treasure. Her essential personality can be glimpsed in her radiant disposition, in the charm of her writing style, and in her pure and loving heart, wholly centered on God.

The only direct historical reference found in the history of Norfolk, says: "In 1393 Lady Julian, the anchoress, was a strict recluse here and had two servants to attend her in her old age. This woman was in these days esteemed one of great holiness."[3] Prior to entering the anchorage, Julian was probably trained and consecrated as a Benedictine nun at the adjoining Convent of Carrow. Her revelations took place in a house or cell built on to the little Church of Saint Julian in Norwich. It is still in use today and beside its foundations the outlines of the ruined anchorage can be traced.

We look in vain in her book for particulars about her parentage, home, friends, interests, and education. To compensate for these omissions, she supplies the most careful descriptions of her condition (physical, mental, spiritual) on the occasions of her visions, including dates and times. Best of all, she withdraws the veil from her inner life and lets us see the secrets of her soul.

Julian's book comes to us in two forms: the *Short Text* written soon after the revelations, which began on May 13, 1373, had ceased; and the *Long Text* that was composed when the revelations ended and Julian committed herself to explore their hidden meaning and to elucidate their "misty" teaching. By ever deepening fellowship with Christ, she sought keener insight and clearer knowledge into what had happened to her. Twenty years later she gave to her fellow Christians the fruits of her disciplined inquiry. The result is one of the most valuable documents of ascetical experience in the whole range of mystical literature.

Gifted Character of Julian's *Showings*

The Showings came to Julian as an answer to prayer. In them we find an admirable synthesis of mystical experience and theological reflection, ranging from "bodily visions" of the passion of Christ to "intellectual visions" of the Trinity; from reflections on creation and Divine Providence to intuitions penetrating the innermost secrets of redemption, mercy, and forgiveness. Julian had long desired three gifts of God:

1) to be granted the *mind of Christ's Passion*: a bodily sight, that is to say, to suffer with Christ as did those who were present at the foot of the cross;

2) to endure *bodily sickness*: an illness that would be so severe as to procure for her the detachment proper to death and to obtain this sickness so as to be entirely purified and afterwards to live for God alone; and

3) to have *three wounds:* one of contrition (sorrow for sin); one of compassion (for the sufferings of Christ); and one of steadfast longing for God (an absolute and unconditional will to love).

This long and disciplined preparation readied Julian for the wonderful visitations she was to enjoy when she was thirty years old. For three days and nights she laid in serious bodily infirmity. On the fourth night she received the last rites of the Church because she thought she could not live until daylight. She lingered for two more days and nights. On the third night she and those with her were sure the end had come. She confesses that being so young she suffered grievously the intervention of death—not because she was afraid to die or because she craved for life itself but because she wanted to love God better and serve him longer. She endured her pain until dawn, but by that time her body was dead "from the middle downwards."[4]

Unexpectedly there comes a sudden change; her pain leaves her and she feels as well as ever. She attributes this cure to the working of God. She then asks that her body be filled with the mind and feeling of Christ's blessed Passion. In asking for this favor, she did not wish for a bodily sign and showing of God but only for the compassion such a sympathetic soul might have for the Lord. Then the visions began. Fifteen showings succeeded one another, starting in the early morning and continuing until that evening. The sixteenth revelation—which was to be the completion and conclusion of all—took place the following night, but before she enjoyed its fruits, Julian suffered a serious relapse. Her bodily sickness returned with its former violence and the spiritual comforts of the revelation fled.

In this condition she was ready to believe that the visions were the ravings of delirium, but when she spoke of them to a religious person who visited her and was greatly edified, she felt ashamed of her own doubts and failures of faith. She lay until night trusting in God's mercy. When she fell asleep, she had a frightful nightmare, but throughout her account she is careful to stress the difference between dream visitations and divinely illumined spiritual revelations.

The last of her visions comes that night. She describes it as a delectable sight and showing in which the Lord assured her that he was the author of the previous revelations. After this she was conscious of a deep and true peace—but not for long. The devil made one more effort to shake her trust and allegiance, occupying her all that night and morning until the new day dawned. Julian resisted his assaults and brought to conclusion her remarkable experiences, giving herself over, in the silence and solitude of her cell, to prayerful investigations of their contents.

Julian's Doctrine of the Spiritual Life

Julian makes a distinction between the *extraordinary* or *accidental elements* of the spiritual life (sickness, showings) and its *essential components* (contrition, compassion, and longing for God). The latter consists of a sweetly burning wound that will be healed only in heaven; she also distinguishes between *unitive prayer*—union of wills—and *contemplative prayer*—beholding what is not a special showing.

It is important to understand that Julian desired sickness so as to be purged of her sinfulness by the mercy of God and afterwards to live in awe of his majesty. This desire for sickness found fulfillment, a grace Julian attributes to a direct divine intervention not to a pathological condition like hysteria.

From a purely medical point of view, it seems probable that her sickness was due to a temporary abnormal condition of her psycho-physical system, not to a purely organic and permanent deficiency already affecting her. One notes in this regard its sudden onslaught and its equally sudden cure. Julian's showings do not rest on their being extraordinary phenomena, for they are intrinsically different from those associated with hysteria, hypnotism, and the like. She contemplates them in the light of her own character and personality as a renown spiritual directress. Considering the immediate and permanent effects of such phenomena on her moral and religious life, one cannot rule out the possibility that her sickness was of divine origin.

A state of hypnosis or trance is excluded since she was highly conscious and able to reason and pass judgment on what was happening to her due to a lifelong habit of mental control *versus* the generally chaotic, unorganized, rambling and digressive character of the hysterical temperament. Nor was her desire for sickness an obsession which could have produced a pathological condition; on the contrary, she sought it only as a means to the attainment of higher spiritual graces, beginning and ending in the Paschal Mystery of Christ's dying and rising.

Julian's account of her sickness is free from all affectation and from any trace of neurotic exhibitionism. She has no desire to impress the reader; rather she wishes to direct attention away from herself to God alone. The strongest indication of the divine origin of her sickness can be found in her behavior during its course and particularly at the epicenter of the crisis. In the midst of sincere pains — she was convinced that she was dying — she remained in an attitude of peace, self-detachment, and readiness to do God's will in suffering and dying. Her stamina, as well as the natural forces of her mind and will, far from being diminished during the sickness, were improved and strengthened. The aim of her prayer — to be purged of every remnant of selfish sensuality and afterwards to live in purer worship of God — seems to have been answered. This is one more indication in favor of a divine *versus* a neurotic origin of her sickness and a warning against interpreting her sights themselves as hallucinations attributed to an overly rich fantasy life.

The same principle must be applied to her sights. It is insufficient to study them in themselves. As with all extraordinary events in the lives of the mystics, it is difficult to determine which are preternatural and which are merely natural. These phenomena are, moreover, intimately connected with the whole physical and physiological make-up of their recipient.

It is best, as a rule, to examine the effects they produce, including an increase of spiritual insight conveyed to her intellect by which she saw and grasped the essentials of Christian living like sorrow for sin and the conviction of God's forgiveness. Through prayer and reflection, she attained the grace of a heightened awareness of how we should progressively unite ourselves to God — not by way of speculative knowledge but by an intimate clinging to the Trinity effected through our love-will.

Julian's attitude towards her sights is to see them as a means for the attainment of higher spiritual goods that last as long as the foundations of our faith. She classifies what she is shown to her in three categories, comparable to the classical treatment of mystical phenomena:

1) Bodily sights or bodily visions (corporeal and imaginative) refer mainly to the fact that they reflect the humanity of Christ, which is perceptible not only to external senses like seeing and hearing but also to internal ones like imagination and memory.

2) Words formed in the mind or understanding comprise an intermediate type of "ghostly sight in bodily likeness" and an imaginative "more ghostly sight" without bodily likeness.

3) Ghostly sights or pure and higher intellectual visions are effected in the understanding and not perceived by the senses.[5] In this case, the visionary's understanding is lifted up or elevated by a special intervention of God. It takes place suddenly without any indication of a connection with what has been seen previously. It causes a feeling of "great marvel," for, as she says, "I saw that he is to us everything which is good and comforting for our help."[6] She also beholds suddenly a "sight" of the Creator's loving and active presence, depicted in the image of a hazelnut, lying in the palm of her hand.[7] Another "sight" granted immediately to her by Christ is that of our Lady in her spiritual glory and excellence.[8] The Lord opens her "all of a sudden" to the truth of Jesus dwelling in her soul; of the Godhead that rules and sustains heaven and earth; and of the Divinity in its own proper life and activity.[9] All of these revelations culminate in the simple yet profound message: "You will not be overcome."[10]

"Ghostly sight" of this sort is a vision granted freely by God himself without any direct or intrinsic connection with one's sense-experiences. It is exclusively concerned with purely spiritual objects, which, though perfectly present, cannot be described in detail. In her words, "And about the spiritual vision, I have told in part, but I can never tell it in full."[11] Ghostly sight is ineffable because of its spiritual nature whereas bodily sight, because of its connection with the visible and tangible, can be described in more pictorial terms. Ghostly sight or spiritual vision is communicated directly by God, who leads the intellect to perceive or slowly to understand the special meaning hidden behind what is beheld in "bodily likeness." More ghostly sight without bodily likeness (intellectual vision) goes beyond "ghostly sight in bodily likeness." The "more ghostly" is not a sudden but a gradual transition which leads her understanding passively from lesser to greater seeing. Not only does each type of showing occur frequently but often two sights or even all three kinds may occur in one and the same showing.

Julian is insistent that bodily sight or corporeal vision is a means to a higher end and that her showings in whatever form do not convey new revelations nor do they communicate hidden truths not already contained in the Revelation entrusted to the Church. Her attitude is that of a humble child of God, who is always ready to reject what she conceives to be a light from him if it is not in full accord with the teaching of the Church.

In Chapter 34 of the *Long Text*, Julian affirms the divine purpose of private revelations, which touch on points of doctrine: "For everything which is profitable for us to understand and know our good Lord will most courteously show to us by all the preaching and teaching [the faith and formation traditions] of Holy Church."[12] Though Julian considers her showings to be of divine favor and origin, she does not consider them to be of essential importance for the life of mystical union with God. She insists that her showings were gratuitous gifts which did not make her better by the mere fact that they were given to her.[13] She emphasizes that they are not essential for a life of love and union. The condition of those who seek God in pure faith without the help of these extraordinary favors is as good as the condition of those who are granted the grace of beholding God in special showings.[14]

These favors must not be asked for to satisfy curiosity or our natural desire for knowledge. Their aim is to facilitate our perception of spiritual truths since it is the love with which they are received that matters, not the sights themselves.

Although Julian received her showings with gratitude and humility, she does all that she can to convince us that they are not the only, or even the best, means to advancement in the love of God. Rather they were channels of insight given to her by the sheer grace of God to be used with great prudence and always in full accord with the will of God who granted them and with the authority of the Church that protected her.

Julian counsels us to see each period of pain or purgation in our lives as a movement towards transfiguration. If we immerse ourselves in the Paschal Mystery, we will proceed as naturally and sanely as possible through life to death to eternal life. To see suffering and even the prospect of death from the perspective of transfiguration, is what Julian refers to as "naughting," a disposition which views all that happens to us with the eyes of love and which sees nothing in this life as ultimate. Our final rest can only come in God, whose promise never wavers: "I will make all things well, I shall make all things well, I may make all things well and I can make all things well; and you will see that yourself, that all things will be well."[15]

CHAPTER 18

Teachings from a Contemporary Master

The form of the soul is God who must imprint himself there like the seal on wax, like the stamp on its object. Now this is not fully realized unless the intellect is completely enlightened by knowledge of God, the will captivated by love of the supreme good, and the memory fully absorbed in contemplation and enjoyment of eternal happiness. "And as the glory of the blessed is nothing else than the perfect possession of this state, it is obvious that the initial possession of these blessings constitutes perfection in this life." To "realize this ideal" we must "keep recollected within ourselves," "remain silently in God's presence," "while the soul immerses itself, expands, becomes enkindled and melts in him, with an unlimited fullness."
  — *Saint Elizabeth of the Trinity*

Evelyn Underhill (1875-1941), a renowned British mystic, writer, and retreat leader, was born into a middle-class family in which there was no particular emphasis on religion. Even in her early writings she was drawn to the imagery and sensitivity of the Christian spirit. After a visit to a convent in 1907, she converted to the faith. Although at first she felt inclined to join the Roman Catholic Church, she remained with the Church of England, but it would be several more years until she acknowledged the fullness of her commitment. In one major work of hers she emphasized the importance of worship; in another, she demarcated the course and spirit of Western mysticism. No matter what she taught, she stressed the need to embody in practical ways the Christian rhythms of contemplation and action, of prayerful deepening and charitable giving.

Under the guidance of Baron Freidrich von Hügel (1852-1925), her spiritual director, Evelyn became one of the main architects of the mystical revival following World War One in Western Europe and America. Among its proponents, in addition to Evelyn, would be C. S. Lewis, John Henry Cardinal Newman, and the Quaker spiritual writer, Rufus Jones. Evelyn embraced the task to craft a spirituality of adoration and action, intrigued as she was by an observation of the English poet William Blake, who wrote in "The Marriage of Heaven and Hell," that "...if the doors of perception were cleansed everything would appear to [us] as it is: Infinite."[1] In 1911, at the age of 36, she wrote what would become her most famous book, *Mysticism*. It was rapidly followed by *The Mystic Way* (1913) and *Practical Mysticism* (1914). Two later works that also reveal her to be a serene, calm, reassuring, and lucid woman as well as a gifted guide for the journey to God are *Worship* (1936) and *The Spiritual Life* (1937).

Underhill's teaching in *Practical Mysticism* offers an excellent summary of her commitment to contemplation in action. For her the life of the spirit has to be ordered towards the mystery of God's grace at work in our whole formation field. We need to let the doors of our perception stay open to the transcendent amidst the demands of daily life. The presence of the Divine Spirit in our human spirit readies us for ordinary contemplation characterized not by ecstatic uplifts or blissful departures from the demands of real life but by concrete acts of charity or self-giving. It is always false to reduce mysticism, in her words, to "the status of a spiritual plaything." Contemplation ought not to "wrap its initiates in a selfish and other-worldly calm [or] isolate them from the pain and effort of the common life. Rather it gives them renewed vitality..."[2] This means that a mystical or contemplative outlook on life involves each of us in a unique spiritual adventure to which the nearest human analogy is the experience of falling in love. To fall in love with God, wholly, passionately, and joyfully, is to be drawn by grace beyond the mediocrity of a Sunday-only spirituality to the maturity of a life of intimacy with the Divine. According to Evelyn, women as diverse as Joan of Arc and Florence Nightingale acted under the same "mystical compulsion." She believes that "their intensely practical energies were the flower of a contemplative life."[3]

Fidelity to our faith and formation tradition has a social, not merely a self-fulfilling aim in that it enables one to uphold at all costs the eternal dignity of others. The path to such a mature spirituality proceeds, in Underhill's appraisal, through five distinct phases.

The first is *awakening* in which one makes a commitment to seek God with all of one's heart. It begins with an awakening of the self to a consciousness of Divine Reality. This experience may be of relatively brief duration, but it is accompanied by feelings of intense joy. Conversion to a life committed to holiness may result, often following a crisis experience. Underhill cites the example of Francis of Assisi, who went into the church of San Damiano to pray and came out a different man, one who had surrendered totally to God with passionate love and a commitment to serve the Absolute in poverty, chastity, and obedience.

What follows this depth of conversion is a time of *inner purification* in which one seeks to become detached from all sensible things through discipline and mortification comparable to the spirit of Saint Francis' embrace of Lady Poverty. Purgation begins with a person-to-Person encounter between us and God in which we realize the depth of our own sinfulness and self-will.

Underhill cites Richard of Saint Victor, who said that the "essence of all purification is self-simplification."[4] This perpetual process has both negative and positive implications. The "negative" entails detachment or the stripping away or negating of all that is superfluous, illusionary, or distracting. The essence of the evangelical counsel pertaining to poverty of spirit entails a deliberate withdrawal of attention from the "bewildering multiplicity of things."[5] The more "positive" side of mortification involves a reorientation of our heart in which anything less than God no longer captivates our attention. We begin to form new habits like surrendering ourselves to God in moments of humility and joy, astonishment and ardor. We discover behind our formerly "fractious conflicting life of desire"[6] a call to freedom from our prison of self-will.

In the third stage of *illumination*, God gives the soul various consolations or revelations of a deeper union with what is Really Real. These glimpses of Divine Reality vary from person to person, for in this game of love (*ludus amoris*) God treats each soul uniquely. Some experience a total oneness with nature. Others hear voices or see visions. Still others note only a quiet intensity of belief. What matters to Underhill is that all true mystics seek God alone and not spiritual phenomena that only point to the Uncreated Light. The purpose of illumination is to call the soul onward in its quest since one's hunger for the eternal will never be satisfied with lesser expressions of transcendence. The illumined soul attunes itself to recollection, inner stillness, and the calming power of remaining in attentive presence to God. This state may deepen into ordinary contemplation, leading to a wholly receptive openness to and union with God in which our personality is not lost; only its hard edge of willfulness and ego-arrogance undergoes a notable softening.

Now the soul enters into the fourth stage in which all sense of God's presence vanishes, and one must struggle onward guided by *pure faith*. As one travels towards union, one must cross the desert of inner aridity and enter a place of grace identified in classical Christian literature as the dark nights of sense and spirit, so aptly named by Saint John of the Cross. Consolations cease. The sense of God's presence seemingly disappears. One may be assailed by doubts and temptations that arise from within. This is the final stage of purgation of the self as center. Replacing it is a sense of one's nothingness without God. Awareness of one's imperfections weighs heavily on one's psyche, together with a feeling of total mental and emotional exhaustion and lingering aridity. Those who persevere through this period of faith testing may enter into the unitive life, which is a gift of God's grace, not the result of any human effort.

The fifth and final stage, in which the soul is united with God, is often described as a *spiritual marriage* between the soul and God. The soul, having been plunged into the living flame of divine love, is wholly transformed. The result is not passive exaltation but energetic action. As our tradition testifies, Catherine of Siena became a peacemaker between warring papal stages; Teresa of Avila reformed her order; and Francis of Assisi rebuilt God's troubled Church. All of these and other exemplary mystics from earliest times to the present age led productive lives of love and service amidst the most intense commitment to contemplative prayer.

Characteristics of *Practical Mysticism*

In response to the key question, "What is mysticism?", Underhill answers by saying that it is not a philosophy, an illusion, a kind of religion, a disease! It does not mean having visions, performing conjuring tricks, leading an idle, dreamy, selfish life, neglecting one's business, wallowing in vague spiritual emotions, being pious or posturing a special attunement to the Eternal. She defines mysticism as the art of union with Reality or with the Really Real. Mysticism, quite simply, opens us to the mystery of God's love; it cleanses the channels of our perception and prevents our senses from being locked into only a measurement mentality. It lifts us through the grace of God to another plane of consciousness that is primarily transcendent and secondarily functional and vital. Her exact definition is this: *Mysticism is the art of union with Reality. The mystic is a person who has attained that union in a greater or lesser degree; or who aims at and believes in such attainment.*[7]

According to Underhill, we begin to enter this higher plane of awareness when we experience some dissatisfaction with the world we have hitherto attempted to control. A crisis of transcendence lifts us beyond the stagnant plane of complacency. We find that we cannot reduce life to a series of static routines submissive to our own willful orders. A crisis of this sort compels us to rearrange the pieces that up to now have formed the tapestry of our life. What we had thought to be of ultimate or absolute importance — our pleasures, our possessions, our powers — now becomes merely relative. What we desire most is to enter into a richer, more holistic world of meaning, one that rises above calculation and functional control and is in tune with transcendent truths and their fruit-bearing potential.

The final chapters of *Practical Mysticism* take up the theme that, as baptized souls, we are all potential contemplatives. Underhill identifies contemplation as *the* characteristic human activity, prompting us to seek to know God through love and to let this love flow outward to others.

Underhill also sees us as poised between two orders of Reality or, in other words, between two ways of apprehending existence.[8] These are: being and becoming; eternity and time; unity and multiplicity; the spiritual and the natural worlds. The contemplative is the person who grasps these two orders at once, and tries to respond fully to both of them. For the contemplative the seeming disharmony between the parts and the whole is an illusion. Freedom from vital drives and functional ambitions as ultimate results in freedom for a transcendent vision of all things in God and of God in all things. This outlook prompts our focal mind to be open to our transfocal consciousness and to its plenitude of spiritual aspirations and inspirations.

The purifying formation and illuminating reformation that ready us for unifying transformation presuppose the disciplining and simplifying of our attention, this being in Underhill's teaching the essence of recollection. These inner movements of the soul are meant to be more than periodic occurrences; they are to become permanent features of our personality, gathering together its disunified fragments and "making 'the inner and outer worlds together to be indivisibly One.'"[9] We move from looking at the world through windows coated with the grime of dusty, idle, and disintegrated thoughts and narrow self-interests to seeing a new heaven and a new earth (cf. Revelation 21:1).

Underhill reminds us that *recollection* begins with the deliberate and regular practice of *meditation* or mental prayer. Once we commit ourselves to taking a closer look at the meaning of the essential beliefs and devotions of our faith and formation traditions, it ought not to surprise us that our ill-educated attention will waver, but we ought not worry. It is wise to trust that progress is being made and that we are entering a fresh place of perception. It may soon strike us that every aspect of life appears to be more significant. We are less inclined to take things for granted. We find ourselves becoming as appreciative as children are of the wonders of daily life. While acknowledging shame and sorrow for our sins, we become more resourceful in disciplining our attention when it wavers and in renewing our search for simplicity of heart.

What matters most on this contemplative journey to God is intuitive love illumined by our transcendent faith and formation traditions. These are the true agents of our encounter with the Really Real. The result of this kind of seeing is that the sense-world becomes for us a "theophany" of the Most High and an "epiphany" of the Mystery. We perceive in the Many the actual presence of the One just as Julian of Norwich, gazing upon a hazelnut, found in it the epitome of creation and a pointer to the transcendent character of life.

Urging us towards this explicit longing for the Infinite is our "transcendence dynamic," described by Underhill as an "inward push" and by the anonymous author of *The Cloud of Unknowing* as a "sharp dart of longing love." To enter this place of silence where we rest in the Lord, we must begin humbly *where we are*. The outward journey begins on the road closest to home.

Our direct participation in this quest for the Eternal gives the world of time its validity and meaning. We experience a change of atmosphere within and a reprioritizing of our actions without. Our consciousness of the Really Real may be fleeting, but its effects remain utterly transforming.

A shift now occurs from the so-called *active* effort of our will by means of self-discipline, control of thoughts, and longing love to *infused* or effortless contemplation. One lets go. One seeks nothing but God's will while becoming conscious of the constricting force of one's selfishness. Final abandonment to the Mystery makes us feel as if everything is being taken away whereas in truth a transformation beyond words occurs in which God's action takes the place of our activity. This ecstatic realization, whether it is accompanied or not by rapturous feeling, is at the heart of our mysterious contact with Divine Love, whose visitations are beyond our control. Asked of us is that we eradicate the last traces of self-interest, even of a spiritual nature, and wait upon what has been given to us: a still awareness, a cessation of striving, and a resting in the arms of the Absolute.

Exercise of Christian Commitment

As Underhill observes, this steady growth in transcendence does not impoverish our sense-life in exchange for a super-sensual existence; rather, in response to grace, we widen and deepen not only the field of meaning over which our attention can play, but also the powers of our purified sense-life itself. We move from the quiet of contemplative union to a life of active service in a graceful rhythm of being and doing that adds to rather than subtracts from our practical efficiency. We live the life of Eternity in the midst of the world of time. Contemplation flows into action complimented by a keen sensitivity to the abundance of practical work we have yet to do.

Such a clear vision enables us to fulfill our calling to bring eternity into time and to give the invisible flow of grace concrete expression in everyday life. We accept in humility that the vocation of the practical mystic is to heal the periodic disharmony between what our faith teaches and what the pledge to uphold our formation traditions entails.

Our life's aim is to draw the scattered worlds of love, thought, and action into one exercise of Christian commitment — perhaps by great endeavors but more likely through the perpetual give-and-take of daily duty and dedication. We have no choice but to work towards the realization of justice, peace, and mercy, of order, beauty, and freedom in an always broken world.

What "practical mysticism" offers is not a new state of consciousness but a total consecration of our life to the Really Real, whatever sacrifices this commitment may entail. Whether we are aware of the felt absence of God or granted a moment of intense presence, our inward certitude that "God is love" (cf. 1 John 4:8) remains the same, until, at last, "like the blessed ones of Dante's vision, the clearness of [the mystic's] flame responds to the unspeakable radiance of the Enkindling Light."[10]

Chapter 19

Social Conscience and Traditional Formation

When all becomes silent around you, and you recoil in terror — see that your work has become a flight from suffering and responsibility, your unselfishness a thinly disguised masochism; hear, throbbing within you, the spiteful, cruel heart of the steppe wolf — do not then anesthetize yourself by once again calling up the shouts and horns of the hunt, but gaze steadfastly at the vision until you have plumbed its depths.
— *Dag Hammarskjöld*

According to formation anthropology, formative social conscience represents the "ought" dimension implied in our focal, prefocal, and transfocal consciousness. It tells us what we ought to do socially in the light of our unique-communal calling in Christ. It focuses our attention on the expression of our own and others' pledge to foster social justice, peace, and mercy for all.

Fidelity to this Christian formation ideal emerges from the consciousness of our responsibility for the wellbeing of society and its members. This other-oriented dimension of conscience gives rise to such dispositions of Christian consciousness as social apprehension, appraisal, and appreciation. We apprehend what we, in fidelity to our unique-communal call and in consonance with our interiorized pyramid of traditions, ought to do or omit. We appraise how we — within the reasonable limits of our providential situation — can congenially, compatibly, compassionately, and competently protect, promote, and facilitate the communal and personal rights and dignity of ourselves and others. We appreciate the way in which our formative social conscience mirrors our Spirit-enlightened, Christ-formed "ought" conscience. It guides in turn the effective and wise implementation of our catechetically illumined moral conscience by instilling in our hearts a sense of what is right and wrong and why we must try always to choose the former path.

As Christians, our social conscience ought to be formed and informed: 1) by scripture; 2) by the infused theological virtues of faith, hope, and charity; 3) by the gifts of the Holy Spirit; 4) by the doctrines and rituals of our Christian faith and formation traditions; 5) by the inspirations and aspirations of our transfocal consciousness as open to the pneumatic-ecclesial dimension of our life; 6) by the mystery of interforming love flowing from the Trinity; and 7) by our Christian character and personhood insofar as we have assimilated and tried to articulate the social implications of the Gospel message. These channels of guidance align our situatedness in society with our preformation in the abyss of the Trinity. From this bottomless ground there wells up, as from a fresh spring, our call to be a spiritual and social presence in the light of the Christ-form of our soul.

Our social conscience is a specialized form of our moral conscience. Operating together, these two modes of doing what is right enable us to focus on the practical details and experiential decisions demanded of us in imitation of Christ. These may not be as minutely treated by the general considerations offered to us by a theology of morality alone. We need its formational complement to act always as the Christ-centered, Gospel-oriented people of God we were meant to be.

Appraisal in Service of Christian Fidelity

Fidelity to Judeo-Christian doctrines, such as those embodied in the Commandments and the Beatitudes, has to be rooted in the pneumatic-ecclesial dimension of our life. Only through the power of the Holy Spirit can we persevere in our following of Christ. Lasting fidelity presupposes our willingness to subject ourselves to ecclesial correction and enrichment while being open to new inspirations. The key to humble appraisal of our faith and formation journey is to pay close attention to the almost silent whispers of the Spirit in the transfocal region of our consciousness. Through no power of our own we witness the impact they have on the unfolding of our call to be disciples of our Master in times of labor and leisure. With God's grace, we may also begin to apprehend and appraise dissonant thoughts, feelings, remembrances, and desires that are incompatible with the call to discipleship.

A crucial task facing us is to examine prayerfully how dissonances at the level of our heart may be related to underlying focal or prefocal images. To what degree are these images influenced by alien formation traditions? Their hold on us can only be weakened if we seek conscientiously to replace them by consonant images from our scriptural, doctrinal, and liturgical traditions. Such form-traditional confirmation heightens vigilance of heart the moment dissonant images threaten to interfere with our receptivity to the inspirations of the Holy Spirit. Such vigilance goes hand in hand with consonant image-formation. It initiates and sustains our intentional evocation of ideas and ideals supportive of our calling in Christ and the loving demands it makes upon us. Wise use of our Christian imagination awakens us to hitherto undisclosed transformational strivings. Awe arises in us for our eternal preformation in the Trinity as well as for the awesome reality of our existence in time.

The virtue of vigilance makes us more sensitive to the formation opportunity hidden in every obstacle. Initially such attention-direction has to be guided by our focal consciousness. The ascetic coformant of our Christian personality has a preeminent role to play in this regard. Sound discipline, aided by divine grace, enables us to make this gift of attention to direction a lasting disposition of our heart. Gradually, the enlightened prefocal region of our consciousness comes to the fore, enabling our image attentiveness to be more spontaneous. The transforming effect of this disposition benefits us in other ways. We now pay more attention to the directives filtering through our transfocal consciousness.

During our earthly pilgrimage, we sense at our most vulnerable that life is like a passing breeze. We stand between the eternity of our divine preformation and the eternity of our glorification in and with the risen Lord. The Holy Spirit transforms our attention-to-consonant-image-formation into a kind of a transfocal second nature that sharpens our attunement to every epiphany of the Divine in time. Because we have, so to speak, one foot in the finite, the other in the Infinite, we need to follow the lead of the Spirit and make our attentiveness to the mystery as focal as possible. Of major help to us in this regard are the faith and formation traditions that alert us the second our prefocal vigilance begins to wane. We then know it is time to pause a while and remember in faith, imagine in love, and anticipate in hope who we are and who God calls us to be.

Through these incarnational sources of memory, imagination, and anticipation, the Holy Spirit may convey to us new ways of coping with the tensions and stresses bound up with the times of transition in our lives. We sense when a renewed period of focalization is desirable, at least temporarily. At such moments, the ascetical coformant of our image formation keeps its mystical counterpart on the solid footing of obedience to the love-will of the Trinity. We seek the transcendent not in lofty visions but in the nobility of ordinary modes of labor and leisure, living and acting as "members of the household of God, built upon the foundation of the apostles and prophets, with Christ Jesus himself as the cornerstone" (Ephesians 2:20).

Situations as Passing and Persistent

As our life unfolds and matures in Christ, we encounter a variety of situations which lead us to question to what degree we have remained faithful to the traditions we sought with God's help to embody. Such situations may be either passing or persistent. We may find ourselves at a certain period of life, by choice or design, in a place that is meant to be only temporary. At one moment I may be a student facing a decision to go to graduate school or to become a recruit in military service. Change of career choices like these are passing whereas persistent situations involving, for example, our family of origin are always with us in some way.

Persistent or key situations tend to be more formative than passing ones. The situational facets we interiorized during initial formation in childhood may have been formative or deformative, but their influence persists. The traditions that sustain them also uphold ways in which our life call advances in accordance with the phase of human and Christian maturation we have entered. The first and in the end the most persistent situation in which we find ourselves is once again that of initial formation in childhood. Physical dependency, together with a marked absence of sufficient instinctual powers, marks our life as infants. Our survival depends on our being initiated into a collection of life-giving form directives and traditions that slowly but surely lessen our dependence on our parents and significant others.

These early phases of self-disclosure need to be tested by the reality of our successive encounters, by the discovery of our personal gifts, and by the first inklings of the mystery of our life call. Fidelity to it always entails coping with our initial formation situation, which accompanies us from the beginning to the end of our life. As we grow older, we may engage in a more focused and deliberate appraisal of the residues left over from our earliest days. We are in a better position to choose what to retain and what to relinquish. Such appraisal lends itself to free and insightful ratifications or rejections of various parts of this initial situation. Letting go of racial prejudices would be a good example of what an effort it takes to disentangle from deformative traditions we did not choose.

Some of us may, at least for a while, reject the traditions passed on to us by our parents because they were taught to us with words but talk did not follow through with action. The problem is that no sooner do we reject one parental tradition than we replace it with another. We can deny or do battle with its influential effects, but the impact of any early tradition on our social, personal, and spiritual life is likely to persist into adulthood.

Types of Passing Formation Situations

Many situations—familial, social, professional and occupational—are operable in our lives at the same time. On the same day a mother may take her children to school, lunch with the members of her garden club, contact customers she serves as a consultant, play a round of tennis, and join the family after hours to participate in a charitable activity. Surrounding these diverse situations are formation traditions that may exercise minor or major influences on anyone who undertakes a similar variety of occupations.

Many people today move from one career track to the next, some driven by the need for more income, others by the altruistic ideal of being of service to others. Such tasks may prove to be lasting, others passing sources of form-reception and donation. Both types of activity are linked in great measure to our functional talents and skills as well as being in some way transcendently motivated.

The ideal for which we ought to strive is to function effectively in our occupations without becoming merely functionalistic. In this way, we follow the form-traditional wisdom that encourages us to manifest a strong work ethic at all times in all types of formation situations. We respond to transcendent directives as they apply to our occupational life while trying to use our avocational know-how to fulfill our higher aspirations. The professional facet of our life call implies that we literally *profess* in what we do a dedication that goes beyond the minimal demands of the work in which we happen to be employed. We commit ourselves, despite the time, money, effort, and sacrifice involved, to develop the knowledge and skill demanded by a faith tradition that transcends a temporary choice of career. Because of the many benefits a professional life style can have on a society, we should do what we can to help others to follow their heart in matters that have this profound an influence on us and on those whom we serve.

In contrast to foundational situations like family systems that follow us for a lifetime, professional ones only last for a certain period of time. An illness that seriously impairs our ability to function changes our best laid plans, perhaps permanently. Other examples of periodic form-traditions whose influence comes and goes might be those that surround trends in music, exercise techniques and dietary changes, liberal or conservative movements in politics. A sudden emergence of these periodic fashions can rivet public attention for a while. Individuals and whole groups may be predisposed to cling to such a situation, but for the most part, they tend to be more current than persistent. They can produce powerful traditions that continue for shorter or longer spans of time.

Secondary Periods of Formation

Secondary periods of formation following initial formation in childhood may proceed from the decisive changes that mark the start of what it means to find ourselves. The helplessness of our original period of life is over. Personally appraised options compatible with our emerging call may introduce us to new, relatively lasting traditions that sustain our eventual choice of a vocation like marriage, religious life, or single life in the world. Such traditions may also support our dedication to a profession or to a series of avocations compatible with our call. These secondary periods of formation tend to be relatively persistent since they, too, are more amenable to change and adjustment than our childhood tends to be.

It is important for us to distinguish between the foundational formation traditions that aid this period of secondary appraisal and the accretions it may carry with it. Pressures associated with sociohistorical and parental influences may linger despite our attempts to listen to the mystery at the center of our life. Right appraisal of these differences is crucial if we are to let go of what hampers our progress and opt for what helps us to move towards mature commitment to our call.

Flow of Ongoing Formation

As our formation story unfolds, new, relatively persistent situations, accompanied by their complementary traditions, may be added to that of our enduring initial situations in childhood and later life. The instances of ongoing formation include: 1) the socio-foundational; 2) the extended familial; 3) the traditional; 4) the segmental; 5) the vocational; 6) the professional; 7) and the stylistic.

1. Our initial situation of childhood, which is foundational enough to persist over a lifetime, is still capable of being modified later on through personal appraisals and other formative influences. Such modifications may or may not be confirmed by the culture in which we live. We may have to search long and hard for compatible sociohistorical settings supportive of who we are and of what we are called by God to do. If consonance prevails, we can enter into a relatively enduring socio-foundational situation that best sustains our call, vocation, and avocation. Stemming from it will be many implicit and explicit form-traditions that reflect the richness of our faith tradition. Our greatest support may come from the faith grouping to which we belong within our overall cultural setting.

2. An unavoidable but potentially beneficial set of relationships comprises that of our family of origin, our extended family, and

our own personal friends and acquaintances. They add to our initial experiences of formation many traditions that help us to integrate and critique what we have learned of ourselves from our early encounters in the familial and sociohistorical circumstances into which we were born. A certain ambivalence or ambiguity may mark our progress as this familiar background recedes and we create our own extended, truly providential family. In some instances we may have to cope with the tension of being pulled one way or the other without offending parents or old friends. Depending on the depth of our inner attunement to our call, we may find more courageous and candid ways to follow Christ and to allow our Christ-form to come to the fore in relation to our extended family.

3. Our immediate situation is traditional through and through. Layers of already existing sacred and secular traditions line up in our pyramid. It is our responsibility before God to see to it that they stay grounded in our faith tradition. Only then can we discern if the situations in which we find ourselves are compatible with the doctrines and creeds to which we adhere. Traditional formation fosters an ongoing appraisal of sociohistorical pulsations and accretions that could retard our phasic maturation in Christ if they are allowed to slip into our pyramid.

4. Our segmental situation reflects what we still carry with us by way of our familial, cultural, educational, and religious upbringing. For example, if both of our parents happen to be musicians, we may find an affinity with artistic people that others do not share. Segmental influences can have a positive or negative effect on us. They may trigger outright rejection of the formation we received in childhood if we happen to feel more at home with a group of people initially disapproved of by our parents. Beyond the question of life styles, each segment of the population communicates its own preferred sets of directives, pertaining to everything from how we dress to how we ought to address the Divine. These differences may seem at first glance only superficial, but some of them may touch upon the

core dispositions of our heart. In the long run, these factors may point to either consonant or dissonant form-traditional directives. Both may be emphasized by the segment of the population to which we belong initially or towards which we gravitate as we grow up. Its characteristic demands and ideals need to be appraised to determine if they offer realistic avenues to our ongoing human and Christian character formation. Later in life we may shift to an entirely different segment of the population than that in which we were initiated while remaining attached to certain remnants reminiscent of it. Although we adapt well to our new segmental style of life with its form-traditional directives, we never manage to forget entirely from whence we came.

5. In the course of our formation history, there comes a time when we need to opt for one or the other vocation in which to best embody our call insofar as we understand it at this moment. The two most obvious options are marriage or the single life in a community or in the world. Each vocation offers another key to our ongoing formation. The obligations we accept and the directives flowing from them also come under the influence of the traditions that surround us. Each has both foundational and accretional elements. These may be modified by the sociohistorical situation in which we find ourselves as well as by the vocation we choose in dialogue with the graced attractions to it we experience.

6. To profess our dedication to a certain enduring occupation in service of society implies a lasting commitment, combined with the willingness to acquire and deepen the knowledge and skills we need to enhance our professional performance. Anything less would be considered by us to be an insult to the social justice demanded of professionals in a world starving not only for their generous gift of self but also for their expertise. Such enduring social commitments are more likely to be lasting if we find ourselves in compatible situations that support them. Classical Christian and other theistic traditions nourish the ideal of a socially committed pursuit of professional excellence

where our lives as dedicated professionals come together with the professing of our discipleship in Christ.

7. Our style of life is congenial with who we are if it becomes a blessed combination of our call, vocation, and avocation. Attunement to the formation mystery at the center of our field allows us to modulate our personal life by the consonant disposition of congeniality. Our interforming interactions with others become, by the same token, more compatible, compassionate, and competent. Who we are and what we do are reflections of our character as appraised and influenced by the traditions we keep alive in our heart as well as in our cultural and sociohistorical situations. We make every effort, in response to grace, to pass on to others a style of life imitative of Christ and inherently respectful of every person we meet.

CHAPTER 20

Commitment to Our Faith and Formation Traditions

It was as if he [Abba Antony] were a physician given to Egypt by God. For who went to him grieving and did not return rejoicing? Who went in lamentation over his dead, and did not immediately put aside his sorrow? Who visited while angered and was not changed to affection? What poor person met him in exhaustion who did not, after hearing and seeing him, despise wealth and console himself in his poverty? What monk coming to him in discouragement, did not become all the stronger? What young man, coming to the mountain and looking at Antony, did not at once renounce pleasures and love moderation? Who came to him tempted by a demon and did not gain relief? And who came to him distressed in his thoughts and did not find his mind calmed?
— *Saint Athanasius*

In the course of any average day, we are likely to be inundated by wave upon wave of countless formation traditions that may or may not be authentic expressions of our classical faith traditions. Coming to heightened consciousness of their implicit or explicit influence is an essential endeavor of mature Christian living. To walk with the Lord, we must be willing to defend and pass on the foundational tenets of our adhered to faith and formation traditions and their life-giving directives. The more we bring to the base of our pyramid the truths of catechetical theology, the better we will be able to integrate both our passing and our persistent situations with our basic beliefs. In this way, we solidify the link between what we believe and the way we allow these beliefs to affect our present-day life.

This commitment opens us to the wisdom of ages past as well as to the formationally relevant contributions of the proximate human and social arts and sciences. Integration of the perennial truths disclosed by scripture and the masters requires the discipline of daily practice and lessens the risk of our living a split existence that compartmentalizes worship and work and erodes fidelity to our calling in Christ. Our humble reliance on him is the best way to recover our balance when we allow anything less than the ground of our faith to influence every dynamic of daily life and to draw us to deeper conversion.

Influence of Syncretic Formation Traditions

Being committed to a classical faith tradition in word and deed has become something of a rarity in our world. Many people are unwittingly influenced by syncretic amalgations that pull together various sociohistorical pulsations and the fads they engender to suit their interpretation of Christianity, to say nothing of history itself. Alien traditions impacting on our field of life erode the courage and candor that sustain commitment to Christ. It is tempting to follow the comfortable route of success at any price with no semblance of the Cross. What makes this trend toward syncretism so attractive is its corresponding appeal to moral relativism. The legitimate demands we consent to follow in our faith tradition seem foreign to a subjectivistic world that would reduce every divine directive disclosure in our pyramid of traditions to what "feels good" to us.

The alternative we choose—to adhere to and build our life around classical texts and traditions—rests on firm theological foundations that teach us how to integrate catechetical truths so deeply in our heart and mind that we have at our finger tips the tools we need to resist the contemporary allure of syncretism. This wise blending of faith and formation traditions facilitates our ability to cooperate without compromise with other believers and people of good will in an effort to come to greater understanding and mutual respect. Our emphasis on respectful dialogue without undue accommodation has proven to diminish religious prejudice and its devastating effects.

Responding to Formation Traditions

At this point in our reflections, we need to distinguish between *reaction* and *response*. Reactions are really unappraised responses to some forming or deforming influences that throw us off course before we have time to think about them. We can return to a deeper level of response once we pause and appraise why we have reacted in this way. Then we can consider how best to address this situation in a mature and responsible manner.

Three possible responses to diverse formation traditions are: *blind identification; contestation/ratification;* and *consonant modulation*. Before describing each of these modes of response in turn, we need to restate the fact that life is usually a mixture of reacting and responding to the initial, passing, and persistent situations that mark our formation journey. We may treat them with anger or enthusiasm, with impulsive rejection or thoughtful reflection, with sadness or joy, with resentment or resignation, with rebellion or acquiescence, with resistance or cooperation. Each reaction or response leaves its mark on our ongoing formation as believers and seekers. All of these ways can be better understood if we take time to ponder such questions as: Should I identify with what happens blindly, without reflection or appraisal? Should I contest what I have begun to grasp through appraisal? Should I wholly or partially ratify it? Should I come to some consonant modulations of this situation and its implied traditions?

1. *Blind Identification.* The infant in us, however old we are, tends to identify blindly with facets of our initial formation situation that trigger, often for a lifetime, various sets of neuroformational coercive dispositions. We may find ourselves reacting to a person, event, or thing in a prereflective, unappraised manner that enables us at that moment to escape the burden of formative reflection. We may be preconsciously wary of the fact that the appraisal process may mark the start of a necessary but painful reform of dispositions with which we identified thoughtlessly due to childhood happenings over which we had no control. Later on, when we attempt to depict our pre-conversion pyramid of traditions, we may see how powerful their effects really are.

2. *Contestation/Ratification.* Following initial formation in childhood, we ideally launch into personal appraisal of how we want to receive and give form uniquely in our life and world. During this phase of maturation, we may feel an inner tug of war between contestation and ratification. At times the lights we derive from sober appraisal of our situation show us what we must contest if we hope to overcome the coercive dispositions we imbibed through blind identification. Now we question the wisdom of clinging to them. Are they really appropriate for the kind of person we discover ourselves to be? Which of them are still compatible with the providential situation in which we find ourselves and with those with whom we now interact? The latter questions may move us to ratify directives that fit the problems and demands laid upon us today. We see that certain dispositions assimilated in childhood are conducive to growth in compassionate presence. These we ratify while contesting those that led to prejudice and depreciation.

Our post-conversion pyramid points to the ways in which we incarnate the foundational tenets of our faith and formation traditions. We make sure that these foundations are not overshadowed or canceled by personal or sociohistorical accretions that prevailed in our initial formation period. This need for contestation or ratification may arise whenever newly emerging events or circumstances call into question the dispositions with which we have blindly identified. In these and other ways, we decide either to contest these early influences or to ratify them totally or in part. Some may have to be discarded completely.

3. *Consonant Modulation.* The ideal for which we ought to strive is the consonant modulation of what needs to be contested or ratified as we work, under the impetus of grace, to reform our hearts and to be more receptive to divine direction disclosures. We recognize that dispositions acquired through blind identification are open to contesting appraisal, especially in the transition periods of our life. It is legitimate to contest deformative traditions like sheer functionalism or pure erotic hedonism that seem to have eroded the faith foundations by which we ought to live as committed Christians. Our life of discipleship may be strengthened through these courageous acts of contestation. They compel us to seek what in our tradition is worthy of lifelong ratification. The depth dimension of our faith may have been obscured by blind identification. It closed us off from the wholesome power of personal reflection and appraisal. Neither could we come to the liberating experience of appreciative abandonment to the mystery.

Consonant modulation discloses to us what is and remains foundational in the formative traditions passed on to us; it also enables us to identify what is merely accretional. Some personal and sociohistorical ways of practicing the faith, though somewhat accretional, may still be of value for our growth as believers. They may merit being ratified in respect for the segment of the population to which we belong. For example, the laws of fast and abstinence as observed by one ethnic grouping may differ from another. Other accretions may have lost their validity altogether; they no longer offer effective directives for formation in Christ and cannot in all honesty be ratified by us. An example would be the custom in Christianity of women having to cover their heads at all times in church.

We gain in freedom and openness by this appraisal of what is truly foundational and what is not. Consonant modulation convinces us that we can and should let go of accretions that are no longer formationally sound nor ratified by legitimate ecclesiastical authority. We need not feel pangs of false guilt evoked by the mistaken notion that leaving empty accretions behind is a betrayal of our faith tradition as such. The fruit of this process may be the contestation of what is dissonant in our pre-conversion pyramid; it is followed by a ratification of its post-conversion consonance with the faith tradition we seek to revere in all that we are and do. While certain accretions do not disappear completely from our pyramid, they are at least reassigned more accurately to their proper place.

The type, depth, and quality of this contestation/ratification dynamic depends on the phase of human and Christian maturation in which we find ourselves as well as on our consciousness of what changes we really need to make in our life. We know in humility that all form-traditional change reflects our prayerful cooperation with the mystery of formation at work in our lives. Transforming alterations are always the fruit of divine grace.

One sign of lasting transformation is our simultaneous practice of compassionate patience with our own and others' progress combined with the courage to resist whatever blocks our commitment to keep at the base of our pyramid of traditions our adhered to foundations of faith. Another sign is our dying to self-love and its expression in individualism, autonomous personality fulfillment, and absolutized self-actualization. Consonant modulation always implies rejecting selfish sensuality and rising with Christ in self-forgetful love for God and neighbor.

In the familial, social, and ecclesial community to which we belong, we must accept the restriction such love imposes on our out-of-control quest for power, pleasure, and possession. Grace invites us to strive always to follow Christ's example of personal love and care for all who sought his help. There is nothing in this ideal to contest. With a *yes* that wells up from the core of our being, we ratify Christ's exemplary call to comfort those who mourn (cf. Matthew 5:4); to forgive others as the Father has forgiven us (cf. Ephesians 4:32); and, above all, to clothe ourselves with love (cf. Colossians 3:14).

CHAPTER 21

Challenge of Adhering to Our Faith and Formation Traditions

What would the world be without Jesus?...An earth without hope or happiness, without love or peace, the past a burden, the present a weariness, the future a shapeless terror — such would the earth be, if by impossibility there was no Jesus....Besides this, Jesus is bound up with our innermost lives. He is more to us than the blood in our veins. We know that he is indispensable to us; but we do not dream how indispensable he is. There is not a circumstance of life in which we could do without Jesus....But, if he is thus indispensable in life, how much more will he be indispensable in death? Who would dare to die without him?
— *F. W. Faber*

Our lifelong quest for maturity in Christ presents us with many challenges. In our dynamic history of formation, reformation, and transformation every event and encounter matters.

Nothing is without meaning. All spheres and dimensions of our field operate in multifaceted, interactive, and integrational ways with the mystery at the center. As persons-in-formation, we are influenced by a matrix of sociohistorical and linguistic forces that can be understood and utilized in many ways. From vital pulsions to functional ambitions, from transcendent aspirations to pneumatic inspirations, we face a complexity of decisions and actions regarding how best to adhere to our faith and formation traditions.

Inner and outer directives instilled in our heart in childhood may need to be reformed in hitherto unforeseen detail as we approach adulthood. Our lives unfold within a web of situational structures that contribute to the fluidity of our formation field over many maturation phases. Moreover, a mysterious transcendence dynamic moves us continuously to go beyond structures that prevent us from being open to new and much needed ways of giving and receiving form.

As a consequence, the appraisal process challenges us to grow in the art and discipline of apprehension, appreciative abandonment to the mystery, affirmation, and application as we try to comprehend and explain a family tragedy; the collapse of values associated with a moral life and a reliable work ethic; and the rise of secularism as a tradition that erodes our sense of reliance on the Sacred. We wonder in a time of transition like our own if we can reconnect our formation traditions to the solid ground of faith that alone can sustain us.

Acting upon such challenges gives rise to further times of testing. How congenial are we with our inmost calling in Christ? Are we open to what we can learn in interformation with our faith community or are we stubbornly entrenched in our own opinions and prejudices? The new knowledge we attain through the appraisal process can be put to good use, provided we guard against capitalizing on our gifts to sway other people to follow our voice when instead they, too, ought to be listening to the shy whispers of the Spirit. By the same token, our functional skills and talents can offer openings to a deeper attunement to the transcendence dynamic that counteracts this manipulative tendency.

Because of the complexity caused by the fallen state of our human condition, we have to avail ourselves of the insights and findings derived from many differential arts, sciences, and disciplines. No one source of knowledge nor method of research will suffice to shed light on the multi-faceted phases of maturation peculiar to every human and Christian life. We may be tempted to choose one or the other point of view as the exclusive explanation of our formation story as a whole. The aberrations resulting from such a narrow choice sooner or later reveal themselves. By contrast, the tools offered to us by a truly holistic approach to spiritual formation prevent us from forcing a set of solutions of our own choosing to fit whatever challenges daily life brings. That is why, within the comprehensive approach offered by form-theological methods of reflection, we remain open to what we can learn about our socio-vital-functional life from compatible religious traditions and other sources of knowledge.

Linguistic and Traditional Limits

Human formation and our empirical knowledge of it cannot be obtained outside the language systems and recent or long-standing traditions that permeate the field of life in which we participate at any given moment of time. Our approach is always conditioned by our pre-scientific and scientific knowledge in dialogue with the providential circumstances in which we find ourselves.

This field-bound nature of our existence can never be denied or dismissed due to the fact that it is precisely who we are. We have been created by the mystery to live in these intertwining relationships for the duration of our earthly existence. To acknowledge our historicity does not lead to the heresy of determinism because some freedom of choice is always ours. We are granted by God the privilege of appraising the *proximate* and *immediate* directives that open us to the transempirical disclosure of *ultimate* directives. This domain of truth touches us through our faith and formation traditions. Within the restricted frame of reference of our field-bound experiences, we may come to increasing certainty about what the mystery asks of us. Each phase of our formation story opens us to new occasions for inquiry about our unique-communal life call. Each disclosure of its efficacy in the Lord corrects and complements the insights we have already uncovered in former phases of our faith journey.

The positive sciences have been dominated, at least since the Enlightenment, by the mistaken notion that their methods of inquiry would yield absolute certainty. More recent developments in sciences like quantum physics have demonstrated that such absolute certitude is impossible to obtain by any empirical or experiential method in and by itself alone. All have proven to be inadequate; none can reduce the mystery to our controlled measurements. For every answer we obtain, more questions remain.

All methods developed by the empirical sciences, however sophisticated they may be, can only lead to relative, not absolute, certainty. For this reason, formation science as integrational is bound to consider the findings of other sciences, both human and positive, and to explore their valid contributions. We do so not for the sake of coming to a naive certainty that pretends to master the mystery but to recover a humility that seeks to serve the full truth and that depends as much on faith as it does on reason. Thanks to our openness to the possible contributions made by all fields of endeavor, we see formation science, anthropology, and theology as storehouses of reliable directives pertaining to our quest for holistic living and our longing to live in the light of our universal call to holiness.

Physical Sciences in Relation to Our Field of Life

Scientific investigations pertaining to the physical or biogenetic dimension of our existence seem to have gained precedence in our time over experiential explorations of distinctively human or transcendent formation. Correcting the urge to analyze and measure who we are, are the revealed doctrines found in the living treasury of our faith traditions. They invite us to listen to the empirical data collected by the sciences of measurement without accepting them as revelatory of the whole truth. In some quarters we witness a tendency to validate the methods of inquiry developed by the positivistic sciences as if their findings were of more value than those of the sciences of meaning, including sacred sciences like that of formation theology. On our part, we turn to the sources of wisdom and truth found in the Revelation to disclose the meaning of our human life form as held in being by God. We realize that different methods of research and reflection are needed to address the fullness of our formational, reformational, and transformational experiences. Included in the context of our inquiry are: 1) the meaning of formative events; 2) the distinctive yet intertwining unity of the spheres of our formation field; 3) the potential and actual directives emerging from its four quadrants with the mystery at the center; and 4) their possible institutionalization in a variety of formation traditions that defer always to the faith tradition they serve.

Directives not only come to us from on high; they also emerge in the nitty-gritty of our sociohistorical life, understood as the most encompassing coformant of our formation field. Its defining characteristic is to be the transmitter of those directives that invite us to be more responsive to self, others, and God. Our faith and formation traditions depend on the interformative communication systems through which spoken and written directives, humbly received by us, may prove in time to be life-changing.

Functional and Transcendent Directives

Functional directives in our field are meant to be servant sources of the transcendent. What we do can be merely a routine chore or we can identify and honor it as a limited manifestation of the mystery. Our response to formative events is not only to seek their outcomes and satisfy our ambitions but also to find out what they mean in the historical conditions in which we find ourselves.

Many transcendent directives are embedded in our functional dimension; they offer us counsels which benefit the humanization and Christianization of our world. Some light may be shed on them by the tools offered by the measurement sciences but for the most part we have to probe their meaning in faith with respect to our reasoning powers. Their diverse embodiments in the concrete circumstances of our daily life never fail to evoke wonder. Planting a garden, cooking for guests, polishing furniture, decorating a room endless—examples could be given of seemingly trivial chores that make us mindful of the "More Than." In a globally aware world, all of us are more sensitive to the centrality of ultimate directives like respect for human rights, peace-making, and the diminishment of religious prejudice. To uphold such ideals requires continual reformation on our part of what in us personally or socially opposes them. Blatant examples would be mistreatment of the most vulnerable and the misunderstandings arising from racial or ethnic profiling.

Exploration of Directives

Both proximate and ultimate directives are best explored in the context of a detailed description of an event selected for research. Our appreciative apprehension of it is linked not only to our life experience but also to the teachings represented by numerous formation traditions and the religious beliefs underlying them. Traditions and their directives do not come into existence automatically. They are in part the fruit of our sociohistorical pulsations, vital pulsions, functional ambitions, and transcendent aspirations. One or the other of these basic strivings may play a dissonant or consonant role in our response to a particular event, depending on how well we evaluate the importance of these strivings. For example, we must base our appreciation of human rights on the dignity of the person, not merely on the functional advantages of keeping people in their place, satisfying the lowest common denominator, or opting for peace at any price. We recognize the challenge set before us as individuals and as like-minded groups to make sure that the causes promoted within our shared formation field meet the highest standards our traditions have to offer.

Our present strivings for equality may be influenced by past ideals still operative in our here-and-now situation; they are more than capable of generating ultimate directives that address our current concerns. Our responsibility is to appraise how best to act in the light of the divine direction disclosures we do receive. Here we see the reciprocal movement between our human strivings for meaning and the spiritual directives that motivate us to remain faithful to the foundational truths of our religious and ideological traditions.

Actualization of Traditional Directives

Traditional directives can only be fully actualized when we work together to improve our personal and social patterns of interformation. The more we practice compassion, mutual confirmation, and the disposition of concelebration, the more we reinforce our appreciation of *ultimate* directives that are valid and lasting whether or not they are being universally lived at any period of history. Concrete observable directives, as actualized and operative in our personal lives and in our faith groupings, provide the gateway to everyday formation. They illumine what motivates us to act as we do. Such directives emerge from four sources. The first comprises the elementary formation strivings inherent in our individual lives, be they sociohistorical, vital, functional, or transcendent. These innate strivings are like the propellers on an airplane. They lift us up and give us the energy we need to develop and maintain directives that enable us to identify and use our gifts and talents for the greater good of all. Secondly, the interformative relations prevalent in our field of life direct us to draw upon those vertical and horizontal resources in our formation traditions that show us how to posit directives that arise from our basic strivings to move beyond selfish individualism to true community. Thirdly, the unique foundational form or essence of life, shining forth in every person created by God, gives rise to directives that foster our appreciation for the dignity and worth of all people. Fourthly, ultimate directives continually seep through the transcendent and pneumatic-ecclesial dimensions of our call. They offer us a variety of ways by which to appraise the consonance or dissonance of the actual directives we ought to follow as individuals or members of a faith grouping. We attune our listening hearts to the divine directives we receive from the Holy Spirit through our religious traditions.

Ascending Hierarchy of Directives

Life becomes more harmonious and whole to the degree that a proper hierarchy of strivings and directives, like the four described above, creates simultaneously a descending and an ascending pattern, flowing downward from the transcendent into all our "lower-I" dynamics and flowing upward from these dynamics in a fashion that serves our overall wellbeing. Along the way, different kinds of strivings disclose themselves successively at various stages and phases of formation. Each gives rise to new levels of reality-testing.

These processes ought increasingly to be free and insightful. None can be explained away as mechanical forces or constellations of organismic data subject to our control. All entail a variety of movements that are both receptive and donative. All unfold within expanding and changing fields of life over a succession of time frames. These *flowing in* and *flowing out* rhythms of our life are more familiar to us than we may realize. We tend to take them for granted, so much so that it calls for a concerted effort to focus on this process, especially when facets of it or incidents within it become thematic, first in a descriptive, then in a theoretical way. Both of these ways are of benefit to practical formation. Far from being an isolated movement, our ongoing emergence proceeds within the context of the spheres, ranges, regions, dimensions, and provisional integrations of our field in a rich texture of relationships. Helpful in this regard may be those intentional directives that come to us from such formative areas of life as art, literature, music, philosophy, and theology. Any discipline, be it speculative, humanistic, or positivistic, may imply directives for existence that elucidate our life's story. The methods by which we choose to study the mystery of formation and its philosophical and theological ramifications have to be flexible and creative. The key dynamic of transcendence in our life is available to our experience at all moments; it can be affirmed more fully whenever we explore its impact on our individual and social life.

Being present to the directives disclosed in any experience lived in tune with the mystery has the effect of transforming our heart prior to any attempt we may make to transform our world. If certain conditions are fulfilled, we may begin to exercise an intrinsic openness to what goes beyond our sociohistorical, vital, and functional make-up and orients us to the transcendent mystery. The mystery can be and is the object of inquiry of informational, doctrinal, and systematic theology; it is also the focus of our faith and formation traditions and our form-theological reflections. We accept in faith, hope, and love the responsibility to act upon the divine directives we undeservedly receive. As believers and seekers, we embody them within common and particular fields of formation in accordance with what God asks of us, moving past the fear of necessary change to the courage of heart that makes every day the "day of the Lord" (Acts 2:47).

Chapter 22

Heart of Faith Formation

It is therefore quite clear that all Christians in any state or walk of life are called to the fullness of Christian life and to the perfection of love, and by this holiness a more human manner of life is fostered also in earthly society. In order to reach this perfection the faithful should use the strength dealt out to them by Christ's gift, so that, following in his footsteps and conformed to his image, doing the will of God in everything, they may wholeheartedly devote themselves to the glory of God and to the service of their neighbor...

The forms and tasks of life are many but holiness is one — that sanctity which is cultivated by all who act under God's Spirit and, obeying the Father's voice and adoring God the Father in spirit and in truth, follow Christ, poor, humble and cross-bearing, that they may deserve to be partakers of his glory. Each one, however, according to his own gifts and duties must steadfastly advance along the way of a living faith, which arouses hope and works through love.

— *Vatican Council II*
Lumen Gentium

Our current modes of cognition; what we comprehend as meaningful and what remains a mystery; our situational and world conditions; the horizons of our fields of life—all the directives we receive from our faith and formation traditions comprise the heart and soul of our existence on earth. Ordinarily our apprehensions and appraisals are directed to concrete events and to the people and things that comprise our actual field of presence and action. We may be angered by the sudden death of a child, by an illness that leaves us vulnerable to failure, by a promotion we do not really know how to handle or simply by not being able to find a parking place! Processes of formation calling for appreciative appraisal are initiated by both major and minor events.

What matters ultimately is not *that* they happen but that we choose to examine them not as random and disconnected occurrences, but as parts of a greater whole. We seek some order in the chaos of sudden, unwanted, or unexpected change. Our receptive potency reminds us of the importance of being as open as possible to the full meaning of what has occurred until it begins to make some sense to us. In this way we view everything from natural disasters to disastrous relationships not in isolation from but in relation to our overall story of phasic unfolding. We make explicit not only what we apprehend but also the ways in which we decide what it means to us and others. At no moment do we leave behind us the demands of discipleship in Christ. They are in the forefront of our concerns.

Elucidating these dynamics enables us to monitor their consonant or dissonant impact on the traditions that prevent us from falling into the trap of an exclusive vital-functional view of life. Functionalism blocks our perspective. A weak or non-existent Christian critique of formation traditions contrary to our faith leaves us vulnerable to error and less likely to practice what we preach.

Another reason for any lack of courage or "lukewarmness" we feel may be due to unexamined deformations we experienced in the past and perhaps still encounter in the present. We may have suffered the psychological and spiritual side effects of harsh disciplines justified by a leveling mentality that strove wittingly or unwittingly to deplete our personal prayer life and replace it by guilt-evoking rules of religious behaviorism. An understandable overreaction to this imposition may make us vulnerable to any emotion-laden approach to spirituality. We may be easy prey for techniques of self-salvation that do not take into account the need for sound doctrines of faith respectful of each person's unique-communal call. Overreactions against a free-floating spirituality may lead to an idolizing of its opposite: a totally rule-bound religiosity that leaves no room for creativity or humble expressions of genuine piety. Such authoritarian, rationalistic modes of formation neglect the need for loving encounters with God and others in our faith community.

Some believers may be victimized by grab bags of non-integrated courses in theology, psychology, spiritual direction, counseling, group dynamics, mysticism, yoga, transcendental meditation, and various examples of transpersonalism lacking any deference to legitimate authority. Scholars and teachers themselves face great difficulty in attempting to synthesize such a vast variety of insights and data into a coherent, foundational, formative Christian spirituality. One has to be able to assimilate the relevant data found in non-Christian traditions while discerning the difference between contemporary enthusiasms and reflection in depth on the age-old reservoirs of Christian wisdom and experience.

Programs in spirituality that are either ultra-conservative or ultra-liberal ought to arouse our concern. The discipline demanded to develop and maintain our transcendent aspirations and pneumatic inspirations is considerable. Before we know it, external modes of pietism and devotionalism can replace the fruits of transformation of heart.

Functioning in Faith

The heart is the integrative center of our personhood as a whole. We can be warm or cold, distant or involved, gentle or harsh in the way we live and work. The key to healthy and holy functioning is to link our ambitions to what inspires us to go beyond them. The quality of our functioning influences the way in which we live our beliefs. A skillful nurse who is technically perfect but hard as nails will not be remembered with the affection we accord the nurse whose heart is in her professional skills.

The infused virtues of faith, hope, and love open us to the transforming influence of the Holy Spirit, who does this work in us by means of providentially guided sociohistorical, vital, functional, and transcendent directives. When pulsations, pulsions, ambitions, and aspirations meet in the formative core of our life, symbolized by our heart, the inspirations of the Spirit seal this integration. Our core form, moved by divine love, is the source of the inspired meanings we see unfolding in the people, events, and things that constitute our current situation. It follows that our functioning in faith undergoes transformation when what we do passes through the portals of our Christian heart.

Integrative Directives

An overall integrative view of our formation field with its dispositions, dynamics, and directives reveals that the situations in which we find ourselves are increasingly less uniform and more pluritraditional. An African tribe, such as the Masai in Kenya or the Ibo in Nigeria, still enjoy a uniformity unknown to us in the western world, where pluriformity is not the exception but the rule. Many diverse and powerful traditions impinge upon our heart, influence our decisions, and motivate us to make choices with consequences that may or may not conform to the Gospel. In the long run, some contamination from traditions at cross purposes with one another is unavoidable. This happens because we live in proximity to others who may harbor viewpoints about the meaning of life that are radically different from our own.

So entrenched may we become in promoting our own agendas that we refuse to so much as try to understand the traditions, customs, and lifestyles of other people. In focusing on our differences, we neglect to appreciate the kinships we do share. For instance, a fear of respectful dialogue may evoke depreciative critiques of the way others live their faith simply because they look or act differently from what we expect.

If we are to remain faithful to our call, we have to come to a more integrative view of diverse faith and formation traditions. What do they have in common? Is it possible to trace in them basic directives for more holistic living as well as an overall attitude of gratitude for our oneness in the mystery? This commitment to cooperate without compromise of our own religious traditions brings peace to our distraught heart. Transfocal directives break through our consciousness, igniting hope in our own emerging sense of being transformed by grace. A consonant formation tradition protects us against self-enclosure and opens us as much to change as to healthy continuity.

Thematic and Concrete Directives

Thematic directives can be said to represent the leading motifs and meanings of our lives. They become concrete in countless creative variations. These ways of witness incarnate themselves in particular times and places, depending on the areas of life God allows us to nurture in awe and appreciation.

Being surrounded by people abandoned in body and soul may lead us to the realization that we need to foster the thematic directive of social justice. Further directives concerning how to specify this theme may emerge when we are sent to minister to a needy segment of the population. The way we apply these directives will vary if we happen to be adherents of a specific faith tradition. We realize that our care for the physically and spiritually poor has to be not a matter of our efforts alone but a response to the concrete directives asked of us by God. We need to listen to them if we are to implement the virtue of social justice in our hearts and subsequently in our ministry. In due time, we may develop a number of life themes that permeate our formation field. No matter where life leads us, we turn for strength to the cordial heart of Christ. Both our implicit religious orientation and our explicit behavior as just and merciful mirror his life in us. Our service to others becomes a blending of different traditions, all of which converge in our shared devotion to serve the segment of a population the mystery entrusts to our care.

Transformative Foundations

The transformative foundations that comprise the ground of our faith are the reservoir from which grace and goodness flow; they are the most striking expression of God's love for us as manifested in salvation history. They are meant not to destroy but to heal, not to diminish but to elevate, not to deform but to transform the created foundations of our already existing structures, acts, dispositions, and strivings.

These transformative foundations are, first of all, the word of God given to us freely and fully through the scriptures and in the treasury of Christian tradition as found in ecclesial doctrine and in the writings of the spiritual masters acknowledged by generations of Christians. Other transformative channels of grace include our sacramental and liturgical life, our veneration of the saints, our religious exercises. All nourish and strengthen our intention to be faithful to Christ despite the obstacles we encounter. Another transformative foundation of our faith is that of spiritual direction, in private or in common, as given by wise, learned, and experienced souls, who are sent to us by the Spirit to teach us the wisdom of surrendering our will to God's will for us. Word and sacrament formatively assimilated enable us to transform our created formation field into a living temple where the Lord comes to dwell.

Any time we fail to act in fidelity to our founding life form, we forfeit a blessed opportunity to reshape our life and world in the image of God. The force of our pride-form is so strong that it has inflicted a deep wound on all of the dimensions and articulations of our existence. It is impossible to extricate ourselves from this deformative predicament by means of our own efforts alone. That is why the Divine Word emptied himself of the glory of his Divine Form and took on our form in all things but sin. He understands the suffering associated with our fallen condition while himself being sinless (cf. Hebrews 4:15). By his suffering and death he transforms our life of infidelity and disobedience. To believe in his mercy opens us to the splendor of our search for union with God, now understood as a participation in the Eternal Trinitarian Formation and Interformation Event or what the Apostle Paul describes as our having received a "spirit of adoption" (Romans 8:15).

Conclusion

Christ alone is the source of our incarnational life as always illumined and strengthened by his Spirit. Thanks to his grace, our formative transcendent mind and will become united with our functional mind and will. Both foster the incarnation of pneumatic-ecclesial directives in our life. Our incarnational decisions are made on the basis of a faith-filled appraisal of what Christ asks of us now and in the future. Our ordinary life becomes an extraordinary example of co-incarnation with Christ. Similarly, the way we live our faith and formation traditions radiates a love for God that knows no bounds. Our whole being becomes receptive to the sheer grace of living what we believe. We exemplify to a world that at times doubts this truth that ministry in, with, and through Christ is the only way to celebrate the peace and joy that are his gifts to us now and for all times to come.

AFTERWORD
by
Susan Muto

Formation theology builds upon Adrian van Kaam's earlier pretheological formation science and its general pre-and proto-theological anthropology. It relies on the pathways to faith opened up in our human life by the Holy Spirit and on our willingness to embody God's word in the events we encounter on our voyage from birth to death. It challenges us to come of age as fully alive children of God while reminding us that the cultivation of our heart and soul by Christ never stops. The roots of formation theology are Holy Scripture, the apostolic tradition of the Church, and her catechetical teachings. Its fruits are then particularized in how we live what we believe in daily life, on how we become spiritually mature Christians. It looks at doctrinal theology from a particular viewpoint, attentive to the impact of our unique-communal call on the human and Christian unfolding of our life as a whole. If "unique" refers to our deepest transcendent identity in God, then "communal" refers to our oneness with the doctrinal theology of the Church and with the commonalities we share in our quest for everyday human and Christian growth in the Mystical Body of Christ.

Formation theology is also a theology of Christian unity. It inspires us to unfold our unique Christ-form in dialogue with the pluralistic society where Holy Providence places us. Through liturgy, word, and sacrament, the Church calls us to Christianize the human labors that guide our unfolding from the beginning to the end of our life. The Holy Spirit helps us to see any worthy endeavor as a pointer to the sublime elevation by grace of what we may do for the sake of the Lord.

Under the guidance of the Church, the Spirit invites us to share in the inner and outer epiphany or shining forth of the Holy Trinity in our world. This task is at once ages old and ever new. It explains why formation theology has been described in this series as "epiphanic."

The true *light* that *enlightens* everyone coming into the world (cf. John 1:9) is the timeless light of the Eternal Word revealed in time. It is the epiphanic light of Christ manifested in his flesh and blood. It is the light that shone round the shepherds and that guided the Magi to Bethlehem. This light was in the world from the beginning. Through it the world was made, yet the world did not know it. It is the light which came to its own, though its own received it not (cf. John 1:19).

Committed Christians are often the first to admit that the light of Christ has dimmed in our distracted hearts. We live amidst the shadows cast by our fallen condition. We often feel like lost souls speeding through life with little or no time to remember who we most deeply are. In a climate of endless production and consumption, we have to pause, take stock of our lives, and recommit ourselves to Christ. His radiance still beams in the farthest corners of our world despite the diminishment of awe disposition and our sense of the Sacred.

Of this we can be sure: How we appear in our places of labor, love, and leisure must be in harmony with who we are. It is not easy to coform our lives to the life of Christ. Yet, thanks to the grace of baptism, we fallen creatures must be as ready to carry his cross as to enjoy the glory of his resurrection. Our mission entails sharing fully in his guidance of the mysterious destiny of our life and in his call to serve souls abandoned in spirit and in body.

This enigma of God's election inspired the Apostle Paul to call himself the servant of the mystery, a title that encompassed the virtues of faith, hope, and love in their fullness. In his epistles he makes clear that Church doctrine is not only a body of information about our faith. From it flows a wisdom pertinent to the ongoing maturation of our personality. At its infused core is our call to personal and communal transformation in Christ. Its activation is a gift of the Holy Spirit, who forms Christ in us through baptism and through the doctrines and sacraments of the Church. Through the three infused theological virtues, we are called to coform our life in the light of the Eternal Formation and Interformation Event of Father, Son, and Holy Spirit. Our veiled participation in the Epiphany of the Trinity initiates and accompanies the specific maturation processes we undergo. Ceaselessly God calls us to grow in fidelity and charity as members of a community of believers whose hope in the epiphanic stream of God's merciful love never dies.

Of particular importance to this endeavor is the fact that our faith and formation tradition offsets the popular and often "formless" spirituality that shapes our culture and many of its religious expressions. There is no comparison whatsoever between the objective truth taught, for example, by our Judeo-Christian faith tradition and the trends and their proponents that detach themselves from any authority beyond that of their own subjectivistic experiences.

Form-traditional spirituality grounded in Church teaching is on a battlefield with traditionless approaches to spiritual living. Were we afloat at sea without a life raft, it would feel as if we were drowning in conflicting schools of spirituality, in opposing therapeutic and counseling techniques, talk shows and do-it-yourself books on everything from meditation to mind reading. Many profess to speak with authority on how to develop our human and spiritual potential while severing faith from its grounding in solid doctrine and the details of daily life. The vastness of interest in all things spiritual contrasts starkly with the shallowness surrounding us. Many Christians imbibe erroneous ideas and practices from popularized, quasi-spiritual teachings that both challenge and erode their faith tradition.

For over two millennia Christianity has been engaged in an impressive apologetic refutation of attacks upon its tenets. We must not bend in our commitment to the defense of this truth, but by itself alone it is not enough. Unfortunately many seek direction in sources other than their faith. Forebodings of this predicament were already foreseen in Holland when Adrian van Kaam and his friends perceived the silent symptoms of disaffection many Christians felt with their own religious affiliations. This made it difficult for them to imbibe formation theology directly. They had to create a climate where candid conversations in small groups about the roots of this inner discontent could be aired. They felt a certain restlessness invading their spirit. It was as if grace used this climate to make straight the path to a truly formative and foundational Christian spirituality that continues to inspire committed believers today.

The natural wisdom with which the Eternal Father of creation endowed our human existence has been badly obscured by the Fall. We long to be awakened and purified by grace and the Holy Spirit's ongoing disclosure of the Christ-form of our soul. Principles at odds with the Revelation are packaged and promulgated in many media outlets. They may be hidden within developmental counseling methods or in the educational approaches found in college courses as well as in elementary and secondary schools. What poisons the soul of adults and children is often not at all obvious since people appreciate that they are at least being helped and taught. Yet the subliminal messages conveyed can carry seeds of ideas incompatible with the truth of faith and reason. The time to articulate a theology of Christian empirical formation is upon us. Such a theology can ready us to interact with the universes of meaning represented by education, human development, management and problem solving techniques without losing our faith. For this gift we pray that the Holy Spirit will grant us:

1. A whole-hearted acknowledgment of the beneficial elements of the human and social sciences without obscuring the need for a creative, critical vigilance of the same developmental

approaches since these insights may be used wittingly or unwittingly to demean religious commitment. Blessings and curses can exist side by side, and we dare not lose our faithful outlook on what is best for Church and society.

2. A gentle yet firm pointing to what is deformative in these approaches and in the deceptive visions of human destiny they may promote.

3. A clear demonstration of where we Christians stand in relation to teachings that may reduce human emergence and meaning to sociohistorical, vital, or functional levels of life only.

4. A realization that popular fads, when imbibed uncritically, as from the media, can result in an anti-Christian view of life, foster a culture of narcissism and death, and taint our vision to such a degree that we no longer feel at home in our own traditions of faith formation.

5. A spontaneous sensitivity that helps us to pinpoint the benefits and deficits of any merely secularistic developmental training and teaching in the context of the *Summa Forma Theologica* represented in the four volumes of this series.

NOTES

Chapter 6
Integrating Our Christian Faith and Formation Traditions

1. *The Collected Works of Saint John of the Cross*, trans. Kieran Kavanaugh and Otilio Rodriguez (Washington, DC: ICS Publications, 1991), No. 100, 92.

2. Cited in "Theology and Spirituality" by Harvey D. Egan in *The Cambridge Companion to Karl Rahner*, ed. Declan Marmion and Mary E. Hines (New York, NY: Cambridge University Press, 2005), 23. See also Karl Rahner, *Foundations of Christian Faith: An Introduction to the Idea of Christianity*, trans. William V. Dych (London: Darton, Longman & Todd, 1978), 303.

3. See Peter L. Berger and Thomas Luckmann, *The Social Construction of Reality: A Treatise in the Sociology of Knowledge* (Garden City, NY: Doubleday and Co., Inc., 1967), for a discussion of the social foundations of knowledge and the necessity of interformative discourse to maintain the plausibility of a symbolic world.

Chapter 7
Symbolic Transmission of a Living Tradition

1. See David Tracy's analysis of this notion as it applies to the classics of human, religious, and Christian living in *The Analogical Imagination: Christian Theology and the Culture of Pluralism* (New York, NY: Crossroad, 1981), 99-304.

2. A corroborating discussion of the concept of a classic can be found in Hans-Georg Gadamer, *Truth and Method*, trans. Garrett Barden

and John Cumming (New York, NY: The Seabury Press, 1975), 253-258.

3. Tracy, op. cit., 233.

4. Yves M. J. Congar, *Tradition and Traditions*, trans. Michael Naseby and Thomas Rainborough (London: Burns & Oates, 1966), 427.

5. Ibid., 429.

6. Ibid., 438.

7. See Susan Muto, *A Practical Guide to Spiritual Reading* (Petersham, MA: St. Bede's Publications, 1994), 6-9. An extensive annotated and bibliographical exposition of exemplary texts in these four categories can be found on pages 201-275. For further background reading, see also Louis Bouyer, *The Spirituality of the New Testament and the Fathers*, trans. Mary P. Ryan (New York, NY: Desclee, 1963); Louis Bouyer, *Orthodox Spirituality and Protestant and Anglican Spirituality*, trans. Barbara Wall (New York, NY: Desclee, 1969); Jean Leclercq, Francois Vandenbroucke, and Louis Bouer, *The Spirituality of the Middle Ages*, trans. The Benedictines of Holme Eden Abbey (New York, NY: Desclee, 1968); Urban T. Holmes, *A History of Christian Spirituality: An Analytical Introduction* (New York, NY: *The Seabury Press,* 1980).

Chapter 8
Traditions and Transformation

1. For a taste of Saint Catherine's formation story, see, among others, Alice Curtayne, *Saint Catherine of Siena* (Rockford, IL: Tan Books, 1980); Raymond of Capuda, *The Life of Catherine of Siena*, trans. Conleth Kearns (Wilmington, DE: Michael Glazier, Inc., 1980); and Igino Giordani, *Saint Catherine of Siena: Doctor of the Church*, trans. Thomas J. Tobin (Boston, MA: Daughters of Saint Paul, 1975).

2. Catherine of Siena, *The Dialogue*, trans. Suzanne Noffke (New York, NY: Paulist Press, 1980), 33-34.

3. Ibid., 118.

4. Ibid., 70.

5. *I Catherine: Selected Writings of Saint Catherine of Siena*, trans. Kenelm Foster and Mary John Ronayne (London: Collins, 1980): Letter 18 (March 1376), 105-106.

6. Ibid., *Letter 13* (May 1375), 85-86.

7. *The Dialogue*, op. cit. 185.

8. Ibid., 188-189.

9. Ibid., 193.

10. Ibid., 197.

11. Ibid., 127-128.

12. Ibid., 130-131.

13. Ibid., 133.

14. Ibid.

15. Ibid., 238-239.

16. Ibid., 276.

17. In *The Ascent of Mount Carmel*, Book One, Chapter 14, Saint John of the Cross says: "In this nakedness the spirit finds its quietude and rest. For in coveting nothing, nothing tires it by pulling it up and nothing oppresses it by pushing it down, because it is in the center of its humility. When it covets something, by this very facet it tires itself." See *The Collected Works of Saint John of the Cross*, trans. Kieran Kavanaugh and Otilio Rodriguez (Washington, DC: ICS Publications, 1991), 151.

18. Ibid., 365.

Chapter 15
Integrative Field of Our Faith and Formation Traditions

1. For a thorough treatment of *eros* and *agape*, see Pope Benedict XIV, *Deus Caritas Est* (Encyclical Letter...on Christian Love), ©2006 Liberia Editrice Vaticana in the special supplement to *Inside to the Vatican* (February 2006), 1-22. The encyclical, issued to bishops,

priests, deacons, men and women religious, and all the lay faithful, was first published on January 25, 2006, on the feast of the Conversation of Saint Paul.

2. Ibid., Paragraph 39:20.

Chapter 16
Teaching the Classics in Service of Our Traditions

1. See *The Mystical Theology* in *Pseudo-Dionysius: The Complete Works*, trans. Colm Luibheid, in *The Classics of Western Spirituality* (New York, NY: Paulist Press, 1987) 133-141.

2. Ibid., 137.

3. Anticipation of these themes can be seen in Saint Gregory of Nyssa, *The Life of Moses*, in *The Classics of Western Spirituality*, trans. Abraham J. Malherbe and Everett Ferguson (New York, NY: Paulist Press, 1978).

4. *The Mystical Theology*, op cit., 135.

5. Ibid.

6. See Jaroslav Pelikan, "The Odyssey of Dionysian Spirituality," in *Pseudo-Dionysius: The Complete Works*, 16.

7. See Dom Jean Leclercq, "Influence and Non-influence of Dionysius in the Western Middle Ages," Ibid., 26-29.

8. Ibid., 30.

9. See Karlfried Froehlich, "Pseudo-Dionysius and the Reformation of the Sixteenth Century," Ibid., 43.

10. *The Mystical Theology*, op. cit., 135. See also Pope John Paul II, *Fides et Ratio* (Encyclical on Faith and Reason), October 15, 1998. Reprinted in *Inside the Vatican* (Rome, Italy, 1998), 1-41. ©*Urbi et Orbi Communications*. In the words of the Holy Father, "Faith and reason are like two wings on which the human spirit rises to the contemplation of truth; and God has placed in the human heart a desire to know the truth—in a word, to know himself—so that,

NOTES / 267

by knowing and loving God, men and women may also come to the fullness of truth about themselves" (Opening Salutation, 3).

11. Ibid., 140-141.

12. Ibid., 138.

13. Ibid., 139.

14. bid., 141.

Chapter 17
Teachings from a Medieval Master

1. *Julian of Norwich, Showings,* trans. with an Introduction by Edmund College and James Walsh in *The Classics of Western Spirituality* (New York, NY: Paulist Press, 1978), 158.

2. Introduction, *Showings*, 26-27.

3. Ibid., 20.

4. *Showings*, Short Text, 128; *Long Text*, 179.

5. These three ways are summarized in the *Long Text*, 192.

6. Ibid., 183.

7. Ibid.

8. See *Long Text*, 221-223.

9. Ibid., 312-315.

10. Ibid., 315.

11. Ibid., 322.

12. bid., 235.

13. See Chapter 6, *Long Text*, 133-135.

14. See Chapter 10, 193-196.15. *The Short Text*, 151.

Chapter 18
Teachings from a Contemporary Master

1. Cited in Evelyn Underhill, *Practical Mysticism* (Columbus, OH: Ariel Press, 1942), 141.

2. Ibid., 13. Thomas Merton makes a similar claim in regard to the life of a priest, whose task is "to spiritualize the world" and who "prepares for the coming of Christ by shedding upon the whole world the invisible light that enlightens every [person] that comes into the world. Through the priest, the glory of Christ seeps out into creation until all things are saturated in prayer." *The Sign of Jonas* (New York, NY: Harcourt, Inc., 1953), 301.

3. Ibid., 14. In our time, a new saint, Mother Teresa of Calcutta, readily comes to mind.

4. Ibid., 57.

5. Ibid., 64.

6. Ibid., 76.

7. Ibid., 23.

8. Ibid., 61.

9. Ibid., 188.

10. Ibid., 191.

BIBLIOGRAPHY

à Kempis, Thomas. *The Imitation of Christ.* Ed. Donald E. Demaray. Staten Island, NY: Alba House, 1996.

A Year with John Paul II: Daily Meditations from his Writings and Prayers. Ed. Jerome Vereb. New York, NY: K. S. Giniger, 2005.

Anonymous. *The Cloud of Unknowing and The Book of Privy Counseling.* Ed. William Johnston. New York, NY: Doubleday Image Books, 1973.

Anthropology of the Love of God from the Writings of Evelyn Underhill. Eds. Lumsden Barkway and Lucy Menzies. London, 1953.

An Aquinas Reader: Selections from the Writings of Thomas Aquinas. Ed. Mary Clark. Garden City, NY: Image Books, 1972.

Armstrong, Christopher J. R. *Evelyn Underhill (1875-1941): An Introduction to her Life and Writings.* Grand Rapids, MI: Wm. B. Eerdmans, 1975.

Armstrong, Karen. *A History of God: The 4,000-Year Question of Judaism, Christianity, and Islam.* New York, NY: Ballantine, 1994.

Athanasius. "On the Incarnation of the Word" and "Prolegomena." *Nicene and Post-Nicene Fathers,* 2nd ser. Vol. 4, *Athanasius: Select Works and Letters.* Ed. Philip Schaff, Henry Wace. Peabody, MA: Hendrickson, 1994.

Athanasius: The Life of Antony and the Letter to Marcellinus. Trans. Robert C. Gregg. *The Classics of Western Spirituality.* New York, NY: Paulist Press, 1980.

Augustine, Saint. *Teaching Christianity.* Hyde Park, NY: New City Press, 1996.

Aumann, Jordan. *Christian Spirituality in the Catholic Tradition.* San Francisco, CA: Ignatius Press, 1985.

Barron, Robert. *Thomas Aquinas: Spiritual Master.* New York, NY: Crossroad, 1996.

Benedict XIV, Pope. *Deus Caritas Est* (Encyclical Letter on Christian Love). Liberia Editrice Vaticana, 2006. Special supplement to *Inside the Vatican* 2006.

Berger, Peter L. and Thomas Luckmann, *The Social Construction of Reality: A Treatise in the Sociology of Knowledge.* Garden City, NY: Doubleday and Co., Inc., 1967.

Bonhoeffer, Dietrich. *The Cost of Discipleship.* New York, NY: Macmillan, 1961.

___. *Meditating on the Word.* Trans. David Gracie. Cambridge, MA: Cowley Publications, 1986.

Bouyer, Louis. *Orthodox Spirituality and Protestant and Anglican Spirituality.* Trans. Barbara Wall. New York: NY: Desclee, 1969.

___. *The Spirituality of the New Testament and the Fathers.* Trans. Mary P. Ryan. New York, NY: Desclee, 1963.

Brother Lawrence of the Resurrection. *The Practice of the Presence of God.* Trans. Salvatore Sciuba. Washington, DC: ICS Publications, 1994.

Campbell, Thomas L. *The Ecclesiastical Hierarchy.* Washington, DC: University Press of America, 1981.

Carroll, James. *Constantine's Sword: The Church and the Jews*. New York, NY: Houghton Mifflin, 2001.

Carroll, William J. "Pseudo-Dionysius the Areopagite–A Bibliography: 1960-1980," *The Patristic and Byzantine Review* 1 (1982):225-234.

The Catechism of the Catholic Church. English Translation. Second Edition. United States Catholic Conference. Liguori, MO: Liguori Publications, 1997.

Catherine of Siena: The Dialogue in *Classics of Western Spirituality*. Trans. Suzanne Noffke, O.P. New York, NY: Paulist Press, 1980.

Chittister, Joan. *The Rule of Benedict: Insights for the Ages*. New York: Crossroad, 1996.

Ciszek, Walter J. with Daniel Flaherty. *He Leadeth Me*. Garden City, NY: Image Books, Doubleday, 1975.

Clement of Alexandria. Fathers of the Church Series. Trans. Simon P. Wood. Washington, DC: Catholic University of America Press, 11954.

Coleman, T.W. *English Mystics of the Fourteenth Century*. London: Epworth Press, 1938.

The Collected Works of Saint John of the Cross. Trans. Kieran Kavanaugh and Otilio Rodriguez. Washington, DC: Institute of Carmelite Studies, 1991.

Colledge, Eric. *The Medieval Mystics of England*. New York, NY: Scribners, 1961.

Congar Yves M. J. *Tradition and Traditions*. Trans. Michael Naseby and Thomas Rainborough. London: Burns & Oates, 1966.

Confessions of Saint Augustine. Trans. John K. Ryan. Garden City, NY: Image Books, 1960.

Davis, Charles, Ed. *English Spiritual Writers*. New York, NY: Sheed and Ward, 1962.

de Caussade, Jean-Pierre. *Abandonment to Divine Providence*. Trans. John Beevers. Garden City, NY: Image Books, 1975.

De Sales, Francis: Finding God Wherever You Are. Ed. Joseph F. Power. Hyde Park, NY: New City Press, 1993.

de Sales, Francis. *Introduction to the Devout Life*. Trans. John K. Ryan. Rev. Ed. New York, NY: Image Books, Doubleday, 1972.

Devotional Classics: Selected Readings for Individuals and Groups. Ed. Richard J. Foster, James Bryan Smith. San Francisco, CA: HarperSanFrancisco, 1993.

Dionoysius the Areopagite. *The Divine Names*. Surrey: The Shrine of Wisdom, 1957.

____ . *The Divine Names and The Mystical Theology*. Trans. C. E. Rolt. London: SPCK. 1977.

____ . *Mystical Theology and the Celestial Hierarchies*. Surrey, England: The Shrine of Wisdom, 1965.

The Documents of Vatican II. Trans. Joseph Gallagher. Chicago, IL: Follett, 1966.

Doherty, Kevin F. "Toward a Bibliography of Pseudo-Dionysius the Areopagite, 1900-1955," *The Modern Schoolman* 33 (May 1956): 257-68, and "Pseudo-Dionysius the Areopagite: 1955-1960," *The Modern Schoolman* 40 (November 1962), 55-59.

Doing the Truth in Charity. Ecumenical Documents I. Ed. Thomas F. Stransky, C.S.P., John B. Sheerin, C.S.P. New York, NY: Paulist Press, 1982.

Dupuis, Jacques. *Toward a Christian Theology of Religious Pluralism*. Maryknoll, NY: Orbis Books, 1997.

Egan, Harvey. *The Cambridge Companion to Karl Rahner*. Ed. Declan Marmion and Mary E. Hines. New York, NY: Cambridge University Press, 2005.

Elizabeth of the Trinity. *The Complete Works*. Vol. I. Trans. Sister Aletheia Kane. Washington, DC: ICS Publications, 1984.

Faber, Frederick William. *All for Jesus: The Easy Ways of Divine Love*. Manchester, NH: Sophia Institute Press, 2000.

The Fifty-Two Christians Who Most Influenced Their Millennium. Ed. Selina O'Grady, John Wilkins. Mahwah, NJ: Paulist Press, 2002.

Foster, Richard J. *Streams of Living Water: Celebrating the Great Traditions of Christian Faith*. New York, NY: HarperCollins, 2001.

From Glory to Glory: Texts from Gregory of Nyssa's Mystical Writings. Trans. by Herbert Musurillo Crestwood. New York, NY: Saint Vladimir's Seminary Press, 1979.

Gadamer, Hans-Georg. *Truth and Method,* trans. Garrett Barden and John Cumming. New York, NY: The Seabury Press, 1975.

The Gift of Faith: A Question and Answer Version of The Teaching of Christ. Ed. Donald W. Wuerl, Thomas Comerford, Ronald Lawler. Huntington, IN: Our Sunday Visitor Publishing, 2001.

Gladwell, Malcolm. *The Tipping Point*. New York, NY: Time Warner, 2002.

Gregory the Great: The Life of Moses. In *The Classics of Western Spirituality*. Trans. Abraham J. Malherbe and Everett Ferguson. New York, NY: Paulist Press, 1978.

Hall, Christopher A. *Reading Scripture with the Church Fathers*. Downers Grove, IL: InterVarsity Press, 1998.

Hammarskjold, Dag. *Markings*. Trans. Leif Sjoberg, W. H. Auden. New York, NY: Ballantine Books, 1964.

Hathaway, Ronald F. *Hierarchy and the Definition of Order in the Letters of Pseudo-Dionysius*. The Hague: Martinus Nijhoff, 1969.

Hay, Malcolm. *The Roots of Christian Anti-Semitism*. New York, NY: Freedom Library Press, 1981.

Hodgson, Geraldine E. *English Mystics*. London: Mowbray, 1922.

Hebblethwaite, Peter. *Paul VI: The First Modern Pope*. New York, NY: Paulist Press, 1993.

___. *In the Vatican: How the Church is Run – Its Personalities, Traditions, and Conflicts*. Bethesda, MD: Adler and Adler, 1986.

Hellwig, Monica. *Tradition: The Catholic Story Today*. Dayton, OH: Pfaum, 1974.

Holmes, Urban T. *A History of Christian Spirituality: An Analytical Introduction*. New York, NY: Seabury Press, 1980.

Huddleston, Dom Roger. Ed. *Julian of Norwich: Revelations of Divine Love*. Westminster, MD: Newman, 1962.

Hughes Alfred. *Spiritual Masters: Living a Life of Prayer in the Catholic Tradition*. Huntington, IN: Our Sunday Visitor Publishing, 1998.

Hurtado, Larry W. *Lord Jesus Christ: Devotion to Jesus in Earliest Christianity*. Grand Rapids, MI: Eerdmans Publishing, 2003.

John Paul, II. *Memory and Identity*. New York, NY: Rizzoli International Publications, 2005.

Jones, John D. *The Divine Names and Mystical Theology*. Milwaukee, WI: Marquette University Press, 1980.

Jones, Rufus Matthew. *Rufus Jones: Essential Writings.* Maryknoll, NY: Orbis Books, 2001.

Julian of Norwich: Showings. Trans. Edmund Colledge and James Walsh. New York, NY: Paulist Press, 1978.

Juliana of Norwich: Revelations of Divine Love. M.L. Del Mastro, trans. Garden City, NY: Doubleday, Image Books, 1977.

Kelly, Thomas R. *A Testament of Devotion.* New York, NY: Harper & Row, 1992.

Knowles, David. *The English Mystical Tradition.* New York, NY: Harper and Row, 1961.

Leclercq, Jean, Francois Vandenbroucke, and Louis Bouer. *The Spirituality of the Middle Ages.* Trans. The Benedictines of Holme Eden Abbey. New York, NY: Desclee, 1968.

Lent with Evelyn Underhill: Selections from Her Writings. Ed. G. P. Mellick Belshaw. New York, NY, 1964.

The Letters of Evelyn Underhill. Ed. Charles Williams. London: Longmans Green, 1943.

Lewis, C. S. *Mere Christianity.* New York, NY: McMillan, 1943.

Llewelyn, Robert. *All Shall Be Well: The Spirituality of Julian of Norwich for Today.* New York, NY: Paulist Press, 1982.

Lossky, Vladimir. *Orthodox Theology.* Trans. Ian and Ihita Kesarcodi-Watson. Crestwood, NY: Saint Vladimir's Seminary Press, 1978.

Manschreck, Clyde L. *A History of Christianity in the World.* 2nd Ed. Englewood Cliffs, NJ: Prentice-Hall, 1974.

Matsagouras, Elias. *The Early Church Fathers as Educators.* Minneapolis, MN: Light and Life Publishing, 1977.

McGinn, Bernard. *The Doctors of the Church: Thirty-Three Men and Women Who Shaped Christianity*. New York, NY: Crossroad Publishing, 1999.

Merton, Thomas. *The English Mystics* in *Mystics and Zen Masters*. New York, NY: Dell Publishing Co., 1969.

Merton, Thomas. *The Sign of Jonas*. San Diego, CA: Harcourt Brace (Harvest Book) 1981.

Molinari, Paul. *Julian of Norwich: The Teaching of a 14th Century English Mystic*. London: Longmans Green, 1958.

Muto, Susan. *John of the Cross for Today: The Ascent*. Pittsburgh, PA: Epiphany Books, 1998.

____.*John of the Cross for Today: The Dark Night*. Pittsburgh, PA: Epiphany Books, 2000.

____ *Dear Master: Letters on Spiritual Direction Inspired by Saint John of the Cross*. A Companion to *The Living Flame of Love*. Pittsburgh, PA: Epiphany Books, 2004.

____.*Deep Into the Thicket: Soul Searching Meditations Inspired by* The Spiritual Canticle of Saint John of the Cross. Pittsburgh, PA: Epiphany Books, 2001.

____. *Pathways of Spiritual Living*. Pittsburgh, PA: Epiphany Books, 2004.

____. *A Practical Guide to Spiritual Reading*. Petersham, MA: Saint Bede's Publications, 1994.

____. *Late Have I Loved Thee: The Recovery of Intimacy*. New York, NY: Crossroad, 1995.

____ . *Renewed at Each Awakening: The Formative Power of Sacred Words*. Denville, NJ: Dimension Books, 1979.

____ . *Steps Along the Way: The Path of Spiritual Reading*. Denville, NJ: Dimension Books, 1975.

____. *Womanspirit: Reclaiming the Deep Feminine in Our Human Spirituality*. Pittsburgh, PA, Epiphany Books, 2000.

Newman, John Henry. *Heart Speaks to Heart: Selected Spiritual Writings*. Ed. Lawrence S. Cunningham. Hyde Park, NY: New City Press, 2004.

Obbard, Elizabeth Ruth. *Introducing Julian: Woman of Norwich*. Hyde Park, NY: New City Press, 1996.

O'Meara, Thomas Franklin. *Thomas Aquinas: Theologian*. Notre Dame, IN: University of Notre Dame Press, 1997.

Pseudo-Dionysius, The Complete Works, Trans. Colm Luibheid. *The Classics of Western Spirituality*. New York, NY: Paulist Press, 1987.

Pioneers of the Spirit: Julian of Norwich. Vision Video: Parish of Trinity Church, Gateway Films, 1996.

Protestant Spiritual Traditions. Ed. Frank C. Senn. Mahwah, NJ: Paulist Press, 1986.

Rahner, Karl. *Foundations of Christian Faith*. Trans. William V. Dych. New York, NY: Seabury Press, 1978.

Rahner, Karl and Joseph Ratzinger. *Revelation and Tradition*. New York: NY: Herder and Herder, 1966.

Readings in Christian Thought. Ed. Hugh T. Kerr. Nashville, TN: Abingdon Press, 1966.

Ricoeur, Paul. *History and Truth*. Trans. Charles A. Kelbley. Evanston, IL: Northwestern University Press, 1965.

Rorem, Paul. *Biblical and Liturgical Symbols within the Pseudo-Dionysius Synthesis*. Toronto: Pontifical Institute of Medieval Studies, 1984.

The Rule of Saint Benedict. Thomas Fry, Ed. Collegeville, MN: Liturgical Press, 1981.

Smith, Huston. *Why Religion Matters: The Fate of the Human Spirit in an Age of Disbelief.* New York, NY: 2001.

Squire, Aelred. *Asking the Fathers.* New York, NY: Paulist Press, 1973.

Steere, Douglas V. *Kierkegaard: Purity of Heart is to Will One Thing.* New York, NY: Harper Torch Books, 1956.

____. *Prayer and Worship: A Contemporary Quaker Classic.* Richmond, IN: Friends United Press, 2000.

Szulc, Tad. *Pope John Paul II: The Biography.* New York, NY: Scribner, 1995.

The Story of Christian Spirituality: Two Thousand Years, from East to West. Minneapolis, MN: Fortress Press, 2001.

Tarnas, Richard. *The Passion of the Western Mind.* New York, NY: Ballantine Books, 1993.

The Teaching of Christ. Eds. Donald W. Wuerl, Ronald Lawler, and Thomas Comerford Lawler. Huntington, IN: Sunday Visitor, 1991.

Ten Boom, Corrie. *The Hiding Place.* With John and Elizabeth Sherrill. Grand Rapids, MI: Chosen Books, 1998.

A Testament to Freedom: The Essential Writings of Dietrich Bonhoeffer. Ed. Geoffrey B. Kelly, F. Burton Nelson. San Francisco, CA: HarperSanFrancisco, 1987.

Thomas Aquinas: The Gift of the Spirit. Ed. Benedict M. Ashley. Hyde Park, NY: New City Press, 1995.

Tracy, David. *The Analogical Imagination: Christian Theology and the Culture of Pluarlism.* New York, NY: Crossroad, 1981.

Tracy, David. *Blessed Rage for Order: The New Pluralism in Theology.* Chicago, IL: University of Chicago Press, 1996.

Underhill, Evelyn. *Abba. Meditations Based on the Lord's Prayer.* London: Longmans Green, 1940.

_____. *Mysticism: A Study of the Nature and Development of Spiritual Consciousness.* London: Methuen & Co., Ltd., 1993.

_____. *The Mystic Way: A Psychological Study in Christian Origins.* London: J. M. Dent & Sons, Ltd., 1913.

_____. *The Mystics of the Church.* New York, NY: Schocken Books, 1971.

_____. *Practical Mysticism.* New York, NY: E. P. Dutton & Co., 1943.

_____. *The Spiritual Life.* Australia: The Society of St. Paul, 1976.

_____. *Worship.* Ed. W. R. Matthews and H. Wheeler Robinson. New York, NY: Harper Brothers, 1957.

van Kaam, Adrian. *Formation of the Human Heart.* Formative Spirituality Series. Volume Three. Pittsburgh, PA: Epiphany Books, 2002.

_____. *Fundamental Formation.* Formative Spirituality Series. Volume One. Pittsburgh, PA: Epiphany Books, 2002.

_____. *Human Formation.* Formative Spirituality Series. Volume Two. New York, NY: Crossroad/Continuum, 1985.

_____. *Scientific Formation.* Formative Spirituality Series. Volume Four. New York, NY: Crossroad, 1987.

_____. *Traditional Formation.* Formative Spirituality Series. Volume Five. New York, NY: Crossroad, 1992.

_____. *Transcendence Therapy.* Formative Spirituality Series. Volume Seven. Pittsburgh, PA: Epiphany Books, 2004.

_____. *Transcendent Formation.* Formative Spirituality Series. Volume Six. Pittsburgh, PA: Epiphany Books, 2003.

___ . *The Transcendent Self: Formative Spirituality of the Middle, Early and Later Years of Life*. Pittsburgh, PA: Epiphany Association, 1991.

van Kaam, Adrian and Susan Muto. *Christian Articulation of the Mystery*. Formation Theology Series. Volume Two. Pittsburgh, PA: Epiphany Books, 2005.

___ and Susan Muto. *Dynamics of Spiritual Direction*. Revised Edition. Pittsburgh, PA: Epiphany Books, 2003.

___ and Susan Muto. *Formation of the Christian Heart*. Formation Theology Series. Volume Three. Pittsburgh, PA: Epiphany Books, 2006.

___ and Susan Muto. *Foundations of Christian Formation*. Formation Theology Series. Volume One. Pittsburgh: PA: Epiphany Books, 2004.

___ and Susan Muto. *The Power of Appreciation: A New Approach to Personal and Relational Healing*. Pittsburgh, PA: Epiphany Books, 1999.

Von Hügel, Friedrich. *Letters from Baron Von Hügel to his Niece*. Washington, DC: Regnery, 1955.

Williams, Paul. *The Unexpected Way: On Converting from Buddhism to Catholicism*. London: T. & T. Clark, 2002.

Wojtyla, Karol. *Faith According to Saint John of the Cross*. Trans. Jordan Aumann. San Francisco, CA: Ignatius Press, 1981.

Woods, Thomas E. *How the Catholic Church Built Western Civilization*. Washington, DC: Regnery Publishing, 2005.

Wuerl, Donald W. *Fathers of the Church*. Huntington, IN: Our Sunday Visitor, 1975.

INDEX

à Kempis, Thomas, 39, 167
abandonment in faith, hope, and love, 53
activism, 152, 154
actual life form, 55
adhered to: faith traditions, 58; faith and formation traditions, 69, 232
adherence to Christ, 95
Aelred of Rievaulx, 103
aestheticism, 71
agapic love, 40, 183, 184
agnosticism, 71
alien traditions, 80, 232
Allport, Gordon, 24
almsgiving, 93
analysis of pluritraditional cultures, 69
Angyal, Andreas, 23, 24, 28
Ansbacher, Heinz, 24
anthropological psychology, 29, 30
anticipation, 44
apophatic: theology, 189; way, 194
apostolic and patristic tradition, 93
appraisal, 224
appraisal: of our situation, 234; of sociohistorical pulsations and accretions, 227
appraisal process, 153, 240
appreciative abandonment to the mystery, 75, 235, 240
Aquinas, Thomas, 187, 192

articulation method, 31
articulation of classical formation, 171
aridity, 212
asceticism, 173, 188, 194
Athanasius, 231
atheism, 71
atheistic-materialistic formation traditions, 73
attention-to-consonant-image-formation, 222
Augustine of Hippo, 49, 142, 167
author of *The Cloud of Unknowing*, 200, 215
awe, 159, 193, 203, 253, 258

baptism, 76
battlefield of our heart, 143
becoming more like Christ, 58
belief systems, 72, 75, 93
Benedict of Nursia, 197
Bernanos, Georges, 105
Bernard of Clairvaux, 103, 191, 200
bio-erotic passion, 183
Blake, William, 210
blind identification, 234
Bloom, Anthony, 105
body of formative wisdom, 91
Bol, Gerard, 15, 16
Bonaventure, 191
Bonhoeffer, Dietrich, 97, 168
Book of Genesis, 40
Bouyer, Louis, 104

bridge between essence and existence, 65
Brother Lawrence of the Resurrection, 166
Butler, Dom Cuthbert, 104

call, vocation, and avocation, 229
call to: discipleship, 141, 221; ecclesial holiness, 16; ongoing conversion, 145
calling in Christ, 80, 221, 232, 240
candor, 75
capitalism, 71
careerism, 75
Carretto, Carlo, 104
Cassian, John, 103
cataphatic theology, 193
catechetical theology, 91, 168, 232
Catherine of Siena, 58, 110, 167, 199, 213
centrality of the ecclesial community, 94
Chaplain Corps of the United States Navy, 37
charitable service, 116
charity, 77, 103, 210
chastity, 211
Chesterton, G. K., 104
Christ-form of our soul, 53, 55, 60, 109, 220, 260
Christian: classics, 100, 167; Revelation, 172
classical faith traditions, 232
classics of Christianity, 94
Clement of Alexandria, 79, 103
Clement of Rome, 102
climate of pluriformity, 80
cloud of unknowing, 190, 194
coformation, 92
coforming power of traditions, 179

co-incarnation with Christ, 255
commitment to follow Christ, 166
communications of faith of reason, 99
compassion, 110, 111, 116, 198, 201, 245
compatibility, 51, 72, 75
compulsion to be current, 80
consciousness of Divine Reality, 211
conflicting directives, 80
conformity to Christ, 167
congeniality, 41, 51, 54, 65, 87, 108, 109, 229
conservatism, 181
consonance in Christ, 55
consonant: image-formation, 221; modulation, 235; or dissonant form-traditional directives, 228;
traditions, 77
consumerism, 74, 75, 179
contemplation, 190
contemplation in action, 210
contemplative prayer, 213
contestation/ratification, 234
contrition, 198, 201
convergence of faith and formation, 159
conversion of heart, 82
cooperation with grace, 146
core: dispositions, 64; form, 112, 180, 252; of our being, 65; of our faith and formation traditions, 52
Coulson, William 25, 26
courage, 75
Crashaw, Richard, 105
credal systems, 168
crises: of transcendence, 20; of transition, 43

coercive dispositions, 234
cult paganism, 176
cultural pulsations, 75
culture of narcissism and death, 261
customs of formation, 58

dark nights of sense and spirit, 212
de Caussade, Jean-Pierre, 107
deification, 190
Denis the Carthusian, 192
detachment, 103, 201
determinism, 241
devotionalism, 87, 152
devotions, 87, 215
dialogical frame of reference, 76
Dickinson, Emily, 105
differentiation-integration dynamic, 53
differentiations of our Christian traditions, 54
direction-in-common, 19
direction-ability, 41
directives for formation in Christ, 235
discipleship in Christ, 229, 250
discipline of reverential listening, 108
disillusions of eros, 184
disobedience of legitimate authority, 181
disposition of concelebration, 245
dispositions of Christian consciousness, 220
divine direction disclosures, 235, 244
Divine Forming and Preforming Mystery, 41
divine life direction, 81
docility, 52

doctrinal: foundations of the Revelation, 54; truths, 85, 172; theology, 257
doctrinal truths, 85
donative formation, 92
Donne, John, 105
Dostoyevsky, Fyodor, 105
Dreikurs, Rudolf, 24, 28
Duquesne University, 22, 31
Dutch Life Schools of Formation for Young Adults, 22, 32
dynamic of transcendence, 246

Eckhart, Meister, 192
ecological formation traditions, 72
ego-desperation, 75
elementary formation strivings, 245
Eliot, T.S., 105
Elizabeth of the Trinity, 209
English spiritual writers, 198
Epiphany Academy, 36
Epiphany of the Trinity, 259
erratic heroism, 160
Eriugena, John Scotus, 191
essence-existence structure, 27
essence of our faith tradition, 158
essential texts, 102
essentials of Christian living, 204
Eternal Trinitarian Formation and Interformation Event, 41, 52, 84, 255
eucharists of everydayness, 67, 107
Evagrius Ponticus, 103
excess of meaning, 99
exhibitionism, 204
existential psychology, 27
existentialism, 178
experience of really feeling understood, 31

experiences of faith, hope, and love, 101
extended family, 227
extraordinary phenomena, 116

Faber, F. W., 239
faith: community, 251; foundations of the Gospel, 76; in the Christian Revelation, 189
false: guilt, 236; irenicism, 180
family of origin, 226
fasting, 93
field of presence and action, 151
fields: of meaning, 43; of presence and action, 74
focal consciousness, 109, 145, 222
followers of Christ, 61
form-theological: anthropology, 188; reflection, 188
form-tradition pyramid, 71; 74, 144
form-traditional: articulations, 167; directives, 46, 70
form-traditional disassociations, 37
formability, 40, 41, 44
formation: anthropology, 188, 219; conscience, 145; counseling, 58; energy, 51; field, 55, 72, 145, 152, 176, 210, 240, 243; in Christ, 171, 180; mystery, 40; science, 189; theology, 37, 58, 91, 172, 173, 182, 242, 257, 258, 260; theory of personality; 26; tradition, 93
formation of a Christian life, 81
formative: event, 30, 83, 84; evolution, 42; reading, 51, 85, 104, 166, 167; social conscience, 219, 220; spirituality, 24; symbols, 97; thinking, 14
forming, reforming, and transforming plan of God, 107
foundational: faith directives, 91; faith formation, 17; faith traditions, 37, 64; tenets of our faith and formational traditions, 235; themes of faith deepening, 161;
foundations: of Christian formation, 169, 188; of our faith, 205; of our faith and formation traditions, 51; of spiritual formation, 111
founding form of life, 64, 254
Francis de Sales, 103, 149
Francis of Assisi, 211, 213
Frankl, Viktor, 24, 28
Freudian libidinal viewpoint, 177
from-through-to pattern of change, 54
fruits: of the Holy Spirit, 53; of transformative participation, 150
full field appraisal, 75
functional; ambitions, 178, 244; symbols, 45
functionalism, 71, 147, 173, 192, 235, 250

Gallagher, Vernon, 22
generational collaboration, 46
gifts: of divine mercy and forgiveness, 109; of memory, intellect, and will 113; of reception and donation, 152; of the Holy Spirit, 220
global internet of nations, 69
gnosticism, 180
Goldstein, Kurt, 23, 24, 28
gospel truths, 75
Greene, Graham, 105

Gregory of Nyssa, 103
guardians of our faith, 54
guidance of grace, 151
Hadewijch, 15
hallucinations, 204
Hammarskjöld, Dag, 219
hedonism, 71, 235
Herbert, George, 105
hidden life of Jesus Christ of Nazareth
hierarchy of needs, 177
Hilton, Walter, 200
historical analysis, 52
history: of humanity and Christianity, 69; of spirituality, 61
Hitler, Adolf, 180
Holy Spirit, 55, 85, 86, 92, 100, 142, 145, 150, 154, 199, 221, 245, 252, 257, 259, 260
Hopkins, Gerard Manley, 105
horizontal: interformation, 94; transmission, 98
human and Christian character formation, 182
humanism, 181
humanistic formation traditions, 180
humanity of Christ, 205
humility, 83, 103, 159, 184, 190, 207, 212, 216, 236
Hunger Winter, 13, 16, 20, 21
hymnology, 105
hypnosis, 203

Ignatius of Antioch, 102
Ignatius of Loyola, 160
illuminating reformation, 107, 214
illuminative way, 112
image of Christ, 80
imagination, 44

imitation of Christ, 163, 220
incarnational sources of memory, imagination, and anticipation, 222
incarnation of Christ, 53
indifferentism, 161
individualism, 71, 76, 236, 245
Industrial Revolution, 72
informational theology, 17, 58
infused theological virtues, 84, 220, 252
initial formation in childhood, 223
instinctual directives, 59
Institute of Formative Spirituality, 36
integrative heart, 145, 150
intellectual visions, 205
interconsciousness, 92, 97
interformative relations, 245
intermingling of cognition and affection, 114
intimacy with the mystery of the Trinity, 50, 104, 196
intraformative assimilation, 98
intraspheric existence, 151
invisible flow of grace, 216
Islam, 177

Jesus Christ, 86, 91, 92, 100, 101, 102, 110, 196
Jesus as our true Mother, 198
Joan of Arc, 211
John of the Cross, 86, 90, 103, 170, 189, 192, 212
Johnson, William, 28
Jones, Rufus, 210
Jorgensen, Johannes, 104
Jourard, Sidney, 24
joy of intimacy, 160
Judeo-Christian faith and formation traditions, 58

Judaism, 177
Julian of Norwich, 197, 215

Kelly, Thomas R., 105, 141
key situations, 223
Kierkegaard, Søren, 105
Knox, Ronald A., 104
Koren, Henry, 27

Langelaan, Adriaan, 15
Leclercq, Dom Jean, 104
Leninist-Stalinist regime, 73
leveling mentality, 250
Lewis, C. S., 210
liberalism, 181
Libermann, Venerable Francis, 22, 160
light of formation theology, 182
lightning speed appraisal, 59
literature of spirituality, 90, 189
longing for God, 198, 201
love-will: of the Father, 87, 93; of the Trinity, 177
love of Father, Son, and Holy Spirit, 65
"lower-I" dynamics, 246
luminous presence of the Spirit, 100

Mary, Virgin and Mother, 49
masters of formation, 102, 173
maturation: in Christ, 16, 108; in obedience, 152
maturity in Christ, 87, 239
Mauriac, Francois, 105
Maximus the Confessor, 191
May, Rollo, 24, 28
meditation in motion, 154
memory, 44
metalanguage, 160

metalanguage of formation science, 32
materialism, 75
meaning of the Revelation, 92
mental prayer, 215
Merton, Thomas 104
method of elucidation, 32
methods: of articulation and elucidation, 21; of measurement, 35, 162
Middle and Far Eastern traditions, 76
modes: of articulation, 166; of form-reception and donation, 71; of functional-transcendence, 173
monolithic society, 69
Montini, Giovanni Baptista, 22
moral relativism, 232
mortification, 212
Moustakas, Clark, 24
Muto, Susan, 104
mystery: of creation, redemption, and sanctification, 65; of formation, 246; of the Revelation, 91;
of transforming love, 46, 94, 150
mystical: literature, 201; union, 115; union with God, 206
mysticism, 188, 191, 193, 210, 213

narcissism, 161, 179
Nazi regime, 73
negative theology, 193
neo-gnosticism, 176
neuroform, 159
new age spirituality, 176
new life in Christ, 143
New Testament, 109
Newman, Cardinal John Henry, 210

Nicholas of Cusa, 192
Nightingale, Florence, 211
non-Christian traditions, 53
non-focal consciousness, 61

obedience: 80, 87, 103, 145, 211; to a higher authority, 142; to the love-will of the Trinity, 222
obstacles: to bodily chastity, 195; to Christian discipleship, 103; to living our faith, 163
O'Connor, Flannery, 105
one-on-one spiritual direction, 115
ordinary contemplation, 210, 212
Origen, 103
original sin, 183

Paschal Mystery, 109, 167, 204
passing sources of form-reception and donation, 224
patterns of comportment, 85
peace and joy, 255
Percy, Walker, 105
perennial truths, 44
perfectionism, 154
phases: of our Christian maturation, 55; of maturation, 177; of self-disclosure, 223
phasic unfolding, 250
phenomenological method, 30
pietism, 87, 152
philosophy, 182
plurality of traditions, 71
pneumatic-ecclesial directives, 255
pneumatic inspirations, 251
pop-spirituality, 173
Pope Benedict XVI, 184
Pope John Paul II, 67
Pope Paul VI, 89
positivism, 181
positivistic sciences, 70, 242

potency for transformation, 87, 110
Potok, Chaim, 105
poverty, 211
poverty of spirit, 212
power: of religious and ideological traditions, 62; of sociocultural pulsations, 181; of transforming love, 44
practice: of Christian formation, 95; of therapy, 62; of virtue, 190
pragmatism, 192
pride-form, 254
prayer, 93
prayers of intercession, 154
pre- and post-conversion experiences, 72
prefocal: presence to the mystery, 152; region of our consciousness, 222
preformation in the Trinity, 221
pretheological disciplines of human development, 17
pretranscendent; counseling, 181; development, 172; "I", 159
process of selectivity, 68
proto-theological anthropology, 188
psychodynamics of human experience, 34
psychology as a human science, 23, 24, 27, 33
Pseudo-Dionysius, 189
pseudo-spiritual movements, 158
purgation, 211
purgative way, 112
purification, 194
purifying formation, 107, 214
purity of heart, 102, 115

pursuit of professional excellence, 228
pyramid of traditions, 220, 233
pyramids of formation, 179

quest: for God, 59; for justice, peace, and mercy, 179; for power, pleasure, and possession, 236

racial or ethnic profiling, 244
racism, 144, 180
Radical Mystery, 160, 178
Rahner, Karl, 91
reading skills, 172
reality-testing, 246
realization of justice, peace, and mercy, 217
reception and donation of form, 40
receptive: formation, 92; potency, 250
recollection, 212, 215
redeeming love of the Son, 100
redemptive love, 86
regions of our consciousness, 43
religion and personality, 24
religious and ideological faith and formation traditions, 34
religious behaviorism, 251
renunciation, 194
reservoirs of Christian wisdom, 251
response to formative events, 243
rhythms of contemplation and action, 210
Richard of Saint Victor, 211
Rilke, Rainer Maria, 105
rituals, 45, 90, 94, 161
Rolle, Richard, 200
routine religiosity, 150

Rogers, Carl, 23, 24, 28
Ruysbroeck, Blessed John, 192

sacrament of reconciliation, 181
sacraments of initiation, 141
scholasticism, 191
Scholtes, Marinus, 14
Schouwenaars, Maria, 22
science: of engineering, 34; of formation, 20, 21, 25, 33; of meaning, 242; of measurement, 242
scientism, 192
schools of spirituality, 17, 172, 259
Second Vatican Council, 95
secondary periods of formation, 225
secularistic formation traditions, 62
secularism, 182, 240
secularistic propaganda, 80
segmental influences, 227
self-actualization, 25
self-centered eros of childhood, 184
self-direction, 153
self-disclosure of the Father, 100
selfish sensuality, 111, 113, 163, 184, 204, 236
sexism, 180
simplicity of heart, 215
social: commitments, 228; conscience, 220; pulsations, 178
socio-foundational situation, 226
sociohistorical pulsations, 51, 244
socialism, 71
soul-form of our human life, 52
source of peace, 87
special schools of spirituality, 15, 170

spirit of Christ-like surrender, 115
spiritual: direction, 58, 181, 254; masters, 102; revelations, 202
Steere, Douglas V., 157
story of salvation history, 100
Strick, Henri, 22
structures of our empirical self, 54
study of demographics, 62
subhuman directives, 59
sublimation, 183
substitutes for the transcendent, 80
super-essential darkness, 195
suppression of passions, 190
Suso, Henry, 192
symbolic: form-directives, 98; pointers, 46
syncretism, 232, 233
system of spirituality, 188
systematic theology of formation, 82

Tauler, John, 192
teaching of the classics, 187
teachings of our faith, 81
Ten Boom, Corrie, 176
Teresa of Avila, 103, 160, 199, 213
threefold path of purgation, illumination, and union, 112, 190
thematic directives, 253
theology: of divine grace, 70; of morality, 220
Thérèse of Lisieux, 103
Thomistic philosophy, 21
Tolstoy, Leo, 105
traditions: of faith deepening, 153; of form- reception and donation, 42
Traherne, Thomas, 105
transcendence: dynamic, 176, 215, 240; therapy, 32, 181

transcendent: anticipation, 45; aspirations, 178, 244; faith and formation traditions, 215; identity, 257; imagination, 45; memory, 45; transformation, 172
transfocal: consciousness, 145, 214, 219, 220, 222; directives, 253; region of our consciousness, 108, 221
transformed eros, 184
transformation, 190
transformation in Christ, 87, 150, 259
transformation of heart, 112, 146, 251
transforming union, 158
transformative: channels of grace, 254; directives, 153, 161; spirituality, 161
transhuman epiphany of the formation mystery, 100
transinstinctual directives, 42
transmission: of form-traditions, 98; of our Christian faith tradition, 90
transmitters of a tradition, 98
transpersonal psycholgism, 176
transpersonalism, 251
Trinitarian mystery, 84, 103

ultimate directives, 245
Underhill, Evelyn, 209
undisclosed transformational strivings, 221
unifying transformation, 107, 214
union with the Trinity, 190
union of wills, 203
unique-communal call, 110, 167, 178, 241
universal call to holiness, 242

van Kaam, Adrian, 104, 260
veneration of the Sacred Heart, 87
vertical: interformation, 94; transmission, 98
vigilance, 222, 260
vital: eros, 183; pulsions, 178, 244
von Hildebrand, Dietrich, 104
von Hügel, Baron Freidrich, 210

way: of affirmation, 192; of negation, 196
Wesley, John, 170
Western and Eastern Spirituality, 105
Western: civilization, 63, 79; mysticism, 210
William of Saint Thierry, 191, 200
wisdom and truth of Christian formation, 102
world peace, 37
World War II, 13
wounded eros, 184
writings of the spiritual masters, 93

Zen Buddhism, 28

About the Authors

Father Adrian van Kaam, C.S.Sp., Ph.D., is the originator of formation science and its underlying formation anthropology. These new disciplines serve his systematic and systemic formation theology. Taken as a whole, all three fields comprise the art and discipline he named *formative spirituality.*

He inaugurated this unique approach in Holland in the 1940's. Upon coming to the United States in 1954, he went to Case Western Reserve University in Cleveland where he received his doctorate in psychology. Shortly thereafter he became an American citizen.

From 1954 to 1963, he taught his original approach to psychology as a human science at Duquesne University. Then in 1963 he founded the Graduate Institute of Formative Spirituality, received the President's Award for excellence in research, and taught there as a professor in this field until its closing in 1993. He is also the recipient of an honorary Doctor of Christian Letters degree from the Franciscan University of Steubenville, Ohio.

The author of numerous books on spiritual formation, an inspiration to many, a renowned speaker, a prolific poet, Father Adrian's work enjoys worldwide recognition.

Susan Muto, Ph.D., executive director of the Epiphany Association, and a native of Pittsburgh, is a renowned speaker, author, teacher, and Dean of the Epiphany Academy of Formative Spirituality. A single lay woman living her vocation in the world and doing full-time, church-related ministry in the Epiphany Association, she has led conferences, seminars, workshops, and institutes throughout the world.

Professor Muto received her Ph.D. in English literature from the University of Pittsburgh, where she specialized in the work of post-Reformation spiritual writers. Beginning in 1966, she served in various administrative positions at the Institute of Formative Spirituality (IFS) at Duquesne University and taught as a full professor in its programs, edited its journals, and served as its director from 1981 to 1988. An expert in literature and spirituality, she continues to teach courses on an adjunct basis at many schools, seminaries, and centers of higher learning. She aims in her teaching to integrate the life of prayer and presence with professional ministry and in-depth formation in the home, the church, and the marketplace.

As coeditor of *Epiphany Connexions, Epiphany Inspirations,* and *Epiphany International,* as a frequent contributor to scholarly and popular journals, and as herself the author and coauthor of over thirty books, Doctor Muto keeps up to date with the latest developments in her field. In fact, her many books on formative reading of Scripture and the masters are considered to be premier introductions to the basic, classical art and discipline of spiritual formation and its systematic, comprehensive, formation theology. She lectures nationally and internationally on the treasured wisdom of the Judeo-Christian faith and formation tradition and on many foundational facets of living human and Christian values in today's world. Professor Muto holds membership in numerous honorary organizations and has received many distinctions for her work, including a Doctor of Humanities degree from King's College in Wilkes Barre, Pennsylvania.